THE PORTUGUESE IN CAN.

Second Edition
Diasporic Challenges and Adjustment

Edited by Carlos Teixeira and Victor M.P. Da Rosa

Although the Portuguese have settled relatively recently in Canada, they have played a major part in the country's cultural mosaic. This second edition of *The Portuguese in Canada* features many new and updated essays and continues to fill a gap in the scholarly literature on multiculturalism in Canada.

The volume's international group of contributors represents a variety of disciplines – anthropology, geography, history, literature, linguistics, sociology, and urban planning. The essays cover such topics as industry and commerce, cultural retention and adjustment, language and identity, citizenship and politics, the urban experience, and literature. Together the essays convey the multifaceted contribution the Portuguese have made to Canada and consider future directions for the preservation and promotion of Portuguese-Canadian culture and heritage.

CARLOS TEIXEIRA is an associate professor in the Department of Community, Culture and Global Studies at the University of British Columbia, Okanagan.

VICTOR M.P. DA ROSA is a professor in the Department of Sociology and Anthropology at the University of Ottawa.

SECOND EDITION

The Portuguese in Canada

Diasporic Challenges and Adjustment

Edited by

CARLOS TEIXEIRA and

VICTOR M.P. DA ROSA

UNIVERSITY OF TORONTO PRESS
Toronto Buffalo London

© University of Toronto Press Incorporated 2009
Toronto Buffalo London
www.utppublishing.com
Printed in Canada

ISBN 978-0-8020-9833-7 (cloth)
ISBN 978-0-8020-9560-2 (paper)

Printed on acid-free paper

Library and Archives Canada Cataloguing in Publication

The Portuguese in Canada : diasporic challenges and adjustment / edited by
Carlos Teixeira and Victor M.P. Da Rosa. – 2nd ed.

ISBN 978-0-8020-9833-7 (bound). ISBN 978-0-8020-9560-2 (pbk.)

1. Portuguese – Canada – History. 2. Portuguese Canadians – History.
I. Da Rosa, Victor M.P. II. Teixeira, José Carlos, 1959–

FC106.P8P67 2009   971′.004691   C2008-907711-3

University of Toronto Press acknowledges the financial assistance to its
publishing program of the Canada Council for the Arts and the Ontario Arts
Council.

University of Toronto Press acknowledges the financial support for its
publishing activities of the Government of Canada through the
Book Publishing Industry Development Program (BPIDP).

Contents

Figures and Tables

Figures

Tables

Acknowledgments

It is impossible to acknowledge all our intellectual debts in the space available. Our thanks go in particular to Professors John Warkentin and Robert A. Murdie of York University for their support and encouragement over the past years. We also thank the editors at the University of Toronto Press: Virgil Duff, for believing in this project; Anne Laughlin, for being a great liaison between us and the rest of the team; and Camilla Blakeley, for her thorough copy editing. We also thank Peter Collins for his valuable editorial aid and Carolyn King for her assistance in drawing the maps.

We also appreciate the encouragement and generous financial support provided by Dr Alzira Maria Serpa Silva, Directora Regional das Comunidades, Direcção Regional, Azores. She never questioned the importance of this project. The editors wish to express their gratitude to the following members of the Portuguese community: Gabriela Cavaco (Banco Santander Totta SA), Rui Ferreira (Banco Espirito Santo), and Virgilio Pires (Merit M.I.). Without their friendship and added support it would have been more difficult for this publication to come to fruition.

Finally, we wish to thank the Portuguese communities in Canada that we visited over the past three decades, for sharing with us their immigrant experiences. It is to them that we dedicate this book.

Contributors

Luís L.M. Aguiar
University of British Columbia – Okanagan

Onésimo Teotónio Almeida
Brown University, Providence, Rhode Island

Jean-Pierre Andrieux
St John's, Newfoundland

Irene Bloemraad
University of California, Berkeley

Peter Collins
Toronto

Victor M.P. Da Rosa
University of Ottawa

Priscilla A. Doel
Colby College, Waterville, Maine

Susana P. Miranda
York University, Toronto

Robert A. Murdie
York University, Toronto

Manuel Armando Oliveira
Universidade Aberta – CEMRI, Portugal

Isabel Nena Patim
Universidade Fernando Pessoa, Portugal

Maria Beatriz Rocha-Trindade
Universidade Aberta – CEMRI, Portugal

Carlos Teixeira
University of British Columbia – Okanagan

John Warkentin
York University, Toronto

THE PORTUGUESE IN CANADA:
DIASPORIC CHALLENGES AND ADJUSTMENT

1 A Historical and Geographical Perspective

CARLOS TEIXEIRA AND VICTOR M.P. DA ROSA

This book is about the Portuguese in Canada: their history, problems, aspirations, and challenges, and their impact on the receiving society. It aims at a better understanding of an important segment of the Portuguese diaspora. In 2003 the Portuguese-Canadian community commemorated the fiftieth anniversary of the arrival of the first group of immigrants to Canada from Portugal. It all started on 13 May 1953, when eighty-five Portuguese immigrants landed in Halifax aboard the *Saturnia.* Since then Canada has become a major destination for the Portuguese diaspora.

The origins of this project are associated with an earlier event, the 1997 celebration in Newfoundland of the 500th anniversary of John Cabot's arrival in North America. This event coincided with the 1997 annual meeting of the Canadian Association of Geographers in St. John's, at which two sessions examined the Portuguese presence in Canada dating back to the fifteenth century. This is the second edition of the book that resulted, and although we have replaced some contributions with new ones and revised others extensively, rearranging materials in order to achieve a better coverage of the Portuguese presence in Canada, the basic themes remain the same as those of the first edition. That being said, anyone who attempts to publish a book such as this one, dealing with multiple aspects of an ethnocultural minority, is challenged to meet the expectations of academic researchers while remaining accessible to the general reader. Since the first edition of this volume was published, Canada, Portugal, and the Portuguese-Canadian community have all changed substantially. We hope this effort will represent an important addition to the growing bibliography on this component of the Canadian mosaic.

The contributors to this volume – some of them participants in the 1997 sessions – come from a variety of disciplines: sociology, anthropology, urban planning, geography, history, languages, literatures, and linguistics. As a result, they use a diversity of disciplinary/interdisciplinary approaches. Moreover, by including contributions by scholars born in both Canada and Portugal, we hope to give readers a deeper understanding of Portuguese Canadians from both 'insider' and 'outsider' perspectives.

Historical Contacts and Migration

Portugal's history has been deeply influenced by lands beyond the sea. In the fifteenth century, 300 years after the founding of Portugal in 1143, the period of its discoveries and colonial empire began. The Atlantic Ocean became the main route for its explorers and navigators of the fifteenth and sixteenth centuries to reach other parts of the globe. This ocean, which transformed Portugal into a commercial and naval power, became in the nineteenth and twentieth centuries the main route for a massive exodus of its population to other countries and continents. Indeed, emigration has been a constant of the Portuguese people (Higgs 1990; Rocha-Trindade et al. 1995; Garcia 1998). In the last hundred years, some 4 million people have left the country – an exodus that affected the islands (Madeira and the Azores) first and foremost, followed by the northern, and then the central, regions of mainland Portugal (Figure 1.1).[1]

For most of this century successive Portuguese governments did not hinder this emigration, recognizing, first, that the future transfer of emigrants' remittances back home was essential to the country's balance of payments and, second, that the exodus eased the problems of unemployment and its attendant social tensions. The origins of emigration lay primarily in the underdevelopment of the country and its lack of resources. Other contributing factors included high population density, inadequate housing, poor use of land, and scarcity of jobs. As the Portuguese sociologists Almeida and Barreto observed some three decades ago, 'Hunger, misery, life's oppressions and total insecurity bring about emigration' (1974: 251). This no longer applies to the majority of Portugal's population, including those in Madeira and the Azores islands, but even today thousands of citizens live far below the poverty level according to European Union standards (Bacalhau 1984; Leeds 1984; Feldman-Bianco 1992; Manuel 1998; Fonseca 2005).

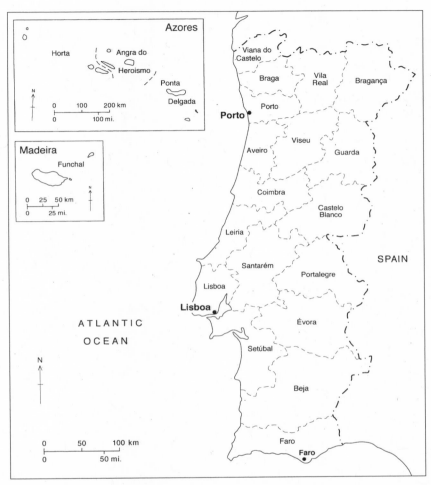

Figure 1.1. Districts of mainland Portugal, Azores, and Madeira

Modern Portuguese immigration to Canada began in the early 1950s (Table 1.1). However, historical contacts with Canada date back to the fifteenth century, when Portuguese navigators are believed to have reached the Atlantic coast (Allen 1992). While the Portuguese did not settle the land, their presence is preserved today in the place names along this coast (Brazão 1964; Alpalhão and Da Rosa 1980; Mannion

Table 1.1
Portuguese immigration to Canada, 1950–2007

Year	Arrivals
1950–9	17,114
1960–9	59,677
1970–9	79,891
1980–9	38,187
1990–9	19,235
2000–7	2,894

Sources: Canada, Department of Citizenship and
Immigration 1955; 1957; Canada, Employment and
Immigration Canada 1960–90; Statistics Canada
2007.

and Barkham 1987). Names of Portuguese origin dot the capes, head-
lands, offshore islands, and large harbours. Labrador, for example,
probably derives from the Portuguese explorer João Fernandes, a
lavrador (farmer) of the island of Terceira (Azores). Other place names
of Portuguese origin in the region include Bacalhaus (Baccalieu
Island), Cabo de Sao Jorge (Cape St. George), Cabo Rei (Cape Ray),
Fogo (Fogo Island), Frey Luis (Cape Freels), Ilha Roxa (Red Island),
Santa Maria (Cape St. Mary's), and Terra Nova (Newfoundland) – all
testimony to the historical presence of the Portuguese in the north-
western Atlantic.

As noted in Table 1.1, however, the early Portuguese settlers in
Canada arrived mainly during the 1950s, when Canada was promoting such immigration in order to meet its need for agricultural and
railway construction workers (Anderson and Higgs 1976). Sponsorship and family reunification accounted for the acceleration of the
process, mainly through the 1960s and 1970s. From the mid-1970s on,
numbers diminished considerably, partly because of changes to Canadian legislation in 1973. Another factor may have been Portugal's
accession to the European Community. This created prospects of better
and more remunerative jobs and higher standards of living for the Portuguese at home. With respect to the Azores, geographical position
and strong historical and family contacts with the United States and
Canada explain the attraction of Azoreans to these areas. Therefore,
North America rather than Europe will probably continue the preferred destination for Azoreans.

Table 1.2
Portuguese-Canadian institutions, by region, 2007

Type of institution	Western Canada	Ontario	Quebec and Atlantic provinces	Total
Businesses	400	5,000	₋719	6,119
Clubs/associations	65	100	46	211
Community schools	7	20	5	32
Churches	7	23	4	34

Sources: Portuguese consulates in Montreal, Toronto, Winnipeg, and Vancouver; for Ontario businesses, Portuguese Telephone Directory, 2007; for Quebec and Atlantic businesses, Aliança dos Profissionais e Empresários do Quebec; for western Canada businesses, authors' estimation.

In fact, from the early 1950s to the present, 60 per cent to 70 per cent of Portuguese living in Canada have come from the Azores, particularly from the island of São Miguel, or are descendants of Azorean families. The lack of disaggregated data concerning the regions of origin of Portuguese immigrants makes it difficult to determine the percentage of Azoreans and their descendants in Canada. Similarly, estimates of the Portuguese population in Canada vary. Estimates by 'key' community leaders such as consular authorities in Canada as well as journalists point to between 500,000 and 600,000 first-, second-, and third-generation Portuguese in Canada, although the 2001 census recorded 357,690 people of Portuguese ethnic origin 'officially' living in Canada (Statistics Canada 2001; Teixeira 2001–2).

Settlement

Today, five decades after the arrival of the first immigrants in Canada, we can find Portuguese communities from coast to coast. Most Portuguese Canadians live in Ontario, Quebec, British Columbia, Alberta, and Manitoba (Figure 1.2), particularly in the urban centres (Figures 1.3, 1.4, and 1.5). Indeed, most of the contributions to this volume deal with Portuguese in Canadian urban settings. Curiously, despite the rural roots in Portugal of most immigrants, there is a notable lack of large Portuguese-Canadian settlements in rural areas (see Joy 1982; Cole 1997, 1998).

Portuguese-Canadian urban settlements date back to the end of the 1950s, and their concentration in particular immigrant neighbour-

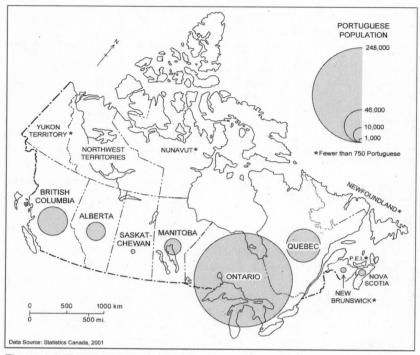

Figure 1.2. Population of Portuguese ethnic origin, Canada, 2001
Source: Data from Statistics Canada 2001.

hoods is therefore not surprising. In Toronto, Montreal, Vancouver, Winnipeg, and Edmonton we can identify a 'core' or 'centre' of self-contained and self-sufficient Portuguese communities.[2] The high degree of 'institutional completeness' in these communities is demonstrated by their appreciable number of social, cultural, and religious institutions, as well as their wide range of ethnic businesses (Table 1.2). Portuguese settlement shows distinct spatial patterns, which translate into spatial and social isolation from the host society. This segregation has been a barrier to the blending of first-generation immigrants into Canadian society. By 2001 Portuguese Canadians were among the most segregated groups in these cities (Qadeer and Kumar 2006; Teixeira 2006).

In the last two decades, however, residential patterns have changed (Teixeira 2006), and the Portuguese are now spreading over a larger

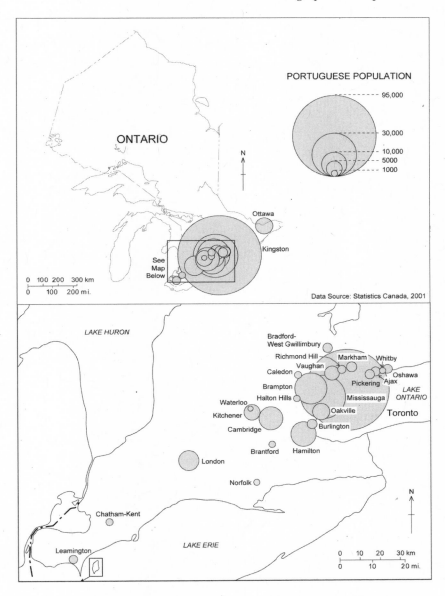

Figure 1.3. Population of Portuguese ethnic origin, Ontario, 2001
Source: Data from Statistics Canada 2001.

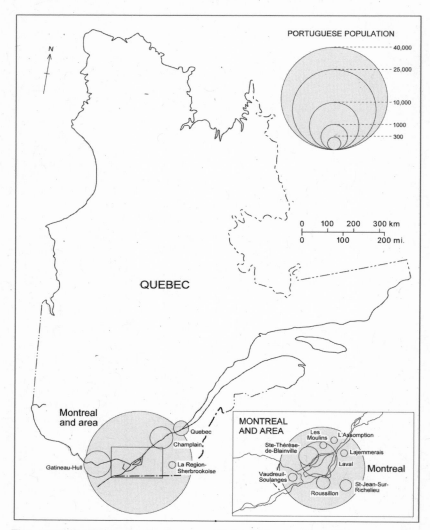

Figure 1.4. Population of Portuguese ethnic origin, Quebec, 2001
Source: Data from Statistics Canada 2001.

territory than ever before, spurred by the improved economic positions of some Portuguese families and their wish to acquire a 'dream'
house, preferably in the suburbs. The slow dispersal of Portuguese
Canadians is a fairly recent phenomenon, with movement out of the

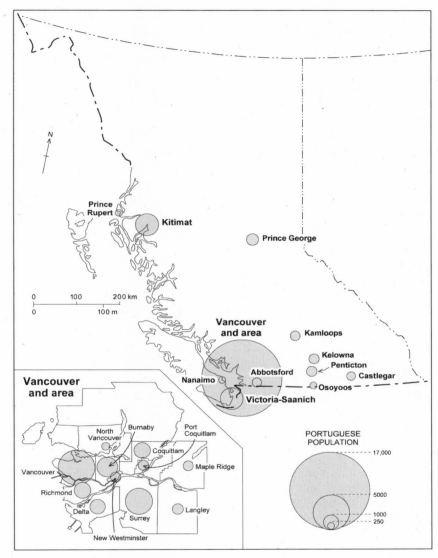

Figure 1.5. Population of Portuguese ethnic origin, British Columbia, 2001
Source: Data from Statistics Canada 2001.

'core' being clearly reflected in the 1976, 1981, 1991, and 2001 censuses. If this trend continues the next censuses may show a weakening of their concentration within the 'core.' Within this context lies the dilemma of the Portuguese in Canada – communities in transition.

Introduction to the Essays

This collection of essays is an attempt to examine the Portuguese presence in Canada comprehensively, from the early Portuguese explorers, through the later Portuguese fishery on the Grand Banks and the Portuguese cultural impact on the people of Newfoundland, to the state of contemporary Portuguese immigrant communities in Canada. The perspective is at once broad and particular, ranging from historical analysis of the Portuguese diaspora over centuries to the stories of individual Portuguese immigrant women in Toronto.

Maria Beatriz Rocha-Trindade (chapter 2) presents an overview of the historical antecedents, as well as the nature and causes, of emigration from Portugal and the situation of the Portuguese diaspora today. She does not forget the new phenomenon of return migration by Portuguese nationals and the significant increase in the number of African immigrants settling in Portugal.

The Portuguese maritime presence in Atlantic Canada was renewed in the twentieth century with the annual sailing, from the 1930s to the 1970s, of the famous White Fleet to the fishing grounds of the Grand Banks. This friendly armada and the relations of its members with Newfoundland and its people form the subject matter of part 1. Priscilla A. Doel (chapter 3) examines the history of the Portuguese codfishing fleet. In particular she discusses how government and corporate authorities used icons of nationalism aboard key ships of the White Fleet to assert state control over the fishermen. Jean-Pierre Andrieux (chapter 4), who has spent his life commuting between St-Pierre and St John's, provides us with an insightful view by a contemporary observer of how Portuguese state and business interests collided in the organisation, and eventual destruction, of the White Fleet. Finally, the cultural and social impact of the White Fleet on the people of Newfoundland is examined by Peter Collins (chapter 5), a young Canadian literary scholar who still remembers with great *saudade* the presence of the White Fleet in his native St John's. He discusses representations of the Portuguese in Newfoundland literature and journalism and concludes the volume's treatment of the singular moment in Portuguese–Canadian relations that was the White Fleet.

The history of the Portuguese in Canada today is a story of immigration, citizenship, adjustment, and some conflict, and these are the primary themes of part 2. These issues are all explored by Manuel Armando Oliveira (chapter 6) in his analysis of cultural retention among Portuguese of Azorean background in Toronto and Montreal. In particular Oliveira highlights the complex, and often conflicted, relationship between the two primary subgroups of Portuguese immigrants in Canada – those originating from mainland Portugal and those who come from the Azores – and how the long and complex relationship between these two populations shapes Portuguese culture in Canada today. Discussion on the themes of citizenship, adjustment and conflict is continued by Susana P. Miranda (chapter 7), who examines the remarkable history of labour activism by Portuguese immigrant women in Toronto. Her study highlights the degree to which the struggle of the women for social justice and fair wages, which pitted them against major corporate interests and even provincial governments, was influenced in many respects by their cultural values and practices. These proved to be sources of strength and an essential resource for the women to draw upon during their years of labour action. Portuguese immigrant activism is also the focus of Luís Aguiar (chapter 8), who examines the increasingly prominent role of deportation as an aspect of Canadian immigration policy. With reference to a recent controversial case in which the Portuguese-Canadian community united to successfully resist attempts by the Canadian government to deport one of its members, Aguiar explores how the discourses of citizenship and anti-immigrant hostility are configured within an increasingly neo-liberal political-economic context. Finally, complementing this analysis is the work of Irene Bloemraad (chapter 9). She discusses the 'political invisibility' of the Portuguese-Canadian community in which, apart from notable examples of activism to address isolated problems, the lack of sustained engagement with mainstream Canadian political life has long been cited as a fundamental concern. This being said, in contrasting the experiences of Portuguese Canadians and Portuguese Americans, Bloemraad notes how the Canadian context – and in particular the Canadian policies of multiculturalism – seems to foster higher levels of political visibility among Portuguese immigrants than does the American context.

In part 3 Carlos Teixeira, first in association with Robert A. Murdie, then Victor M.P. Da Rosa, and then on his own, describes 'Little Portugals' in Canada: in Toronto (chapter 10), in the province of Quebec (chapter 11), and in the Okanagan Valley (British Columbia), respectively. Chapters 10, 11, and 12 challenge the long-held assumption about the immutability of these communities. Political and economic changes taking place in Canada in general, and in Quebec and Ontario in particular, are affecting new Canadians' view of Canada. These three chapters are particularly interesting for how they highlight commonalities in the Portuguese experience in Canada despite differences in contexts – francophone Quebec, in urban Toronto, and in rural British Columbia. In all of these cases the changes that Portuguese communities will experience in the near future – particularly with respect to cultural retention by new generations of Portuguese Canadians raised and educated in Canada – will be crucial to the survival and integrity of the group, its cohesion, its culture, and its traditions.

Part 4 examines the cultural retention, literature, and sense of history of Portuguese Canadians. Value conflicts form the main theme of the work of Onésimo Teotónio Almeida (chapter 13), in which he compares and contrasts the Portuguese in Canada with those in the United States in terms of the struggle for cultural adjustment and adaptation between community involvement and knowledge of the Portuguese diaspora. Isabel Nena Patim (chapter 14) writes about the new literature of Portuguese background in Canada, and explores how the themes of survival and identity are represented in works such as Erika De Vasconcelos's *My Darling Dead Ones*. Central to this literature are attempts to answer what Patim foregrounds as the primary question of cultural identity for this immigrant community: 'Who am I now that I am here?' Finally, the contribution of John Warkentin (chapter 15), a living institution in the field of historical geography in Canada and a friend of Portuguese communities in this country, presents fascinating insights into issues and themes discussed in this volume from the perspective of a scholar who has reflected on issues of ethnicity and identity over the course of a long and eminent career. His work contextualizes the Portuguese-Canadian experience within a broader social and cultural frame and allows us to understand issues – such as the controversial tension between Azoreans and mainland Portuguese in Canada – through parallels in the wider Canadian experience. We simply could not imagine a more appropriate way to conclude this volume than with John Warkentin's work.

Finally, it should be noted that, as one of the editors of this volume wrote some thirty years ago, the Portuguese brought to Canada not only their labour but also their unique cultural values, which were destined to become part of our common Canadian heritage. All the contributors to this volume therefore agree that the dedication of this book belongs properly to the Portuguese communities explored and represented in its pages. In this context we would like to reiterate our sincere hope that *The Portuguese in Canada* will serve as both a guardian of our past and a beacon for the future.

NOTES

1 Portugal has an area of 91,985 square kilometres. Its population of approximately 11 million (2007) is distributed among eighteen continental and four island districts. Madeira has one district (Funchal). As Figure 1.1 shows, the islands of the Azores are divided into three districts: Angra do Heroísmo (islands of Graciosa, São Jorge, and Terceira); Horta (Corvo, Faial, Flores, and Pico); and Ponta Delgada (Santa Maria and São Miguel).

2 The areas identified as 'core' or 'centre' reflect relatively homogeneous and compact socio-spatial units within cities, where a large number of Portuguese live and where most of their institutions, businesses, and services are located.

REFERENCES

Allen, J.L. 1992. 'From Cabot to Cartier: The Early Exploration of Eastern North America, 1497–1543.' *Annals of the Association of American Geographers* 82 no. 3: 500–21.

Almeida, C., and A. Barreto. 1974. *Capitalismo e emigração em Portugal*. Lisbon: Prelo.

Alpalhão, J.A., and V.M.P. Da Rosa, 1980. A *Minority in a Changing Society: The Portuguese Communities of Quebec*. Ottawa: University of Ottawa Press.

Anderson, G.M., and D. Higgs. 1976. *A Future to Inherit: The Portuguese Communities of Canada*. Toronto: McClelland & Stewart.

Bacalhau, M. 1984. 'Regional Distribution of Portuguese Emigration According to Socio-Economic Context.' In *Portugal in Development: Emigration, Industrialization, the European Community*, ed. T. Bruneau, V.M.P. Da Rosa, and A. Macleod, 53–63. Ottawa: University of Ottawa Press.

Brazão, E. 1964. *La découverte de Terre-Neuve*. Montreal: Les Presses de L'Université de Montréal.

Canada, Department of Citizenship and Immigration. 1955. *Report of Immigration Branch*. Ottawa: The Department.

–. 1957. *Report of Immigration Branch*. Ottawa: The Department.

Canada, Employment and Immigration Canada. 1960–90. *Report*. Ottawa: The Department.

Cole, S.C. 1997. 'Género e família na construção das identidades portuguesas no Canadá.' *ANTROPOlógicas* 1: 3–19.

– 1998. 'Reconstituting Households, Retelling Culture: Emigration and Portuguese Fisheries Workers in Canada.' In *Transgressing Borders: Critical Perspectives on Gender, Households, Culture*, ed. S. Ilkan and L. Phillips, 75–92. Westport, CT: Bergen and Garvey.

Feldman-Bianco, B. 1992. 'Multiple Layers of Time and Space: The Construction of Class, Ethnicity, and Nationalism among Portuguese Immigrants.' In *Towards a Transnational Perspective on Migration*, ed. N.G. Schiller, L. Basch, and C. Blanc-Szanton, 145–74. New York: New York Academy of Sciences.

Fonseca, M.L. 2005. 'The Changing Face of Portugal: Immigration and Ethnic Pluralism.' *Canadian Diversity/Diversité Canadienne* 4: 57–62.

Garcia, J.L. 1998. A *emigração Portuguesa: Uma breve introdução*. Lisbon: Secretaria de Estado das Comunidades Portuguesas.

Higgs, D. 1990. 'Portuguese Migration before 1800.' In *Portuguese Migration in a Global Perspective*, ed. D. Higgs, 7–28. Toronto: Multicultural History Society of Ontario.

Joy, A. 1982. 'Accommodation and Cultural Persistence: The Case of the Sikhs and the Portuguese in the Okanagan Valley of British Columbia. PhD diss., University of British Columbia.

Leeds, E. 1984. 'Salazar's "Modelo Económico": The Consequences of Planned Constraint.' In *Portugal in Development: Emigration, Industrialization, the European Community*, ed. T. Bruneau, V.M.P. Da Rosa, and A. Macleod, 13–51. Ottawa: University of Ottawa Press.

Mannion, J., and S. Barkham. 1987. 'The 16th Century Fishery.' In *Historical Atlas of Canada*. Vol. 1, *From the Beginning to 1800*, ed. R.C. Harris, 58–9, plate 22. Toronto: University of Toronto Press.

Manuel, PC. 1998. 'The Process of Democratic Consolidation Portugal, 1976–1996.' *Portuguese Studies Review* no. 1: 33–47.

Qadeer, M., and S. Kumar. 2006. 'Ethnic Enclaves and Social Cohesion.' *Canadian Journal of Urban Research* 15: 1–17.

Rocha-Trindade, M.B., A.P. Cordeiro, A.P.B. Horta, A.J. Madeira, M.C. Rego, and T. Viegas. 1995. *Sociologia das migrações*. Lisbon: Universidade Aberta.

Statistics Canada. 2001. Citizenship, Immigration, Birthplace, Generation Status, Ethnic Origin, Visible Minorities, and Aboriginal Peoples. www.statcan.ca.

– 2007. Table 051-0006. Immigrants to Canada by country of last permanent residence, quarterly (persons). www.statcan.ca.

Teixeira, C. 2001–2. 'The Portuguese Presence in Canada: An Overview of Five Decades.' *Gávea-Brown: A Bilingual Journal of Portuguese-American Letters and Studies* 22–23: 5–28.

– 2006. 'A Comparative Study of Portuguese Homebuyers' Suburbanization in the Toronto and Montreal Areas.' *Espaces, Populations, Sociétés/Space, Populations, Societies* 1: 121–35.

2 The Portuguese Diaspora

MARIA BEATRIZ ROCHA-TRINDADE

Analysis of emigration movements was originally rooted firmly in demography. Wherever researchers noted a significant population flow between a country of origin and a country of destination, they counted the people in transit and duly classified them according to gender, age group, educational level, and professional profile. Later, more economy-oriented studies of emigration patterns explored the reasons underlying emigration through analysis of the differentials of demographic pressures, economic level, and job opportunities between the two ends of the journey. This led to the formulation of theories that were based on the dual concept of attraction and repulsion (Rocha-Trindade 1995, 57–104).

However, such indicators were not in themselves sufficient to explain the complexities of collective movements, and so researchers began to consider other aspects of migration relating to sociology, social psychology, and cultural anthropology. Later, considerations of an economic, political, and social nature came into the analysis of migration questions and problems; nowadays, a number of important matters are frequently considered in the field of social intervention, such as integration, inter-ethnic relations and conflicts, plural identities, ethnic networks, and so forth. These aspects are often linked to issues concerning such as motivation, the circulation of information, and the sometimes stereotypical images constructed about both the country of origin and the country of destination. This approach was developed in the large receiving countries, where it was extended to the analysis of settlement and integration of the various waves of immigrants. In contrast, governments in the countries of origin were concerned more with securing guarantees in terms of employment, social insertion, and respect for the rights of the workers and families settled abroad.

Today, the globalization of communications and the continuing international circulation and settlement of peoples render the study of emigration and immigration movements of particular importance in government, social, and urban planning. Spatially dispersed diasporas – such as that of the Portuguese – can have a cultural and economic impact on a global level by linking such otherwise disparate societies as Canada's and Brazil's. Thus the study of the historical migrations of this group serves as a good example of the value of migration studies to our understanding of contemporary societies.

This chapter first looks at Portuguese emigration up to the nine-teenth century. Second, it examines emigration since the last century until today. Third, it analyses return migration and immigration to Portugal. Finally, it synthesizes the characteristics of the Portuguese diaspora.

Historical Antecedents

Colonial Emigration

Situated in the extreme south-western corner of Europe, in close contact with both the Mediterranean and the Atlantic, Portugal has been a stopover on journeys of peoples throughout history. Visited by Greeks and Phoenicians, occupied by Romans, invaded by 'barbar-ians' from northern and eastern Europe, conquered by Moors, and made independent by its first Christian king in 1143, Portugal pos-sesses the oldest frontiers of any country in Europe. The multiple ethnic and cultural influences that have been the products of this his-torical process, leading to what is today a rather homogeneous national culture, may be one explanation for the Portuguese inclina-tion to seek contact with other peoples and places.

This predilection has in fact characterized the whole of Portuguese history over the last five centuries. In the fifteenth and sixteenth cen-turies Portuguese overseas expansion established a trade network and military domination on a worldwide scale, extending from the north and west coasts of Africa to India and from the Straits of Malacca to China and Japan. In the western hemisphere, possession of the Atlantic archipelagos reinforced Portuguese military and economic power over the South Atlantic and Brazil.

Accompanying this overseas expansion were the first waves of emigrants from Portugal. Some sources refer to the departure of about 2,400 individuals per year to the fortified towns of the Indian Ocean in the early sixteenth century (Serrão 1971). This movement grew in the second half of the century with emigration to Brazil, which received some 3,000 emigrants a year. As a result the Portuguese population resident in that colony, estimated at some 57,000 in 1576, quadrupled between 1580 and 1600.

At the end of the seventeenth century departures for Brazil increased, owing to the discovery of mines of precious metals and gems. A massive migration ensued, primarily from north-west Portugal. Improvements in the shipping connections to Brazil also account for the annual departure at this time of over 2,000 Portuguese – who set sail from the ports of Viana, Oporto, Lisbon, and Vigo in Galicia, Spain – heading for Pará, Pernambuco, Bahia, and Rio de Janeiro. This flow of people was made up of those seeking to make their fortunes quickly, especially in trade, since agricultural tasks would continue for some time still to be done by slaves of African extraction. These emigrants included not only individuals of the humbler classes but also nobles and men of letters invested with official duties who, once there, became involved in liberal professions (Sérgio 1956).

The subsequent decline in Portuguese power in India and southeast Asia led to larger contingents of emigrants being sent to Brazil, thereby encouraging a colonial policy that essentially transferred the focus of emigration from the Indian to the Atlantic Ocean.[1] The fact that interest in Brazil persisted is clear from the high number of annual departures (between 8,000 and 10,000) recorded during the first two-thirds of the eighteenth century. Although figures dropped off slightly later in the eighteenth century, they picked up again during the nineteenth, following the transfer of the Portuguese crown to the colony in 1807. After Brazil gained independence in 1822, ending the Portuguese colonial presence in that region, demographic movements from Portugal to the new country became in effect international – as opposed to colonial – emigration. Although the Portuguese empire survived until recently in India (1961), Africa and Timor (1975), and Macao (1999) – this in spite of its becoming progressively more limited and weakened – the movement of people to these colonial destinations never reached a scale comparable to the Portuguese migration to Brazil.

The Nineteenth-Century Transatlantic Emigration Cycle

Following the pattern of the previous century, the Portuguese in the nineteenth century settled primarily in north-eastern Brazil, again in Pará, Pernambuco, and Bahia, where they were involved in the growing of cotton and sugar cane. Later there was a movement toward the centre of the country, thanks to the growth of the mining industry after the discovery of large deposits of gold and precious stones. This led to the spread of Portuguese settlement as far as Goiás, Minas Gerais, and Mato Grosso. Some settlers quickly acquired spectacular wealth, which was responsible for the birth of the *O Mineiro* (the Miner) figure in Portuguese folk tradition: an image that faded only with the impoverishment of the gold and diamond beds and a consequent sharp drop in emigration.

The next phase of the Portuguese emigration to Brazil, which occurred in the second half of the nineteenth century, was connected to new economic conditions (extensive coffee and cotton plantations in the São Paulo region) and social and political changes (independence and an end to slavery through progressively liberating legislation, culminating in *Lei Áurea* – the Golden Law – which in 1888 decreed its abolition in Brazil).[2]

Meanwhile territories populated and colonized earlier by the Portuguese – primarily the Atlantic archipelagos of Madeira, the Azores, and Cape Verde – changed from 'receiving' to 'sending' regions when many of their natives left in search of a better life beyond national borders. Initially they headed for Brazil (settling particularly in the southern states of Paraná, Santa Catarina, and Rio Grande do Sul) and for Africa (Mozambique and the Angolan Plateau). At the end of the nineteenth century Madeirans also headed for the Pacific, to the Sandwich Islands, now Hawaii (Felix and Senecal 1978; Dias 1981; Rocha 1983), as well as for British Guiana (Demerara) and the Dutch Antilles (Curaçao) – all places that could be reached only by a long and hazardous voyage.[3]

The Azoreans, however, preferred the American continent. The first Portuguese immigrants probably came to the east coast of the United States as fishermen and sailors. Some of them became farmers, miners, or worked at railroad building; a growing number progressively reached the opposite coast of America. In the words of Martins, 'The [Portuguese] colony in California is Azorean, for American whaling ships go to the

Azores to recruit seamen. Whaling ... is to a part of the Azorean people what Brazil is to people from the northern Minho province' (1956: 234). For these migrants, after fishing as an employee on someone else's boat or as a self-employed fisherman, jobs in factories and on farms were the most common occupation. Factory jobs were mostly on the east coast (Massachusetts and Connecticut), and farming employment largely in California, particularly in the San José and San Joaquin valleys.

Another North American destination, Canada, is insufficiently documented over the nineteenth century. While the role played by Portuguese navigators in the discovery of Newfoundland, Labrador, and the eastern seaboard of continental Canada is widely recognized, there are only a few isolated references to the Portuguese names of families settled there since the sixteenth century. This is unusual, since the intensive fishing activity carried out by Portuguese boats in these regions is well known and would naturally have given rise to a fair, though limited, number of settlers (Moura 1992). However, Canada seems to have become a major important destination for Portuguese emigration only after 1950. The celebration of the fiftieth anniversary of the arrival of Portuguese in Canada led to a large number of studies related to this event and to the creation of the Pioneers' Museum in Toronto dedicated to it.

In general all these tides of transatlantic emigration became geographically specialized streams, providing a clear example of the demarcation of geographical destination zones, which lasted throughout the following decades.

Contemporary Emigration

Transoceanic Destinations

The two main destinations for Portuguese emigrants in the Americas – Brazil and the United States (Table 2.1) – have one characteristic in common, namely that they both maintained permanent and regular streams of emigrants during the first half of the twentieth century, except during the two world wars. During the First World War the almost total suspension of departures from Portugal was mainly a result of Portuguese involvement in the conflict, which absorbed many in both the young and adult population. During the Second World War the total insecurity of the Atlantic sea crossing, owing to attacks by German submarines, ended shipping.

Table 2.1
Portuguese living abroad, by country, 2007

Country	Number living abroad
Europe	**1,580,298**
Austria	2,000
Belgium	35,000
Czech Republic	160
Denmark	752
Finland	290
France	791,388
Germany	115,606
Greece	494
Ireland	1,798
Italy	4,210
Luxembourg	70,000
Monaco	700
Norway	1,038
Netherlands	17,927
Poland	316
Romania	155
Spain	82,700
Sweden	3,000
Switzerland	189,015
United Kingdom & Channel Islands	250,000
Other	178
Americas	**2,839,521**
Argentina	13,147
Bermuda	11,000
Brazil	700,000
Canada	357,690
Chile	575
Colombia	280
Dominican Republic	153
Dutch Antilles	3,022
Ecuador	269
Mexico	513
Panama	250
Peru	156
United States	1,349,161
Uruguay	3,000
Venezuela	400,000
Other	305
Africa	**376,696**
Algeria	116

Table 2.1 (*continued*)

Country	Number living abroad
Angola	45,000
Botswana	120
Cape Verde	8,834
Republic of Congo (Congo – Brazzaville)	162
Democratic Republic of the Congo (Congo – Zaire)	762
Guinea-Bissau	1,827
Kenya	663
Malawi	308
Morocco	459
Mozambique	13,021
Namibia	1,502
South Africa	300,000
São Tome and Principe	943
Swaziland	1,104
Tunisia	139
Zimbabwe	1,200
Other	536
Asia	**156,611**
China	230
East Timor	400
Hong Kong SAR	10,000
India	4,399
Israel	389
Japan	416
Macau SAR	140,000
Philippines	112
Thailand	120
Other	545
Oceania	**15,730**
Australia	15,440
New Zealand	290
Total	4,968,856

Note: Figures are precise or rounded, according to available data.
Source: Ministry of Foreign Affairs 2007.

During peacetime emigrants of Azorean origin dominated migration to the United States, primarily because family members had settled there since the previous century. The main settlement areas continued to be the northern part of the eastern coast and California, where the immigrants enjoyed significant prosperity (Taft [1923] 1969; Pinho 1978; Pap 1981; Monteiro 1987; Baganha 1990; Vicente 1998).[4] A great impetus to migration occurred in 1958 with passage of the Azorean Refugee Act – after an initiative taken by Senator John F. Kennedy of Massachusetts – which allowed entry to persons displaced by the eruption of the Capelinhos volcano in the archipelago. In the 1960s and 1970s Portuguese immigration exceeded 1,000 people a month on average, with more than half of them coming from the Azores. In the next two decades, however, these numbers fell to some 2,000 to 3,000 annually.

Brazil remained the chosen destination for the majority of Portuguese emigrants from the northern half of Portugal. The vast colony of people of northern Portuguese origin in Brazil attracted them, as did language and cultural affinity, which facilitated integration. However, significant movements to other countries began in the second half of the twentieth century.

In the case of Canada, Portuguese emigration became significant only after 1953. This was the year when 550 Portuguese – all male – were recruited from the mainland, the Azores, and Madeira in a process coordinated by the Portuguese and Canadian authorities. Ever larger contingents followed in subsequent years, until the maximum annual figure of 16,300 was reached in 1974. Today it is estimated that the number of residents of Portuguese origin in Canada is about 360,000, of whom about 60 to 70 per cent come from the Azores (see Table 2.1). The largest Portuguese community is in Toronto, where more than half of the total reside, with significant numbers also in Quebec, British Columbia, and Manitoba (Da Rosa and Teixeira 1996; Teixeira 1999; Moura and Soares 2003; Oliveira and Teixeira 2004; Coelho 2007).

Another new destination in the late twentieth century has been Venezuela, as a result of the surge of wealth created by the oil fields in the southern part of the Gulf of Mexico. Family migration to Venezuela came primarily from the district of Aveiro, in north-central continental Portugal, and from Madeira. Several large Portuguese communities sprang up, which prospered in the wholesale and retail trade and in the service industry, especially urban and intercity transport. Despite the international oil crisis of the 1970s, the internal economic crisis in Venezuela in the late 1980s, and some degree of civil insecurity in more recent years, the community has grown and prospered and is now estimated at 400,000 people.

Although it was much smaller emigration to Argentina also took place in the postwar period, expanding on an initial nucleus of Portuguese who had settled there in the 1920s. This new group came mainly from the eastern half of the Algarve province in the south of Portugal (Ferreira 1976; Borges 1997), as well as from the Cape Verde islands, then under Portuguese sovereignty (Poteca 1993). Given the seafaring background of these emigrants, it is not surprising that they devoted themselves above all to fishing, boat building, and ship fitting. The community in Argentina is now estimated at about 13,000 people.

The case of Portuguese emigration to South Africa is distinct from the flow to most countries because of its 'accidental' origins. The largest group of such immigrants hailed originally from Madeira, which was on the sea route between Britain and its colonies in Africa; Madeirans were carried along by the stream of Britons, both public officials and colonists, heading for South Africa. Once there the Madeirans dedicated themselves to farming, trade, and services.

South Africa also enjoyed a temporary migration of Portuguese colonists from Mozambique who had moved there to find work in the mines. Because Mozambique shared a common border with South Africa and had easy access to it, when the Portuguese colonies of Angola and Mozambique became independent in 1975, there followed a massive exodus of Portuguese of European origin not only back to Portugal but also to South Africa. In the following decades the tide of emigration from Madeira to South Africa continued, and even intensified, until the total number of people of Portuguese origin in the country reached a maximum of 600,000. However, subsequent civil unrest and lack of security sharply reduced the number of Portuguese residents to about 300,000 at present.

Australia completes this story. Japanese occupation of Timor and the island's subsequent liberation by the Allied armies (of which the Australians were a part) brought to Australia many of the Portuguese who had been serving or living in the Portuguese colony, and many settled there permanently. Others followed, primarily from the Portuguese territory of Macao in south-east China. Australia continues today to be a destination favoured by the Portuguese, given its rapid growth, low population density, numerous job opportunities, and chances to prosper. The community is estimated at 15,440 persons.[5]

Intra-European Emigration

After the Second World War northern Europe experienced a period of explosive economic growth, mostly due to the benefits of the Marshall Plan. This led to the creation of new jobs, especially in the industrial (primarily construction) and service sectors. The movement of local workforces to the more highly skilled and better-paid jobs created a vacuum in the supply of manual labour, which was filled by foreign workers from the Mediterranean basin. Besides the Portuguese were Italians, Spaniards, Turks, Greeks, Yugoslavs, North Africans, and many other nationalities. In competition with these others the Portuguese found open work markets in France, Germany, and other European countries that were hungry for unskilled labour. In the 1960s and 1970s, when more than 1.5 million Portuguese emigrated, representing one-sixth of the Portuguese population, over 1 million of them moved within Europe.

West Germany accepted only legal immigrants, but most destination countries received undocumented immigrants who had crossed the border illegally.[6] Indeed, clandestine emigration, which was not new to Portugal, was predominant in this flow. The fact that one could travel from Portugal to any European country by land made it relatively easy for emigrants to cross borders by interrupting the journey by rail or road and then just walking, generally at night and away from places where lines of communication crossed borders. A vast number of scientific works, newspaper articles, films, and videos have been produced on this subject.

Although movement into France began slowly it grew steadily, and in 1963 overtook emigration to Brazil. Portuguese settlement in France in the 1990s was estimated at around 1 million. Other European destinations have been Germany, Belgium, Britain, Holland, and Scandinavia. German leads this group with about 116,000 Portuguese (Table 2.1). In Luxembourg Portuguese account for almost 15 per cent of the population and one-third of its workforce.

The Swiss have always had a policy of temporary immigration, and historically many Portuguese worked there on a yearly or seasonal basis. Some flexibility in recent legislation has allowed long-term temporary workers to be given permanent work permits, however, and Switzerland has now become the European country with the highest number of Portuguese immigrants after France and the United Kingdom.

The entire European pattern of emigration/immigration changed suddenly in the 1970s with the onset of a widespread economic depression. The downturn not only halted the progress and pace of development of European countries but also severely affected the flow of imported labour, which until then had been a major economic support. Among working populations immigrants were at the bottom of the pyramid of professional skills. Formerly considered productive and useful, they soon came to be seen a dispensable burden. Thus, their host countries came to be referred to as receiving countries (with a somewhat negative connotation).

The oil crisis of 1973–4 changed the fate of the human pieces on the chessboard of international interests, with consequences that lasted throughout the 1970s. Europe experienced widespread unemployment (Pérez 1981; Kubat 1984; Ferreira and Clausse 1986; Rocha-Trindade 1988). At first European governments found a rather simplistic, pragmatic solution: they would send foreign workers home, along with their families. Sending immigrants back to their countries of origin would ensure the financial survival of domestic companies, which claimed that they could not keep employment at its former high levels. Foreign workers would therefore be the first target in staff reductions. However, as we now know, many jobs taken by imported labour are not the type that host nationals would ever accept. This fact, together with the political unpalatability of forced repatriation, led to alternative, more moderate solutions.

In countries of origin such as Portugal, the closing of borders to new emigrants caused concern, aggravated by the failure of recent attempts to open up new markets for Portuguese emigration. The lack of security in Portuguese-speaking Africa (a possible alternative destination) limited the number of emigrants to those countries. Most were people who signed short-term cooperation agreements. Other countries with strong demand for qualified technical personnel (the Maghreb countries and the Middle East) generally offered only fixed-term contracts, as well as living conditions unlikely to attract family emigration.

By the end of this period only some traditional non-European destinations (mainly the United States, Canada, and Venezuela) continued to show some permeability, and of the new destinations only South Africa and Australia were significant. The near end of emigration within Europe did not rule out two possibilities: short- and mid-term temporary emigration for the purposes of agricultural work, construction, and the hotel industry, especially in Switzerland and France; and the reunification of families, which, though severely restricted, still led to a significant number of departures. Portugal's entry into the European Community (EC) in January 1986 changed the legal status of Portuguese residents in member countries, as well as that of those seeking a new labour market, from 'economic emigrants' to 'resident EC citizens.' Later, 1988 saw full implementation of the principle of free circulation of persons within the EC (now with the new designation of European Union, EU).

The change in status removed entries and exits from Portugal to EU countries from migration statistics, making Portuguese intra-European migration difficult to establish accurately. This has not meant the end of Portuguese migration into Europe but a change in the profile of problems to be solved. It is obvious that settling in a different country within the EU requires the individual to possess some visible means of living, be it self-employment, paid work, or access to legitimate financial revenues. However, there is no way to prevent a European citizen from seeking work in a foreign country, even if this migration is kept from the knowledge of both local authorities and those in the country of origin. The 'unofficial' status of such migrants leads easily into exploitation such as reduced wages, excessive working hours, lack of social support, and possibly even unacceptable living conditions.

Destinies such as the United Kingdom, Spain, Holland, and Iceland have been recently favoured by Portuguese irregular emigrants. When cases of work exploitation have been detected and brought to public knowledge in these countries, they have led to the intervention of Portuguese and local authorities, with resulting improvements. The Portuguese government has launched an intensive campaign advising prospective immigrants to EU countries to take suitable precautions to avoid being caught in difficult situations stemming from irregular status abroad.

For a general view of Portuguese migrants living in more than 150 different countries, see Table 2.1. The designation 'Other' refers to the sum of Portuguese in those countries with fewer than one hundred Portuguese residents each. It should be noted that some of the figures in the table are estimates rather than precise statistics; nevertheless, it is fair to assume that 5 million is the right order of magnitude of the Portuguese living abroad – the equivalent to one-half of the resident population of the country.

Immigration and Return Migration to Portugal

We have so far focused on the departure of Portuguese from their European territory to two distinct types of destination: first, dependent territories (Brazil up to 1822 and Portuguese colonies in Africa, Asia, and Oceania up to 1975); and, second, the same territories after their independence, plus other countries. Strictly speaking, movement of the first type was internal migration.

We can now analyse the three types of movements in the opposite direction – from other countries to Portugal – in a similar perspective. First, if immigrants are residents of former Portuguese territories, who have retained Portuguese nationality after independence, their departure for Portugal is the equivalent to a return of nationals. Second, if they are foreign citizens, their movement constitutes international immigration. Third, if they are immigrants to or born in a foreign country but hold Portuguese nationality, their movements constitute a return migration. There are numerous examples of all three in recent history, but they are not always easy to identify and classify.

The Return of Nationals

The return of nationals as a result of Portuguese decolonization in Asia and Africa began in 1961 (Rocha-Trindade 1987, 1995). India's occupation of the Estado da Índia (the Portuguese state of India: Goa, Damão, and Diu) began this process. It led to a sudden influx of refugees of both European and Asian origin into Mozambique, just across the Indian Ocean, and to continental Portugal. The outbreak of wars of liberation in Angola, Mozambique, and Guinea-Bissau also produced a significant influx of residents of European origin, as well as young Africans whose academic training Portugal wished to encourage. Labourers from Cape Verde also arrived to occupy jobs left by Portuguese doing military service (mainly overseas) or by emigrants and came to make up the oldest and largest Portuguese-speaking African community in Portugal (Carreira 1977).

The 1974 collapse of dictatorship in Portugal and the end of the colonial war in Africa and ensuing rapid decolonization helped reverse population movements in and out of Portugal. The turbulent emergence of new African states in 1975 led to the repatriation of at least 500,000 Portuguese – perhaps as many as 800,000, or about 8 per cent of the country's population. Of returnees, 61 per cent came from Angola, 33 per cent from Mozambique, and 6 per cent from other former colonies (Pires et al. 1984: 38). Of those who returned 60 per cent were born in continental Portugal, and the remaining 40 per cent included not only their descendants but also a number of African born or people who had been granted Portuguese nationality.

Returned nationals from East Timor and Macau came to Portugal because of unusual circumstances. In legal terms both territories had formerly been under Portuguese administration but followed different paths after Portugal returned to democracy in 1974. Although the People's Republic of China claimed sovereignty over Macao, it agreed to continued Portuguese administration of the territory until December 1999. East Timor proclaimed its independence in 1975 but was immediately occupied by Indonesia on the argument that it was a part of that country, a situation that was not recognized by the United Nations.

The political and social instability that resulted from the war of resistance throughout East Timor ended only with a referendum that conceded independence to the Timorese people. The referendum took effect on 20 May 2002, and between 1975 and 2002 many Timorese moved to Portugal as refugees. Most have since returned to their home country.

With the return of Macau to full Chinese sovereignty on 20 December 1999, most of the Portuguese civil servants resident there returned to Portugal, as did the portion of the population of Macau that held Portuguese nationality. Whatever the ancestry of people from Macau now living in Portugal, their full citizenship rights have led to an almost complete integration within Portuguese society.

The present relationship of Portugal with these two territories and their populations are excellent, both in political and social terms. Many cooperative initiatives have been established at the level of government and civil society. In the case of East Timor (Timor-Leste) the scope of the cooperation between the two states encompasses police and security forces, education, and justice and civil administration; for Macau, now a Special Administrative Region (SAR) of China, the cooperation extends mostly to commercial, industrial, and cultural exchanges.

Return Migration

As a rule, trans-oceanic Portuguese migration tended to lead to permanent settlement except in two extreme situations: first, complete failure to reach the objectives sought because of bad health or simply bad luck; and second, significant success, encouraging return to the country of origin. In cases of family emigration with children born and brought up in the receiving country, however, such a return has sometimes been difficult because of a lack of motivation on the part of the descendants.

With intra-European migration close proximity allows for regular trips back and forth, and no final decision on permanent residence is necessary. Indefinite postponement of the decision is common, even though the desire to return to Portugal persists and becomes, in the end, a utopian dream (Rocha-Trindade 1983). Serious economic crises and higher unemployment, as occurred in much of Europe during the oil crisis, or outbreaks of xenophobia, as took place particularly in France and Germany in the early 1990s, can, however, make a definitive decision necessary.

That said, advances in transportation technologies allow for inexpensive mass transit over long distances, facilitating temporary return on holidays. This constitutes a new way for Portuguese to retain links with their origins while living their migratory experience.

International Immigration

International migration to Portugal from African Portuguese-speaking countries is closely related to the return of nationals, which by creating a precedent stimulates the emigratory options of citizens living in those former colonies.[7] Knowledge of the language and the presence of family and acquaintances in Portugal facilitate such moves. According to information provided by the Portuguese border control and immigration authorities, 139,828 foreigners from Portuguese-speaking African countries resided in Portugal by the end of 2006, representing 32.1 per cent of authorized foreign residents. Cape Verdeans make up one of the largest communities of foreigners, with 65,485 residents.

In reverse of the former Portuguese emigration to Brazil, many Brazilians are now migrating to Portugal for the same reasons of linguistic and cultural affinity. This immigration consists mostly of young adults, some with professional qualifications and even specialists in professions such as dentistry, design, marketing and advertising, tourism, and show business. Another, less qualified group finds more modest jobs in industry and commerce. Today the size of the rather heterogeneous Brazilian immigrant community ranks high among foreign communities, with 65,423 legal residents: 15 per cent of the foreign resident population. Furthermore, the estimated number of Brazilians staying illegally in Portugal is possibly higher than 40,000, making the overall national group the largest among immigrant populations.

The geographical origin of foreigners settled in Portugal is not limited to Portuguese-speaking countries in Africa and Brazil: a new influx of migrants since the very end of the twentieth century came from eastern European countries, namely Ukraine, Moldova, Romania, and Russia.

The number of immigrants from the European Union, primarily Britain, France, Germany, and Spain, as well as from North America is very significant, with about 20 per cent of total foreign residents. Their socio-economic status is higher than that of the majority of the previously mentioned countries. The underlying motivation for this category of immigrant appears to be the renaissance of political, economic, and social life that followed the consolidation of Portuguese democracy, which attracted new foreign investment aimed mainly at tourism, trade, agriculture, and the service sector. These investments are promoted mainly by Americans and Europeans, some of whom have settled in Portugal.

Numerous immigrants' associations are springing up almost explosively. In light of the economic immigration of unskilled or semi-skilled workers and their relatively recent arrival, these organizations play a crucial role in defending the rights of the respective communities and establishing dialogue and negotiation with Portuguese authorities.[8]

The similarities between the associative movements of Portuguese emigrants abroad (several thousands worldwide) and those of immigrants in Portugal are not coincidental. The flows and counter-flows of people, through their physical, emotional, and cultural intermingling, are but two moments, forever being renewed, of the same wave. For an abridged view of the quantitative aspects of immigration into Portugal, see Figure 2.1.

Characteristics of the Portuguese Diaspora

Adopting the pragmatic principle that it is essential for authors to be faithful to and coherent about the definitions they adopt, I should note the following about my concept of the diaspora: 'The term Dias-

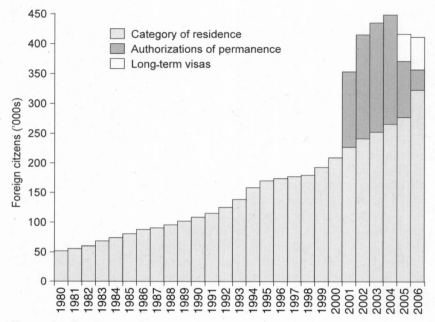

Figure 2.1 Foreign citizens living legally in Portugal, 1980–2006

pora means the dispersion of significant part of a population, concentrated originally on a well-defined cultural/national space, towards different areas of the globe, away from their original territory. It goes further to assume that this dispersion stays besides several generations lives and that, despite that, those groups or expatriated communities continue to manifest the purpose of identifying themselves with its ancestors national origin and to take as reference some of the cultural lines that are their characteristics' (Rocha-Trindade 1995: 141; 2006: 51–73).

It should be mentioned that not all scholars agree about the meaning of diaspora. In particular, those who are rooted in historical-philosophical disciplines will have difficulty extrapolating the concept beyond its classic application to the Jews, especially if they are not familiar with the sociological literature about migrations published in recent years. Divergence also exists among those who consider an essential characteristic of diasporas to be that they are the result of a catastrophic movement of dispersion, with a deep traumatic component and those who consider this to be a simple indicator of a special type of diaspora, not the totality of its typology (Cohen 1997).

From the lay point of view politicians, media communicators, and ethnic communities themselves have adopted the diaspora concept and used it extensively to consolidate the strength of foreign presences in a new country, to emphasize the unity of such groups and communities, and to show their networking potential in transnational terms (Bordes-Benayoun and Schnapper 2006).

Arguments can be invoked in favour of one or another of these positions, which I consider to be restrictive and enlarged, respectively. The supplemental imposition of the catastrophic requirement neither adds to nor modifies either the migrants' eventual motivation or the likelihood that their will keep a sense of belonging, desire to return to their land of origin, and maintain close links with their original culture.

Analysis of the various migratory movements of Portuguese has revealed a series of trends. The first relates to the regular and constant flow of departing Portuguese, beginning in the fifteenth century and continuing until present times, which led historian Magalhães-Godinho (1974) to characterize emigration as 'a structural phenomenon of Portuguese society.' A second characteristic is its extreme dispersion among numerous countries, on all continents where the Portuguese have settled, living in relative harmony with a vast variety of faces, cultures, and religions.

Related to this second point is the Portuguese ability to integrate into different social and cultural contexts, learning the local language, adopting daily practices, and very often intermarrying with people from the majority society. The first generation has usually reached a reasonable level of social insertion into the receiving country after only a few years, and the successive generations generally consider themselves integrated from the beginning. In such circumstances the Portuguese and Luso-descendent communities that have sprung up in foreign countries firmly reject any tendency to self-segregation. However, their integrationism seems to coexist with a deep feeling of identification with their roots – with Portugal – and, particularly within the first generation, with the region of the country from whence their progenitors came. There is a need to visit Portugal to locate family, and to maintain permanent contact with acquaintances in the faraway country of origin. Many emigrants recall or re-create types of behaviour and cultural features evocative of their ancestral legacy, which is thus continued and renewed, sometimes in hybrid and syncretic forms.

Even when the Portuguese language has been lost, there still remains a tendency to seek the company of other people of the same origin, in associative groups that have taken different forms in each place and in each period, have varied purposes, and engage in varied types of activities. Through such associations groups of people of Portuguese origin have sought to identify interests that lead them back to their original common reference points and enable them to construct symbols capable of lending form and expression to such references. Intertwining the flags of the distant country with that of the present one is possibly the most frequent symbol and no doubt the one that best represents shared feeling of belonging among these 'hyphenated Portuguese' (Rocha-Trindade 1989; Nunes 2007).

Recent Portuguese official initiatives related directly to emigration issues have been intended to stimulate the feelings of the general population about this phenomenon. Two public exhibitions were launched in 2007: *Terra Longe, Terra Perto* (Close-by Land, Faraway Land), in the city of Setubal; and *Traços da Diáspora Portuguesa* (Marks of the Portuguese Diaspora), in Lisbon. Both include objects, documents, and images pertaining to the general theme of Portuguese emigration. A television documentary series broadcast in the same year on the general subject of Portuguese emigration (*Ei-los que Partem!*) has experienced considerable success. A week of cinema productions dedicated to similar issues took place in January 2008.

As well, over the last few years a major effort has been put into the creation of the Museu da Emigração e das Comunidades (Museum of Emigration and Portuguese Communities) in the northern city of Fafe, in the district of Minho. In addition to objects directly linked to emigration and return from Brazil and elsewhere, the museum contains a very comprehensive interactive database of genealogies, family and official documents, scientific papers, and books, all of them concerning Portuguese emigration issues (Rocha-Trindade and Monteiro 2007a, 2007b).

It is obvious that Portugal remains, as a country and a national identity, profoundly permeated by the realities of migration. Whether this is emigration, return migration or, more recently, immigration, the Portuguese remain fully aware of the importance of migrations in Portuguese history to this day.

NOTES

1 Many Portuguese writers at the turn of the nineteenth to the twentieth century turned their attention to what was then considered 'the emigration problem.' Among these were Herculano (1879), Costa (1911), and Silva (1917), who left a rich store of information about the phenomenon, situating it within the national and international economic and political context of their times through descriptions that not only indicate the origin of the flow of emigrants but also represent its size. Using macroscopic approaches, they link up the social variables that underlie the causes, growth, and characteristics of emigration. Their works became reference points for the writers who once more took up the theme of global analysis of emigration in the 1960s and 1970s: Serrão (1971), Magalhães-Godinho (1974), and Almeida and Barreto (1974).

2 The abolition of slavery marks the end of one phase and the beginning of another in the immigration process in Brazil. The Aurea Law, or Law of Redemption, which abolished slavery in 1888, was preceded by a series of laws that progressively traced out the path to freedom. First came the Law of Free Womb, known also as the Law of the Unborn, which in 1871 made free the children of slave mothers. The Law of the Sexagenarians in 1885 gave freedom to slaves over sixty years of age.

3 The Sandwich Islands were one of the destinations preferred not only by emigrants from the Atlantic Portuguese archipelagos, in particular Madeira, but also by a significant number of people from the district of Serpa in the Alentejo, in south-central Portugal. In 1910 and 1911 close to 1,000 Portuguese fled drought and the disastrous consequence of a weak attempt at agricultural reform. On a single voyage an English ship carried 500 to Hawaii. As the newspaper *Diário de Notícias* wrote at the time, it was an exodus of the starving. According to *Boletim da Câmara Municipal de Serpa*, April–May 1977, this was the first large-scale emigration from the Alentejo. Dias (1981) wrote about the Portuguese presence in Hawaii and also produced a video about their presence, in both Portuguese and English versions. The images that illustrate his work are based on Felix and Senecal (1978). The technical features of international

means of transport profoundly affected the voyages made by emigrants in the early twentieth century.

4 The writings of many scholars, novelists, and journalists of Portuguese origin – some resident in the United States, others already back in Portugal – provide data on Portuguese emigration to that country, letting us trace chronologically the long and lasting route that connects the two sides of the 'Atlantic River' (Almeida 1997). These analyses present the Luso-American way of life (Almeida 1987) and link the two reference points – a forever present origin and a totally adopted destination – that they do not want to abandon. Among other writers see, for example, Dias 1981, Chaplin 1990, and Freitas 1990.

5 Today both Australia and Canada clearly restrict immigration in terms of age and professional profile.

6 This was legal immigration but was intended to be temporary. For this reason, migrants have always been known there as *Gästarbeiter* (guest workers), which in practice has not been the case.

7 African Portuguese-speaking countries are designated PALOPs, from the initials of the corresponding Portuguese expression, *Países Africanos de Língua Oficial Portuguesa*.

8 The legal existence of associations not only constitutes recognition of the presence of immigrants in their new country but also allows them as a group to present legitimate complaints, which, on an individual basis, might not have been heard by decision makers. The creation of such associations has generally been supported by the authorities of the country of origin, who, through them, establish a connection with the immigrants for political and economic reasons. Portuguese governments after the 1974 revolution have helped these associations of immigrants; in 1996 the government set up a High Commissioner for Immigration and Ethnic Minorities, attached to the prime minister's office. Since 2007 this organization has been called the High Commissioner for Immigration and Intercultural Dialogue/ACIDI.

REFERENCES

Almeida, C., and A. Barreto. 1974. *Capitalismo e Emigração em Portugal*. Lisbon: Prelo.

Almeida, O.T. 1987. *L(USA)LÂNDIA: A Décima Ilha*. Angra do Heroísmo: Direcção de Serviços de Emigração / Açores.

– 1997. *Rio Atlântico*. Lisbon: Edições Salamandra.

Baganha, M.I.B. 1990. *Portuguese Emigration to the United States, 1820–1930*. New York: Garland.

Bordes-Benayoun, C., and D. Schnapper. 2006. *Diasporas et nations*. Paris: Odile Jacob.

Borges, M.J. 1997. 'Portuguese in Two Worlds: A Historical Study of Migration from Algarve to Argentina.' PhD diss., Rutgers University.

Carreira, A. 1977. *Migrações nas Ilhas de Cabo Verde*. Lisbon: Universidade Nova de Lisboa.

Chaplin, M.D.L. 1990. *Retalhos de Portugal Dispersos pelos Estados Unidos da América: Mulheres Migrantes de Descendência Portuguesa*. Farmingdale, NJ: M.D.L. Chaplin.

Coelho, J.M. 2007. *Pequenas Histórias de Gente Grande*. Toronto: Creative 7.

Cohen, M.E. 1997. 'Deconstructing Diaspora Dreams.' MA thesis, University of Toronto.

Costa, A. 1911. *Estudos de Economia Nacional I: O Problema da Emigração*. Lisbon: Imprensa Nacional.

Da Rosa, V.M.P., and C. Teixeira. 1986. 'O Multiculturalismo Canadiano e o Futuro dos Açorianos no Quebec.' *Arquipélago* 9 and 10: 217–37.

Dias, E.M. 1981. *A Presença Portuguesa no Havai*. Lisbon: Separata do Boletim Cultural da Assembleia Distrital de Lisboa.

Felix, J.H., and P.F. Senecal. 1978. *The Portuguese in Hawaii*. Honolulu: Centennial.

Ferreira, E.S. 1976. *Origens e Formas da Emigração*. Lisbon: Iniciativas Editoriais.

Ferreira, E.S., and G. Clausse, eds. 1986. *Closing the Migratory Cycle: The Case of Portugal*. Social Science Studies on International Problems no. 11. Saarbrucken: Breitenback.

Freitas, V.A. 1990. *Jornal da Emigração: A L(USA)LÂNDIA Reinventada*. Angra do Heroísmo: Gabinete de Emigração e Apoio às Comunidades Açorianas.

Herculano, A. 1879. 'A Emigração 1873–1875.' In *Opuscullos*, 105–294. Lisbon: Viúva Bertrand e Ca. Sucessores Carvalho e Ca.

Kubat, D., ed. 1984. *The Politics of Return: International Return Migration in Europe*. Rome: Centro Studi Emigrazione / Centre for Migration Studies.

Magalhães-Godinho, V. 1974. 'L'émigration portugaise du XVe siècle à nos jours: Histoire d'une constante structurale.' In *Conjoncture economique, structures sociales: Mélanges en honneur*, ed. C.E. Labrousse, 253–68. Paris: Mouton.

Martins, J.P.O. 1956. *Fomento Rural e Emigração*. Lisbon: Guimarães.

Ministry of Foreign Affairs. 2007. *General Directorate for Consular Affair and Portuguese Communities*. Lisbon: Ministry of Foreign Affairs.

Monteiro, P. 1987. 'Luso-Americanos no Connecticut: Questões de etnicidade e de comunidade.' *Povos e Culturas* no. 2: 765–913.

Moura, M.A. 1992. *Les Portugais dans l'exploration et la colonisation de l'est du Canada au XVIe siècle*. Montreal: N.p.

Moura, M.A., and I. Soares. 2003. *Pionniers: L'avant-garde de l'immigration portugaise – Montréal, Canada 1953*. Montreal: Privately printed.

Nunes, L.P.S. 2007. *Caminhos do Divino. Um Olhar sobre a Festa do Espírito Santo em Santa Catarina*. Florianópolis: Editora Insular.

Oliveira, M.A., and C. Teixeira. 2004. *Jovens Portugueses e Luso-Descendentes no Canadá: Trajectórias de Inserção em Espaços Multiculturais*. Oeiras: Celta Editora.

Pap, L. 1981. *The Portuguese-Americans*. Boston: Twayne Publishers.

Pérez, J.C. 1981. *Emigración y Retorno: Una Perspectiva Europea*. Madrid: Instituto Español de Emigración.

Pinho, Helder. 1978. *Portugueses na Califórnia: A História e o Quotidiano de uma das mais Vivas Comunidades Lusas no Mundo*. Lisbon: Notícias.

Pires, R.P. et al. 1984. *Os Retornados: Um Estudo Sociográfico*. Lisbon: Instituto de Estudos para o Desenvolvimento.

Poteca, M.M. 1993. 'Los Immigrantes Caboverdeanos en la Argentina, una Minoria Invisible.' *Museo* 1: 1–40.

Rocha, R. 1983. 'Apontamentos sobre a Comunidade Portuguesa de Hawaii.' *Anais do Clube Militar Naval* no. 1–3: 253–83.

Rocha-Trindade, M.B. 1983. *O Regresso Imaginado*. Lisbon: Instituto de Defesa Nacional (Separata).

– 1987. *O Fenómeno Migratório na Região Centro: Regresso e Reinserção na Diocese de Coimbra*. Coimbra: Comissão de Coordenação da Região Centro / Secretaria de Estado das Comunidades Portuguesas / Caritas Diocesana de Coimbra.– 1988. *População Escolar Directa e Indiractamente Ligada à Emigração*. Lisbon: Universidade Aberta.

– 1989. 'A Presença dos Ausentes.' *Sociedade e Território: Revista de Estudos Urbanos e Regionais* 3 no. 8: 8–16.

– 1995. *Sociologia das Migrações*. Lisbon: Universidade Aberta.

– 2002. *Portugal – Brasil: Migrações e Migrantes 1850–1930*. Lisbon: Edições INAPA.

– 2006. 'Un peuple de tradition migratoire: Le cas du Portugal,' In *La Immigració, Una Oportunitat?* 51–73. Andorra: Govern d'Andorra.

Rocha-Trindade, M.B., and M. Monteiro. 2007a. 'Museums Devoted to Migration: The Portuguese Emigration Museum.' *Museum International* no. 233–34: 145–50.

– 2007b. 'Il Museu da Emigração e das Comunidades, Fafe, Portogallo.' *Studi Emigrazione*, 44, no. 167: 588–96.

Sérgio, A. 1956. *Antologia Sociológica*. Lisbon: Privately printed.

Serrão, J. 1971. *Emigração Portuguesa: Sondagem Histórica*. Lisbon: Livros Horizonte.

Silva, F.E. 1917. *Emigração Portuguesa*. Lisbon: Tipografia Universal.

Taft, D.R. [1923] 1969. *Two Portuguese Communities in New England, 1910–1920*. New York: Arno Press and the New York Times.

Teixeira, C. 1999. *Portugueses em Toronto Uma Comunidade em Mudança*. Açores: Direcção Regional das Comunidades.

Vicente, A.L. 1998. *Os Portugueses nos Estados Unidos da América*. Lisbon: Fundação Luso-Americana para o Desenvolvimento.

PART ONE

Newfoundland and the White Fleet

3 The White Fleet and the Iconography of Control

PRISCILLA A. DOEL

This chapter looks, first, at the history of the codfishing fleet up to 1950; second, at the Golden Age of the White Fleet through the 1970s; third, at the iconography of its pride and joy, the *Gil Eannes*; and fourth, at the decline of the fleet and at historical conservation efforts.

Historical Introduction

The Early Years

Cod ... *bacalhau*. For centuries, salt cod was the staple of many a poor country's diet, including Portugal's. Cod was the fish found in almost unlimited quantity from the time that John Cabot in 1497 reported taking them up in abundance by means of weighted baskets. *Bacalhau* was the fish that brought the Portuguese codfishing schooners (*bacalhoeiros*) of Portugal's Great White Fleet to the Grand Banks of Newfoundland – and particularly into St John's harbour – where the fishing captains sought shelter from hurricanes spawned in the Caribbean or for supplies or repairs from the 1940s until the early 1970s.

A reference to cod on the 1529 *Tierra de los bacallaos* map states that 'up until now nothing of value has been found with the exception of codfish which are held in little esteem' (Cortesao and da Mota 1960). Although the cod seemed not to have had value at that time or to that cartographer, three years later another cartographer noted of Tierra Nueva de los Bacallaos that 'this land was discovered by the Portuguese ... there is nothing of value here except for the cod which is a fish and a very good one. Here the Corte Reales [explorers] were lost' (Cortesao and da Mota 1960). The charts of the day spread the news that the Portuguese were in these areas and that codfish was abundant and good to eat.

Portugal's codfishing on the Grand Banks continued on a regular seasonal basis until Portugal, having been annexed by Spain in 1580, was forced to contribute all vessels above a minimum size and burthen to Spain's grandiose preparations in gathering together and outfitting an Invincible Armada to do battle against England (Martin and Parker 1988). Although one of the staples in the diet of the seamen who trained on these ships was cod or tunny, served on Tuesdays, Fridays, and Saturdays (Valadão do Valle 1991), it was to become scarce, for the British defeat of the Armada dealt such a blow to Portuguese maritime activities that significant distant-water sailing stopped for 300 years.

Modern Organization

Not until the 1830s does there appear to have been any sizeable effort to organize long-distance codfishing to the Grand Banks. At that time the Companhia de Pescarias Lisbonense (1830–57) approached Britain for help in organizing, buying, and outfitting six schooners for the Grand Banks fishery (Moutinho 1985). This venture probably taught the Portuguese handlining techniques and the use of various tools, and possibly introduced them to the dory. The dory and tools, some with names of English origin, were to be used in the North Atlantic cod fisheries until 1974, when the last codfishing schooner left St John's harbour, bound for Portugal (Doel 1992).[1]

During the period 1866–1901 two companies controlled all Portuguese codfishing on the Grand Banks with a total of twelve ships. The fleet could not be augmented without tax penalties being levied. Mariano e Irmaos (1866–1903) operated three vessels, and Bensaude & Ca. (1866–1902) nine. The name of the latter changed in 1902 to Parceria Geral de Pescarias (Moutinho 1985).[2]

From 1900 to 1950

The Portuguese codfishing fleet continued to sail to the north-west Atlantic on its yearly campaigns for cod through the First World War, the Great Depression, the Second World War, the forty-year dictatorship of António de Oliveira Salazar and his Estado Novo (new state) corporatism (1926–66), and the '25 de Abril para sempre' (the 25th of April forever) revolution, until the present. During this century the politics surrounding the economics and administration of the fisheries underwent many changes. What started out as a small endeavour on the part of a few fishing companies trying to stay afloat while dealing with problems of supply and demand, foreign competition, taxes, and government instability became a strong and visible presence in New-foundland by the 1950s. By that time, although the fleet had grown, it had not kept abreast of technological advances in ship design. Portugal was slow among fishing nations of the world to introduce a significant number of trawlers, relying instead on handlining. During the First World War era, the necessity of organizing and protecting the growing industry was recognized and discussed by the stakeholder government and controlling companies. Between 1903 and 1914 the number of *bacalhoeiros* had grown from sixteen to thirty-four. By the end of the war there were just eleven, but the fleet expanded steadily until, by 1922, it consisted of sixty-five vessels (Manso and Cruz 1984).

The early twentieth century brought about growth in the size and carrying capacity of the fleet as new companies entered the fisheries, but development continued along unstable administrative and economic lines (Doel 1992). The 1930s saw struggle as the industry, in addition to fighting hard times in general, had to face fisheries-related issues such as low catches and workers' protest against the lack of reasonable contracts and insurance policies.[3] The 1930 campaign to the Grand Banks was so unproductive that the captain of the *Santa Mafalda* decided to set out, without charts, in search of the fabled Banks of Greenland. Although the courageous captain was unsuccessful, he had sown the seed of hope. The following year his vessel was accompanied by the *Santa Isabel*, the *Santa Joana*, and the *Santa Luzia*, with their captains from Ilhavo making their way through the fields of ice to the rich Banks of Greenland. From that time on the Greenland trip became an integral part of the yearly campaign.[4]

As the Estado Novo attempted to upgrade the fisheries in the 1930s, organizational structures emerged in keeping with its corporative policies. The Comissão Reguladora do Comércio de Bacalhau, the CRCB (Regulatory Commission of the Codfish Industry), was founded in 1934 and then restructured in order to control and protect Portuguese codfishing interests more effectively. It regulated prices paid to the supplier, built refrigerated warehouses, stabilized market prices, regulated imports of cod, modernized ships, and sent the first trawler, the *Santa Joana*, to the Grand Banks in the late 1930s. In addition, the Grémio dos Armadores de Navios de Pesca do Bacalhau, or GANPB

(Guild of Shipowners of Codfishing Vessels), was formed in 1935, followed by establishment of its insurance company, Mútua, one year later. The first trip of the first hospital supply ship, the *Carvalho Araújo*, took place in 1923, followed by the earliest voyage of the first *Gil Eannes* in 1927.

Organizational efforts during the following decade brought a serious labour problem to a head when recruitment for the 1937 campaign erupted in a famous strike: a state decree forced all those men participating in the 1936 campaign to enrol immediately for 1937; those who did not sign up were to be considered deserters. Violence and protest erupted but were immediately put down. According to the opinion of the day, the well-being of the Estado Novo – the Portuguese nation – was at stake (Moutinho 1985).

By 1938 the codfishing fleet was in desperate shape as it suffered financial, labour, and physical deterioration. Any significant growth during the Second World War was difficult because of the scarcity of materials and lack of interest by ship owners. In 1942 forty-five ships, duly authorized by the CRCB and full-fledged members of the GANPB, set out for the Grand Banks and Greenland (Manso and Cruz 1984).

Despite the dangers involved in sea travel during the Second World War Portugal continued sending ships to the north-west Atlantic, but they now travelled in convoy, strictly observing blackouts and radio silence. Sailing ships of different hull speed and motor capacity, trawlers, and the hospital supply ship *Gil Eannes* all crossed in silence. It was at this time that the term White Fleet was coined, by the convoy skippers: 'Portugal, who remained neutral during that conflict, had a pact with Germany not to attack its fishing fleet. It was agreed that all the hulls would be painted white with the ship's name in huge letters amid-ships, plus the flag. Prior to the war, our fleet (Parceria Geral de Pescarias, I mean) had oxblood hulls. They continued to be painted white after the war, however' (B.B. Frantz, personal communication, 1989).

During the war the Estado Novo very deliberately began to define and celebrate the role of the brave and God-fearing Portuguese doryman labouring on the Banks for the good of the Portuguese people (*pátria*) and for his own family (*família*). The first concrete example of this type of propaganda was the book written by Portuguese journalist and photographer Jorge Simões in 1942, *Os grandes trabalhadores do Mar*. The GNAPB invited him to accompany the fleet on its 1941 campaign, aboard the *Groenlândia* and the *Gil Eannes*. Through photographs and exciting accounts of storms, a fire aboard, encounters with Inuit, a meeting with the interpreter Pinto Hans, a collision, and many more adventures, his work gave the campaign the visibility and respect that it needed to become an acceptable part of the Estado Novo's social and economic policies.

Codfishing on the Grand Banks continued to prosper after the war, and Salazar, through politics and propaganda, controlled Portuguese society both at home and on the Banks. His Estado Novo was clearly a dictatorial form of government; being a contemporary of Hitler, Mussolini, and Franco, he used similar authoritarian and undemocratic policies such as secret police. The life of the doryman both at home and on the Banks had been characterized by misery, poverty, and repression, as had been the life of many Europeans and Americans during the Great Depression and the two world wars. Patriotism, religiosity, and family all intertwined as Portuguese society became more and more centred on the state, the church, and the family (*pátria, deus, família*) (Doel 1992).

The Golden Age and the *Gil Eannes*

Given Newfoundland's new status as a Canadian province in 1949, the 1950s marked the beginnings of restrictive Canadian policies and resource protection in territorial waters. By the early 1950s the International Commission of Northwest Atlantic Fisheries (ICNAF) was established, and the cod-abundant waters bordering Newfoundland (Canada) and Greenland (Denmark) were to be studied and evaluated with an eye to resource protection. Concomitantly, national territorial rights to the sea were extended from three miles to twelve, and later to 200. At the same time, however, technological innovation with the requisite capital inputs significantly increased the exploitative capacity of the fishery of most nations. Of particular note was the introduction of dragger fishing.

The 1950s also marked the move of the Portuguese codfishing fleet into international visibility and fame through Alan Villiers's 1951 book, *The Quest of the Schooner Argus*, followed by prominent articles in *National Geographic*. Villiers, a celebrated writer and a respected man of the sea, had been invited by the Portuguese ambassador in Washington to sail to Newfoundland and Greenland aboard one of the *bacalhoeiros*. This he did in 1950 aboard the beautiful and modern *Argus*, owned and managed by Portugal's oldest codfishing company, the Parceria Geral de Pescarias. His book took the story of the Portuguese White Fleet to the English-speaking world with a highly romanticized vision of the life of the humble, hard-working, God-fearing Portuguese fisherman. Meanwhile, through the visual and written propaganda of state and church ceremonies, newspaper articles, and the indispensable magazine *Jornal do Pescador*, the dictatorship at home continued to define and celebrate the role of the Portuguese fisherman for himself and for the rest of Portugal.

As Canada began to exert its territorial claims to the waters around the Grand Banks, Portugal, at home and abroad, continued to emphasize both the importance of its codfishing fleet on the Grand Banks and its traditional fishing rights in these waters. Without a doubt it intended the launch in 1955 of the new *Gil Eannes*, a hospital supply ship, to enhance and ensure its place in the Grand Banks fisheries. The editorial 'Welcome to the Portuguese' in the St John's *Evening Telegram* remarked that 'this year also marks the fifth century of the discovery of the Grand Banks by the Portuguese and the fourth century of their participation in the fisheries there.'[5] The new ship, whose medical services were rendered free to all fishermen on the Banks, was a majestic symbol of Portugal's past, present, and future presence in these cod-rich waters. It was fitting that the new *Gil Eannes* graced the period 1950–65: Portugal's Golden Age in the Grand Banks fisheries.

Of all the vessels on the Banks and in Canadian ports, the *Gil Eannes* best symbolized Portuguese pride, having been built in Viana do Castelo with domestic materials by native shipwrights and craftspeople. The glistening white new ship of state embodied the Estado Novo's principles regarding state, church, and family, and its name evoked Portugal's glorious days of exploration and discovery – the days of Gil Eannes rounding Cape Bojador in 1434. The vessel was a symbol of state control over the reorganized long-distance fisheries. This 323 ft, 4,854 ton, state-of-the-art, steel-hulled vessel watched over some 4,000 to 5,000 fishermen from the coastal villages of Portugal and the Azores, who were launched from some sixty to seventy vessels to fish in their one-man dories under the watchful eyes of their captains and officers. Although all ships were privately owned, all were united under the GANPB.

The *Gil Eannes* was designed for multiple functions. In addition to being a seagoing hospital ship, it carried supplies for the fleet: food, water, fuel, bait, and spare parts for repairs. It was also the fleet's communication control centre, with elaborate and powerful external and internal communication systems, and it carried an information-gathering bio-hydrographic laboratory. In addition, the ship housed a small chapel on the aft deck. The commander's quarters were the offi-. cial space for meetings between the commander, representatives of Portugal, ship captains, and dignitaries of other nations in ports of call. Wherever it went, the *Gil Eannes* was the symbol of Estado Novo ideology, reinforcing Portugal's traditional presence in North Atlantic waters, assisting its handlining fleet, and solidifying relations with Canada.

Moreover, while the captain of each ship worked for the owner of that vessel and had great latitude in determining where and when to fish on the Banks, how to treat or discipline his crew, and how to respond to emergencies related to the well-being of ship and crew, he was always subject to the authority of the commander of the *Gil Eannes*. The commander was Portugal's official representative in the North Atlantic – a figure to be respected and feared – a symbol in uniform of the Estado Novo.

When the new *Gil Eannes* came through the Narrows and entered the harbour of St John's in May of 1955, Newfoundland was ready to greet it. One reporter described the arrival as 'probably the most colourful and historic sight that St. John's had ever seen.'[6] On both sides of the Atlantic every detail of pageantry and ceremony had been minutely planned to showcase the Portuguese fisheries on the Grand Banks of Newfoundland. On 27 May, 4,000 Portuguese fishermen clad in their colourful checked shirts, walked fifteen to twenty abreast up the hilly streets of St John's to the Basilica of St John the Baptist, bearing the three-and-a-half-foot-high statue of Our Lady of Fátima, their gift of gratitude and friendship. Our Lady was to be a holy link between the two peoples, and even today worshippers pray before her in the specially prepared alcove to the left of the main altar. The 6,000 men and women who filled the cathedral, along with those who lined the streets, were part of 'one of the most colourful, inspiring, and solemn events ever to take place in St. John's.'[7]

State Icons on the *Gil Eannes*

Given constraints of time and distance related to management of the long-distance fisheries, it was difficult for the Estado Novo to maintain total control over the men of the Portuguese fleet. Fishing vessels moved from one fishing area to another and had frequent contacts with people from other nations in Canadian ports, where fishermen and captains alike experienced a less rigid, more democratic way of life – a challenge to Estado Novo systems of control.

In order to solidify unwavering commitment to *Deus, Pátria e Família*, the new *Gil Eannes* incorporated symbols of these concepts into decorative motifs. The state commissioned the Azorean artist Domingos Rebelo to paint two murals for the ship: one to grace a long wall of the commander's quarters, the other to enhance the altar of the little chapel on the aft deck. In accordance with the Estado Novo's use of moral symbols to justify the institutional arrangements of its political system, 'skill groups [such as artists] ... define and promulgate official images of the world and what is happening in it, official "definitions of the situation"' (Gerth and Mills 1953: 212–13).

The commander's quarters displayed Rebelo's colourful mural. Within the narrative frame of a state-sponsored mural, the artist visually reconstructs the epic story of the life of the Portuguese doryman in order to suppress other versions of that life, which was widely known as one of hard work, sacrifice, deprivation, and physical and psychological abuse (Figure 3.1). Most viewers probably did not analyse structure, style, or content of the image but merely reacted to symbols that they had internalized. Domingos Rebelo, however, guides the viewer/reader through the three narrative scenes surrounding the fisherman. For example, if we start with the fisherman in the foreground, we meet his gaze straight on. We become anchored to the mural with the oar that he holds with both hands. Then the circular motion of his arms lifts our eyes to the top of the oar and then directs our view to the left, letting us see family life at home in Portugal. The right-hand corner of the crib at bottom left redirects our eyes over the head of the boy and his teacher to the iceberg in the background behind the fisherman. We look from left to right and then return, directed by the oar to the other scene at home, where all fishermen, active or aged, are cared for. Through the integration on canvas of different artistic spaces and geographical places, the artist presents the life, idealized through memory, of a typical Portuguese dory fisherman on the Grand Banks (Figure 3.1).

As we consider the images we must ask who this stalwart, emotionless man dressed in the typical plaid flannel shirt is who meets our gaze head on? The message is clear. He is anonymous: the stereotype of the good, humble, obedient, stable fisherman. He is father and

Figure 3.1. Mural from the commander's quarters on the *Gil Eannes*, by Domingos Rebelo, 1955 (courtesy of Priscilla A. Doel)

husband. He is all the fishermen, on whom rest the responsibility for the well-being of *Pátria e Família*. He is the faithful Zé Pescador (José Fisherman) the central figure in a national mission.

The paternalistic role played by the Estado Novo in the life of the fisherman's family during a six-to-seven-month absence each year is seen to the left, where we see buildings representing health, education, and welfare programmes administered by the Estado Novo through the Junta Central de Casas de Pescadores. Prominent in the foreground is the son – the future fisherman – receiving instruction at the school of fishing and navigation. With his teacher he is studying a model of a sailing vessel. Behind the boy is a young girl learning to sew in order to fulfil her future role in the Estado Novo as mother and homemaker. Motherhood and family clearly dominate this scene, with one expectant mother holding a young child, another mother holding her baby, and yet another infant resting in a crib. The Estado Novo took great pride in its programmes to promote nutrition, good hygiene, and health services, as symbolized by the large, official two-storey building. Other social programmes included day-care centres and construction of new homes for the fisherman and his family, as seen in the background.

The scene to our right again shows the protective arm of the Estado Novo as it cares for both the active fisherman when he is at home and for the aged fishermen. The Estado Novo, under the iron hand of Commander Henrique dos Santos Tenreiro, government representative to the GANPB, oversaw many programmes that provided care and services, and they can be seen in the painting: transportation (the Volkswagen), equipment (foul-weather gear, line), health care (the operating table), and homes for the aged (the scene on the far right).

The scene in the background at the horizon shows three evocative memory images of the Grand Banks cod fisheries: the extremely large iceberg in the centre, the large fog bank approaching to the left, and the famous and beloved *Gazela* (now owned by the city of Philadelphia) to the right. All icons are white. The artist does not narrate anything about this scene in detail. It is precisely the hardships that underlie these icons that are absent from this mural – the realities of life on the Banks.

In considering the mural as grand symbolism for the place of the humble fisherman in the nation, we must ask one remaining question. Who saw it hanging in the saloon of the commander's quarters? Fishermen certainly did not enter this space, but officials of state, visiting dignitaries, and captains of the fishing vessels were entertained here or held meetings here. As we have seen above, through the examples of the *Gil Eannes* and the commander of the fleet – whose official title was Representative of the Ministry of the Navy and Chief Officer of Assistance and Supply Services to the Portuguese Cod Fleet – management of symbols within the authoritarian system of the Estado Novo was essential in defining and reinforcing its ideology. Visiting foreign dignitaries would probably bring with them their own internalized symbols, which would be counter-symbols to the authoritarian regime. Also, and of utmost importance, Portuguese captains, most of whom were well educated and spoke English, would be exposed in their travels and personal and professional contacts in Canadian ports to counter-symbols of a more democratic political and social system. So those who might be tempted to consider other systems of state as more viable were controlled through visual imagery in the commander's quarters of the ship of state. The symbols used in this mural also served to evoke Portuguese pride in the doryman and the *campanhas*.

As if to corroborate the role of the *Gil Eannes* as the icon of Portuguese nationalism, and Rebelo's mural as the icon of family and social systems, yet another icon of Estado Novo ideology aboard the *Gil Eannes* represented the presence of *Deus* (omniscient, omnipotent, omnipresent) in the form of a chapel on the aft deck (Figure 3.2). With the chapel doors opened wide, the viewer can see another mural by Rebelo that effectively portrayed the central role of religion (Deus) in the relationship between the *bacalhau*, the dorymen at work on the Banks, and the family at home in Portugal – all united through the mother of God.

The Virgin, arms extended to accept all those paying homage to her, is the focal point of the triangular arrangement of the space. To the viewer's left two dorymen pay their respects to God through the Virgin. One is dressed in the typical flannel shirt, heavy pants, and rubber boots and carries foul-weather gear as he moves toward the Virgin. The other man, dressed in warm sweater and working apron, kneels as he prays with his palms together in symbolic gesture and eyes closed. At the feet of the standing fisherman is a representation of an enormous cod – his reason for being on the Banks and away from family and home. To the viewer's right mother and child (wife and son) in Portugal pray to the Virgin for the well-being and safe return of husband and father. A satchel on the ground, perhaps containing her handiwork or their few items of clothing, complements the *bacalhau*.

Figure 3.2. Mural from the chapel on the *Gil Eannes*, by Domingos Rebelo, 1955 (courtesy of Priscilla A. Doel)

The colours worn by mother and son are sombre, suggesting a mood of mourning, while those worn by the men on the Banks suggest warmth and protection against the elements. The colours surrounding the Virgin – blue and white – separate her from the four worldly figures.

In this state artwork of the Estado Novo era, we have seen that idealized myths surrounding Portugal's postwar codfishing industry were based on three fundamental symbols. First, the *Gil Eannes* was representative of *Pátria* in the modern world, with its advanced technology and social welfare being a source of nationalistic pride. Second, Rebelo's mural in the commander's quarters symbolized the interrelationship between the Portuguese codfishing industry and *Família*, the foundation on which the welfare system rested. Finally the chapel, with its other Rebelo mural, symbolized the presence of *Deus*, long the unifying icon of Portuguese overseas expansion.

However, between the myth of the Estado Novo as it idealized the doryman and the reality of life on the Banks there lay a vast chasm. Within the collective memory of the Portuguese doryman, there still remained memories of earlier periods of near slavery such as those described by Alan Villiers through a conversation he had with ship-mate Pierre Berthoud in 1929, when their ship crossed the outward-bound course of a small fleet of Portuguese schooners headed for the Banks: '"A tough life, you say?" The Frenchman looked fiercely at us. "A dog's life," that's what it is! My God there is no harder life upon the sea! All fishing is tough, but that's the toughest, hardest way to make a living that I know. Those fellows will be lucky to be back home six months from now. Aye, and some of 'em won't be coming. I warn you, shipmates, things are tough all over Europe now, but don't ever ship in one of them! Those Portuguese use one-man dories. Keep out of them!' (Villiers 1951: 17).

Decline and Restoration

In 1972 the *Novos Mares,* the last handlining sailing vessel, left the Banks, never to return. The age of the one-man dory had finally ended, and it was clear that the *Gil Eannes* was no longer needed. With the 25th of April revolution of 1974 and the collapse of the Estado Novo, the already floundering fisheries suffered further blows, from which they never recovered.

Finally, in 1986, following the lead of its European neighbours, Portugal joined the European Community (EC). Until that time Portugal had dealt directly with Canada in setting up bilateral agreements establishing its fishing quotas and access to certain areas. Now, as a member of the EC, it was part of Europe and could deal with Canada only through the bureaucratic channels of Brussels. Portugal continued to fish on the limited basis allowed by European quotas, but the Canadian government banned its ships from Canadian ports, accusing them of overfishing and violating their quota allocations. Times had changed, and with them, the very special relationship shared by the people of Newfoundland and their friends of the Portuguese cod fleet came to an end.

Knowing that codfishing as a viable economic endeavour and as a way of life will never return to the Grand Banks of Newfoundland, both Portugal and Newfoundland are moving toward different goals, each guided by new political, economic, and social systems. That these systems colour the manner in which the two peoples perceive their common past, linked by cod, is evident in the way in which each chooses to incorporate its past into its present and future collective memory.

While the fancy façades of brick and glass in downtown St John's appear to turn their backs on the inactive port beneath them, Canadian officials carefully monitor and study the depleted resources of the Grand Banks and surrounding waters. Resource protection and the assurance of a national sustainable fishery are their prime concern. For most of the inhabitants of St John's, the seasonal presence of Portugal's codfishing fleet is but a remote memory, and they, like the bronze statue of Gaspar Corte-Real that graces their city, turn their backs on the port as they look in other directions for development and well-being. The little Lady of Fátima, a beloved icon, still graces the basilica, where she continues to receive the prayers of worshippers, some of whom know her story, others of whom do not. The small Portuguese immigrant community is well integrated into the city, since its children have grown up there as Canadians and old customs have given way to new.

On the other side of the Atlantic, however, the age of cod is being carefully recorded and celebrated for future generations, as the famous captains of Ilhavo and their families work side by side with government and museum officials to document and thus preserve their rightful place in Portugal's centuries-old seafaring heritage. The famous Rebelo murals, used by Salazar's state to reinforce the values of *Pátria, Deus,* and *Família,* were removed from the *Gil Eannes* in the early 1980s and now serve as icons for a new generation, constituting, as it were, new cultural texts that evoke responses from people who will share the collective memory without having experienced it. The chapel on the aft deck of the Gil Eannes was completely removed and is now a part of the permanent cod fisheries exhibition at the Museu da Marinha in Belém, just outside Lisbon. It is fitting that the mural be housed close to the banks of the Tagus River, the point of departure not only for the ships that sailed to Newfoundland in search of cod but also a major point of departure for all Portuguese seafaring endeavours.

The mural that once adorned the commander's private quarters is now a permanent part of the museum in Ilhavo, a place that was home to many captains of cod and to many of the fishermen who rowed and sailed the dories in search of cod. The museum not only houses most of the archival material related to the cod fisheries but also offers a hands-on experience of codfishing on the Banks through life-sized replicas of fishermen and crew engaged in many typical activities, now part of Portugal's collective memory.

Although Rebelo's murals were removed from the *Gil Eannes* in the mid-1980s, the ship lay for some thirteen years alongside a quay in Lisbon, more or less abandoned and neglected as it deteriorated into a forgotten and disdained past. Plans to renovate it as a restaurant or a cruise ship never materialized. Fortunately, other plans to sell the ship for scrap never materialized either. Recent news brings positive reports that – through the efforts of many individuals and groups – this once-proud ship of state will return to the shipyards of Viana do Castelo, where it was built and launched, to be renovated. Berthed in Viana do Castelo, the hospital supply ship that served not only Portuguese fishermen but also those of other nations will once again enter service, this time as a museum.[8] With new purpose, the *Gil Eannes*, like the icons in Rebelo's murals, will return to its former glory and become a part of the collective memory of past, present, and future generations.

NOTES

1   Moutinho (1985) suggests that various English words associated with the fishing industry made their way into Portuguese, such as *biguane* (a big one); *levas* (livers); *picefoque* (pitchfork); *suevlo* (swivel); *troteiro* (throater).
2   This firm, having modified and modernized its operations, now has headquarters on Rua de Ouro in central Lisbon. It maintains a limited number of codfishing vessels, which use St Pierre as their port of call.
3   An account of these problems is found in 'The Life of Those Who Go Fishing for Cod,' by doryman Marcelino Pires, a 1932 article republished in the newspaper *Comércio da Póvoa de Varzim,* 4 May 1935.
4   An interesting account of this voyage, based on an original logbook entry, was written by Cachim and appears as a chapter in his book *Os Ilhavos, o Mar e a Ria* (1988: 65–71). His account was translated into English by Priscilla Doel (1996).
5   *Evening Telegram* (St John's), 'Welcome to the Portuguese,' 26 May 1955, 4.
6   *Newfoundland's National Weekly* (St John's), 31 May 1955.
7   *Evening Telegram* (St John's), 28 May 1955, 4.
8   *O Ilhavense* 'Gil Eanes em Bom Porto,' 17 Dec. 1997.

REFERENCES

Cachim, A.E. 1988. *Os Ilhavos, o Mar e a Ria.* Estarreja: Camara Municipal de Ilhavo.

Cortesão, A., and A. da Mota Teixeira. 1960. *Portugaliae, monumenta cartographica.* Vol. 5. Lisbon.

Doel, P.A. 1992. *Port O'Call: Memories of the Portuguese White Fleet in St. John's, Newfoundland.* St John's: ISER Press.

–, trans. 1996. 'Os Ilhavos, o Mar e a Ria.' *National Fisherman* 76, no. 12: 56-9.

Gerth, H., and C.W. Mills. 1953. *Character and Social Structure.* New York: Harcourt Brace.

Manso, R., and O. Cruz. 1984. *A epopeia dos bacalhaus.* Porto: Distri Editora.

Martin, C., and G. Parker. 1988. *The Spanish Armada.* New York: W.W. Norton.

Moutinho, M. 1985. *História da pesca do bacalhau.* Lisbon: Imprensa Universitaria.

Simões, J. 1942. *Os grandes trabalhadores do Mar: Reportagens na Terra Nova e na Groenlândia.* Lisbon: Oficinas Gráficas da Gazeta dos Caminhos de Ferro.

Villiers, A. 1951. *The Quest of the Schooner Argus: A Voyage to the Banks and Greenland.* New York: Charles Scribner's Sons.

4 Portuguese Fishermen in Newfoundland

JEAN-PIERRE ANDRIEUX

Since the early sixteenth century Portuguese fishermen have followed in the wake of early Portuguese navigators and travelled to the New Found Land in search of cod (Morison 1971; Abreu-Ferreira 1995, 1995–6). They adopted the Virgin Rocks, one hundred miles east of St John's, as their traditional fishing ground. Portuguese fishing methods changed little over the centuries, continuing a long tradition of labour-intensive fishing methods. Even after 1945, when all other nations fishing in Newfoundland waters gave up traditional handlining operations and converted to modern trawlers, because of the policies of the Salazar dictatorship Portugal maintained the traditional system in parallel with the new, more efficient trawlers (Doel 1992).

This new technology, in particular the invention of the stern factory trawler, brought scores of nations to the Grand Banks. These intense harvesting methods transformed the fishery and led to rapidly diminished cod stocks. In the face of such competition the Portuguese attempted to modernize their ageing and antiquated fleet. However, the three- and four-masted handliners, in spite of being converted from wind power to engines and being fitted out with fish loops, radar, and more modern equipment, were clearly obsolete. Fortunately for the owners, fires of unknown origins would sometimes start aboard these old ships on calm days, and they would go to the bottom in Newfoundland waters. Insured owners could then convert to modern trawlers capable of harvesting fish in deeper waters as the old cod stocks were becoming exhausted (Andrieux 1996).

This chapter is an account of this transitional 'moment' in the Portuguese fishery in Canadian waters. Through conversations with Portuguese fishermen of the White Fleet and photographs from this era, I attempt to shed light on a shadowy area of the history of the fisheries. Portuguese ship owners subsidized the modernization of their fleets through insurance money from a long string of accidents and fires aboard their vessels. Primarily, however, this is the story of the Portuguese fisherman and his struggle to wrest a precarious living from the waters of the North Atlantic. It first offers a brief history to the late 1940s; second, looks at the 'golden age' of the White Fleet; and third, considers its strange demise.

The Portuguese Fishery: A Brief History

The first recorded voyage by the Portuguese to Newfoundland dates back to 1500, when the intrepid navigator Gaspar Corte-Real arrived hard on the heels of John Cabot. With a charter from the king of Portugal he claimed this new land as Terras dos Labradores (Brazão 1964, 1965; Alpalhão and Da Rosa 1980). Immediately after this voyage fishing companies were founded in Aveiro, Viana do Castelo, and Terceira for the purpose of sending vessels on codfishing expeditions to the Terra Nova. It seems that these vessels were sailing as early as 1504. This effort was so profitable that King Emanuel established a tax in the ports of the Douro and the Minho regions on the fish brought back from the Newfoundland Banks.

Portuguese fishermen crossed the Atlantic in sturdy fishing vessels on the spring east wind, to fish on the Grand Banks some 2,000 miles from home. They used hook and line and filled their holds with cod, always in a race with the fierce seas of late autumn and winter off the coast of Newfoundland. Fog, gales, and freezing weather took their toll each year, yet fishermen still sailed. Cod had come to mean the difference between food and hunger in much of southern Europe (Simões 1942; Moutinho 1985).

The number of vessels engaged in the Newfoundland cod fishery grew rapidly. In 1550 Aveiro alone had 150 fishing vessels sailing to Newfoundland, with equal numbers sailing from Oporto and other ports. These vessels sheltered in harbours close to the Bonavista area. In 1620 they were chased out of these ports by the British in a violent encounter. The Portuguese then shifted their fishing effort to the Grand Banks, where they have maintained a presence ever since. The fleet of the early twentieth century consisted of three- and four-masted schooners, whose decks were filled with one-man fishing dories. The

Portuguese fishermen who went to the Newfoundland Banks had passed on their traditional operations from generation to generation, but political changes in Portugal would transform its fishery.

In a military coup in 1926 António de Oliveira Salazar, a young professor from Coimbra University, was asked to put the finances of the country back in order. He soon rose to the presidency and installed a dictatorial government (Wheeler 1993). The government took control of fishing policies, as the industry was an important part of the economy. For example, like their European counterparts, Portuguese owners started to introduce trawlers within the handlining fleet. As the number of trawlers grew it became national policy, dictated by Henrique dos Santos Tenreiro (by then an admiral and in charge of fishing activities), to keep both fleets operating in parallel. This kept large numbers of workers employed in the older, labour-intensive fleet. Thus, while other nations converted exclusively to trawlers, Portugal maintained both methods.

During the Second World War, Portugal remained neutral, and its vessels were able to continue harvesting cod on their traditional fishing grounds. Initially they painted the name of the vessel and its country of origin in large letters on the side, along with a replica of the national flag. Soon, however, the government forced the vessels, which had been painted in various colours, to be repainted white and to sail with full navigational lights during the night, to identify them to German submarine raiders as being neutral. Thus the vessels became known as the Portuguese 'White Fleet,' a name that remained long after the war (Doel 1992; Andrieux 1996).

At the beginning of the war all Portuguese fishing vessels travelled individually, but this, and their neutrality, did not necessarily guarantee them safe passage. There were, in fact, two casualties during the war (Rower 1983). The first was the *Maria da Glória*, a three-master owned by fishing captains Silvio Ramalheira and Belo Morais. On 5 July 1942 the vessel was on its way up from the Newfoundland Banks to Greenland for the summer fishery. After sighting a submarine the captain got on the radio set and told the other Portuguese vessels travelling with him that he had seen this submarine – a fatal mistake. The submarine, despite the vessel's neutrality, immediately sank it and even fired on the crew. The Germans then tried to sink all its dories with cannon fire. The vessel sank so quickly that the Portuguese had no time to get food supplies. Some men died in a storm that followed;

others went insane because of lack of water. After seven long days only two dories of survivors were sighted off the Labrador coast by a Canadian warplane.

Three months later, on 11 September 1942, the three-master *Delaes* was sent to the bottom by *U-96*. This submarine had had a successful twenty-four-hour hunt, having torpedoed three other vessels. Why *U-96* had decided to sink a neutral vessel is unknown. Probably the *Delaes* had been in the wrong place at the wrong time, near an Allied convoy. As a result of these sinkings Portuguese fishing vessels no longer sailed alone to the Banks but were organized into convoys according to their speeds, as some lacked engines.

The war also brought another significant change. Two vessels made a port call in Halifax to pick up bait. So successful was it that all the White Fleet started calling at St John's, after the cessation of hostilities in 1945, for this new herring bait, known in Portuguese as *sardinha*. They changed later to squid (*lula*) and even later to mackerel (*cavala*), which also proved very good.

The Golden Age of the White Fleet

The postwar years marked the high point of the White Fleet fishery off Newfoundland. St John's welcomed thousands of Portuguese fishermen every summer. It was not an easy life for members of the White Fleet (Simões 1942; Villiers 1951). The days were hard and long amid the treacherous winds and waves of the North Atlantic (see Figure 4.1). What the men looked forward to most, besides returning home to their families (Cole 1990; Doel 1992, 1997), was their next visit to St John's.[1] When they were in port they could best be described as colourful, happy, and remarkably well behaved (Doel 1997). These brave, hardworking seamen went about their business and leisure in an unassuming, quiet manner so that their presence did not interrupt residents' lives (see Figure 4.2).

When the fleet was in St John's, harbourside was a forest of masts, the rigging festooned with yellow oilskins, buoy markers, drying stockings, rubber boots, woollen underwear, plaid shirts, and dory sails (Figure 4.3). While in port the fishermen spread everything on deck to air and dry. On the piers they gathered to mend their sails, stretch and repair long lines of hooks, patch their shirts, or just sit and smoke or drink Portuguese wine. They were always noted for their friendliness.

Figure 4.1. Stormy day on the Grand Banks, 1960s (courtesy of J.P. Andrieux)

Figure 4.2. Portuguese White Fleet in St John's Harbour, 1960s (courtesy of J.P. Andrieux)

Few spoke English, but this wasn't a barrier. They would go to the stores and point out what they wanted or carry a note from someone who knew English. Or they might bring a page from an Eaton's or Simpson's catalogue with the item in question on it. Hundreds of fishermen could be seen on Water and Duckworth streets, carrying loads of merchandise. Indeed, given the size of their presence in St John's, it is a tribute to them that their demeanour during these frequent, friendly invasions has kept them in high standing as very welcome visitors.

By the early 1950s other nations had phased out dory fishing operations, which gave way to modern trawlers. In Portugal, however, sailing vessels were still setting out each spring for the Newfoundland Banks. Although time had brought changes in size, shape, and gear, the hardy fishermen were still facing most of the same hazards that their ancestors had. As mentioned, the Salazar government had decided, for political reasons, to keep the handlining dory vessels of the White Fleet operating in parallel with the more modern trawlers (Figure 4.4). This did not please the fishermen of the White Fleet, of course, who had harsh and crowded living conditions on board, often

Figure 4.3. Portuguese fishing vessels sheltering in St John's Harbour, away from Hurricane Blanche, 1969 (courtesy of Ian Brookes)

Figure 4.4. A handliner of the White Fleet on the Grand Banks of Newfoundland, 1960s (courtesy of J.P. Andrieux)

sleeping two to a bunk (Figure 4.5). Toilet facilities were non-existent or basic. Fresh water was rationed, and no showers could be taken. Men had no water to wash themselves or their clothes. Financial rewards were few. Most men would have preferred, if they had a choice, to be on the trawlers, but signing on to the White Fleet for a seven-year term got men out of compulsory military service.

The Sinking of the White Fleet

In 1955 Portuguese fishermen, despite their use of older fishing techniques, led European nations in volume of catches on the rich Banks of

Figure 4.5. Portuguese fishermen of the White Fleet, 1960s (courtesy of J.P. Andrieux)

Newfoundland (Moutinho 1985). A major change would soon revolutionize the fishing industry and ultimately lead to its demise. The British arrived on the Banks with a new ship, a stern trawler called *Fairtry,* which had a self-contained factory that would catch, process, and freeze fish at sea. The USSR immediately copied this technology. The capabilities of the vessel spelled trouble for everyone. As more and more vessels of this type started fishing, stocks were being ravaged.

In order to protect stocks, in 1964 Canada extended its fisheries limits from three to twelve miles. This change, and competition from the new factory trawlers, made the White Fleet less and less profitable. In September 1965 the Portuguese ambassador to Canada, Dr Eduardo Brazão, visiting St John's for the unveiling of the statue of Gaspar Corte-Real, predicted the end of the famed White Fleet; he indicated that its three- and four-masters would gradually give way to modern fishing vessels. What he failed to say was how this replacement was being undertaken.

Figure 4.6. The *Luiza Ribau* on fire at the Virgin Rocks off Newfoundland's coast, 23 August 1973 (courtesy of Capt. Francisco Marques)

Following a 'gentleman's agreement' between the insurers, the owners, and the Portuguese government, much of the White Fleet succumbed to accidental fires during this period. It was said that the owners would not pocket the actual money from losses but that it would go toward the construction of new vessels. Any further cost would be financed by the Foundation for the Renovation and Outfitting of the Fishing Industry (FRAIP) – a government body that lent money at low interest rates over a certain number of years to owners wishing to build modern vessels.

It was rumoured that most of the so-called accidental fires were actually deliberate, started by a short circuit in the engine room. The generators would soon be affected and the electrical supply therefore cut off, making it impossible for water to circulate to fight the fire. Soon the vessel would have to be abandoned (see Figure 4.6) (Andrieux 1996, 1997).

The fishermen would often know, or sense, that their vessel's days were numbered. Consequently, they took few clothes or personal belongings when they left Portugal. If they believed that something was bound to happen during the fishing campaign, particularly if fishing was very poor, they would leave their belongings with friends in St John's. In St John's local people who had a connection with the White Fleet shared these premonitions. The harbour pilots, who were familiar with the handlining fleet, would make comments and bets among themselves over which vessel would next succumb to an engine-room short circuit or some other imaginative scheme.

There were many ways in which fishermen could tell which vessel would next go down. Vessels of the White Fleet by tradition fished together, and their catches would not greatly vary from one vessel to another. Vessels had instructions from their owners to declare their catches by radio each week so that these could be progressively insured. In case the vessel went down, the owner would be compensated according to the fish reported to be on board. The airwaves were unscrambled, and the weekly messages could be intercepted. If a single vessel declared unusually high catches for two or three weeks in a row, listeners realized that the vessel in question would soon go down. Within a few days they would have to answer yet another distress signal and welcome shipwrecked countrymen on their already crowded handliner. They would usually keep them on board until the hospital supply vessel the *Gil Eannes* picked them up to take them to St John's; if it was not in the region they would head to St John's to drop off the crew members, who would then be repatriated to Portugal (Andrieux 1996).

The ship chandlers in St John's had their own way of predicting disasters. The vessels of the White Fleet salted their catches of large cod and had little, if any, refrigeration equipment for meat, fruit, and vegetables. As a result, the *Gil Eannes* went back and forth from St John's to where the vessels were fishing, delivering these fresh staples to the White Fleet, as well as mail and fresh water. If a handliner did not place an order, it was taken for granted that she was the most likely candidate for sinking.

There was little risk of loss of lives from these accidental fires. It was generally agreed, accordingly to rumours of the time, that when plans were made to sink a vessel, weather conditions had to be favourable. Usually a fire would occur on a calm day, when the fishermen were in their dories or were in a position to get off the vessel without difficulty. Another condition was that there be other vessels close by so that the shipwrecked men could quickly be rescued. Many of the dozens of Portuguese handliners that came to grief in Newfoundland waters sank at the Virgin Rocks, about one hundred miles south-south-west of St John's. The Virgin Rocks are a series of outcropping shoals covering about ten square miles; the water around them ranges from two to nine fathoms deep, and the rocks were said to be the most profitable fishing grounds on the Grand Banks.

In the 1960s it was thought that the new technology of factory freezer trawlers could be the only remedy for declining fish catches. No one seemed to realize that the Newfoundland Banks were not an inexhaustible fishing ground. By 1969 numerous non-traditional fishing nations (for instance, Bulgaria, East Germany, Japan, Poland, the USSR) had invaded the Grand Banks and surroundings, and it should have been little surprise to anyone that the fishery was collapsing. Foreign fleets were being blamed for exhausting the Labrador inshore fishery; they had fished 1,400 per cent more cod in 1969 than they had in 1958.

The following year, 1970, was pivotal for the Portuguese fishery. Major changes took place on two fronts. It was the year that Salazar died, and his successor, Marcelo Caetano, was perceived to be weak. The political system that fostered the labour-intensive White Fleet was crumbling, and more modern steel-hulled vessels were converted from their one-man dory operations to longlines and gill nets. The dories were being replaced by a handful of power boats. Steel-hulled vessels were suited for these conversions, but the older vessels were not. With these conversions, crews were reduced from one hundred per vessel to fifty-five.

These changes proved very successful and in the early 1970s additional vessels were converted to this new method of fishing, while the older, unsuitable vessels would continue to fish in their traditional fashion while awaiting their fate by fire. The White Fleet vessels were probably the only ones in the world that still used the 'one dory, one man' system of fishing.

By 1974 fire had decimated the rest of the wooden handliners, and only three of them left Portugal for the fishing campaign. Two days after they sailed, on 25 April 1974, a coup d'état was organized by General António Sebastião Ribeiro Spínola and a group of army captains in Portugal. There was an explosion of popular joy among the Portuguese people, who placed carnations on the tips of the soldiers' rifles in what became known as the Revolution of Carnations (Wheeler 1993). It ended decades of oppressive dictatorship.

Appropriately enough, the revolution took place in the dying days of the White Fleet, which had been kept alive by the regime and its fisheries minister, Tenreiro. As news of the revolution and their newly discovered freedoms spread among crew members of the White Fleet, there was great rejoicing. The men wanted to strike for higher wages, and the three handliners – the last of the White Fleet – headed for St-Pierre, the closest port. They remained there for a few days until coerced by local authorities to leave.

Clearly the owners were unhappy with this situation. A few days later, on 26 June, the *Ilhavense* caught fire and went to the bottom. The *São Jorge* had a similar fate a couple of days later. It was the last vessel of the Portuguese handlining fleet equipped with dories to sink in Newfoundland waters. On 24 July the last remaining member of the White Fleet, the *Novos Mares,* with its dories proudly stacked on deck, sailed for the last time through the Narrows on its way back to Aveiro (Andrieux 1996). This event ended nearly 500 years of traditional handlining in Newfoundland waters by Portuguese fishermen.

Conclusion

At the time of writing, February 1998, I stand on the nearly deserted docks of Gafanha, Aveiro, once the home of the mighty handliners of the White Fleet. It is with great nostalgia that I reminisce about the fleet that graced St John's and St-Pierre for centuries.

Much has changed for the Portuguese fishery in the years since the White Fleet left Canadian waters for the last time. Handliners were replaced by modern factory freezer trawlers, which were harvesting fewer and fewer cod. The 200 mile limit, the withdrawal of codfishing privileges when Portugal joined the European Community in 1986, and quotas all combined to bring to its knees the once-mighty Portuguese fleet (Andrieux 1987). Dozens of old fishing companies have folded or are on the verge of folding. Their fish-drying facilities are empty for lack of cod and have a mournful appearance. Vessels have been sold to the European Union for scrap and for a handsome price for their fishing licences. It is speculated that within a year or two the surviving vessels will be concentrated in the hands of two or three owners.

The presence of the Portuguese in Newfoundland waters is now a historical one. They contributed socially and economically to the culture and history of Newfoundland – and particularly to St John's. The White Fleet now sails only in the memories of those Portuguese and Newfoundlanders who were alive in those hard, wonderful years. The persistence of its memory is a tribute to the warm relationship between the Newfoundlanders and the Portuguese of that era.

NOTES AND ACKNOWLEDGMENTS

I wish to acknowledge the contributions to this research project of numerous active and retired Portuguese captains, officers, fishermen, owners, ship chandlers, technicians, doctors, clergy, and merchants, who shared with me their recollections and experiences of the White Fleet. I gathered this information informally over a number of years on Portuguese vessels that visited the Grand Banks. During their port calls my wife and I would be dinner guests on these vessels, where the stories of yesteryear would always surface. Many of the retired fishermen shared their stories during our numerous visits to Portugal.

I was fortunate in having the assistance of Dr Anna Maria Lopes of the Museu da Marinha de Ilhavo, who supplied me with initial lists and positions of sunken Portuguese vessels in Newfoundland waters. Friends of the museum – Capt. Francisco Marques, Capt. Vitorino Ramalheira, Capt. Francisco Paião, and many others – had extensive knowledge of the fleet and were of great assistance, bringing light to many unanswered questions.

Thanks also to Dr Manuel Lopes and his staff at the Museu Municipal de Etnografia e História (Póvoa de Varzim), the Canadian Department of Fisheries and Oceans, and many others who supplied me with photographs to illustrate these recollections.

1 See the unpublished catalogue "The Portuguese White Fleet, St. John's, Newfoundland 1969," which accompanied an exhibition at the gallery of the Portuguese consulate in Toronto, 15–25 Feb. 1996. This photo exhibition by Ian Brookes, a retired geographer from York University, dealt with twenty-nine ships of the White Fleet that in 1969 sought

refúge in St John's from Hurricane Blanche. The exhibition was also presented at several museums in Portugal, as well as at the annual meeting of the Canadian Association of Geographers in St John's, 20–23 Aug. 1997.

REFERENCES

Abreu-Ferreira, D. 1995. 'The Cod Trade in Early-Modern Portugal: Deregulation, English Domination, and the Decline of Female Cod Merchandise.' PhD diss., Memorial University of Newfoundland.
– 1995–6. 'The Portuguese in Newfoundland: Documentary Evidence Examined.' *Portuguese Studies Review* 4 no. 2: 11–33.
Alpalhão, J.A., and V.M.P. Da Rosa. 1980. *A Minority in a Changing Society: The Portuguese Communities of Quebec.* Ottawa: University of Ottawa Press.
Andrieux, J.P. 1987. *Newfoundland's Cod War: Canada or France?* St John's: O.T.C. Press.
– 1996. *Marine Disasters & Shipwrecks of 'Newfoundland and Labrador.* Vol. 3, *1940–1980.* St John's: O.T.C. Press.
– 1997. 'The Portuguese White Fleet in Newfoundland Waters.' Paper presented at the annual meeting of the Canadian Association of Geographers, St John's, 23 Aug.
Brazão, E. 1964. *La découverte de Terre-Neuve.* Montreal: Les Presses de l'Université de Montréal.
– 1965. 'Les Corte-Real et le Nouveau Monde.' *Revue d'histoire d'Amérique française* 19 no. 1: 3–52; no. 2: 163–202; and no. 3: 335–49.
Cole, S.C. 1990. 'Cod, Cod, Country and Family: The Portuguese Newfoundland Cod Fishery.' *MAST* 3 no. 1: 1–29.
Doel, P.A. 1992. *Port O'Call: Memories of the Portuguese White Fleet in St John's, Newfoundland.* St John's: ISER Press.
– 1997. 'The Spatial and Geographic Identity of the Portuguese White Fleet Fisheries.' Paper presented at the annual meeting of the Canadian Association of Geographers, St John's, 23 Aug.
Morison, S.E. 1971. *The European Discovery of America: The Northern Voyages.* New York: Oxford University Press.
Moutinho, M. 1985. *História da pesca do bacalhau: Para uma antropologia do 'Fiel Amigo.'* Lisbon: Editorial Estampa.
Rower, J. 1983. *Axis Submarine Successes, 1939–1945.* Annapolis, MD: Naval Institute Press.

Simões, J. 1942. Os *grandes trabalhadores do Mar: Reportagem na Terra Nova e na Groenlândia*. Lisbon: Oficinas Gráficas da Gazeta dos Caminhos de Ferro.

Villiers, A. 1951. *The Quest of the Schooner Argus: A Voyage to the Banks and Greenland*. New York: Charles Scribner's Sons.

Wheeler, D.L. 1993. *Historical Dictionary of Portugal*. Metuchen, NJ: Scarecrow Press.

5 Remembering the Portuguese

PETER COLLINS

Records of the Portuguese presence on the eastern coast of Canada – associated largely with the White Fleet, which harvested cod on the Grand Banks of Newfoundland from the 1940s to the 1970s – are surprisingly rare, with few primary documents and little secondary research existing on the subject (Teixeira and Lavigne 1998). This absence is particularly notable with regard to the Portuguese fishermen and their impact on Newfoundland, especially on St John's, even though thousands of them might be in port at one time during the summer fishing season.[1] Priscilla Doel, whose book *Port O'Call* represents a singular exception to this scholarly oversight, notes with astonishment the lack of any substantial documentary evidence of 'this elusive Portuguese presence' (Doel 1992: 5).

In the course of rediscovering these 'elusive Portuguese' for this chapter, I found that a Portuguese word recurred again and again – *saudade* – generally translated as a longing, a homesickness, a nostalgia for something lost, with those who experience this feeling being *saudo-sistas*.[2] Although the term appears most frequently with respect to the Portuguese fishermen's longing for home and family during months at sea, *saudade* has broader resonance in English writing, particularly postcolonial literature and writing on emigration, where it may be read as a metaphor for the emigrant experience and the attempt to reconstruct the past.

As Salman Rushdie observes, 'writers in my position, exiles or emigrants ... are haunted by some sense of loss, some urge to reclaim, to look back ... But if we do look back, we must also do so in the knowledge ... that we will not be capable of reclaiming precisely the thing that was lost; that we will, in short, create fictions, not actual cities or villages, but invisible ones, imaginary homelands' (1991: 10). Rushdie uses the terms 'fictions' and 'imaginary' in reference to 'the partial nature of ... memories' that characterize the history, the story, of the emigrant experience (12). He notes that even 'precise' scientific reconstructions of the past, through history, geography, or archaeology, are always provisional and that therefore the recovery of stories – of past 'voices' – becomes an essential complement to the quotidian, statistical analysis of the world around us.

Rushdie's argument goes to the heart of the problem confronting research into the cultural impact of the Portuguese presence in Newfoundland: namely, the lack of documentary evidence. Configuring this argument in terms of the subject at hand – the Portuguese of the White Fleet – we may argue that while an accounting of the number of Portuguese fishing vessels, the dates of their sailing, the size of their crews and catches, and so on is of obvious use in our task, so too is reclamation of the cultural history of the Portuguese presence, of those 'voices evoking memories' – to use Doel's Rushdiesque language – 'expressed, more often than not, with *saudade*' (Doel 1992: 34).

Moreover, such an exercise serves as more than a sentimental record of a fading past. As Rushdie argues, such reconstructions are 'not merely a mirror of nostalgia' but also 'a useful tool with which to work in the present' – to explicate the workings in 'nation[s] of immigrants [such as Canada] ... of the phenomenon of cultural transplantation, [by] examining the ways in which people cope with a new world' (1991: 12, 20). Therefore, in studying the 'cultural transplantation' of these Portuguese fishermen into the landscape of Newfoundland, I first present my own recollections, next examine the extant documentary record – largely newspapers and journal articles – and finally supplement these sources by examining the representation of the Portuguese in local St John's theatre, as well as in the recorded 'memories and voices' of Newfoundlanders and Portuguese Newfoundlanders. Through close reading of these texts – a mode of literary analysis that foregrounds subtexts and subtextual contradictions – I hope to illuminate this 'moment' in the centuries-old cultural cross-pollination between Portugal and Canada.

Figures in a Landscape

This essay has its origins almost a generation ago, in the mental landscape of a young boy growing up in St John's in the late 1960s and the

1970s. His world was rather small, limited to his working-class down-town neighbourhood, his school, and the nearby Bannerman Park. The figures in his landscape were ethnically and culturally homogeneous – generally poor, Irish Catholic – save for the few Chinese families, which mostly kept to themselves, running restaurants and a laundry.

And then there were the Portuguese.

It is difficult to convey a sense of the place that the Portuguese fish-ermen, who seasonally visited St John's with the White Fleet, occupied in the boy's world. He would see them at Mass every Sunday morning, in the Basilica of St John the Baptist, clustered together near the statue of Our Lady of Fátima to the right of the main altar. On Sunday after-noons, and indeed almost every afternoon in the summer, he would see them playing soccer in Bannerman Park, the closest open space to the St John's waterfront.

To be a Portuguese fisherman, he knew, was synonymous with being poor. This was common knowledge in St John's, deduced from the fact that many of the fishermen could not afford even the cheap running shoes – 'Portuguese sneakers,' schoolchildren called them – that could be bought at the inexpensive Arcade store downtown, but would play soccer barefoot even on gravel and concrete. Yet despite their often darker skin, their foreign language, and their differences, in a strange way the Portuguese 'belonged.' The park had trees, the bandstand, the swimming pool, and the Portuguese ... always the Por-tuguese ... playing soccer rain or shine, very much a part of the land-scape of the city.

In the years that followed, at some point when the growing boy was not looking, the Portuguese seemed to disappear from St John's. Later, as a young academic, he ... I moved to the Canadian mainland and became aware of the complex tapestry that is the story of the Por-tuguese migration and presence in Canada. However, in researching the cultural impact of the Portuguese on the life of St John's, I found that the memories of the Portuguese from a St John's boyhood would reappear to inform and shape the research. While this 'privileging' of subjective memory could be regarded as marring an objective recon-struction of a historical moment, it may be argued that such works are inevitably 'broken mirrors, some of whose fragments have been irre-trievably lost' (Rushdie 1991: 11).

Perception, interpretation, and the assigning of significance are, as Rushdie observes, all informed by our subjectivity: 'Human beings do not perceive things whole; we are not gods but wounded creatures, cracked lenses, capable only of fractured perceptions ... Meaning is a shaky edifice we build out of scraps, dogmas, childhood injuries, newspaper articles ... It would be dishonest to pretend, when writing about the day before yesterday, that it was possible to see the whole picture' (1991: 12–13).

So it is too with my reconstruction of the Portuguese presence in St John's. The Portuguese shown here in the landscape of St John's – whether in memory, newspapers, or drama – are 'representations' from the point of view of Newfoundlanders. This situation presents an opportunity to perceive an annual ethnic 'invasion' – a term indicative of the scale of the Portuguese fishing effort off Newfoundland, which at its height employed dozens of ships and thousands of men – from the perspective of a host culture. Perhaps the most astonishing thing about this meeting of cultures was the warm and friendly atmosphere in which it was conducted, which may be seen to have its roots in a shared experience of poverty and an uncertain livelihood determined by proximity to the ocean.

Memories: Journalism

Newfoundland newspaper accounts of the relationship between the men of the White Fleet and Newfoundlanders again and again attest to the existence of a special relationship. An article by G.A. Frecker in the St John's *Evening Telegram* is representative of these expressions of the shared romance with the sea: the source of life, and all too frequently of death, for those who fished the North Atlantic from their precariously small dories. Frecker writes, 'I was born at the doorstep of the sea and ships are in my blood ... The Portuguese fishing fleet has a special interest for me because it is more than an agglomeration of individual ships; it is a floating community, a society of people who share in common the development of one of Portugal's great industries – the cod fisheries.'[3] The writer goes on to observe that the Portuguese are 'very welcome [in St John's] for they not only bring business but also colour and a cosmopolitan flavour to our city.'

This sense not only of economic ties but of an intimate cultural bond finds echoes several years later in newspaper editorials on the occasion of the Portuguese fishermen's gift of a statue of Our Lady of Fátima to the Catholic basilica. Two editorials in the leading local newspaper – 'Welcome to the Portuguese'[4] and 'Reflections on Portuguese'[5] – note both the size and the friendliness of the seasonal Portuguese invasion: 'Only on few occasions have so many foreigners, in the strict sense of the word, trod our shores at one time. Today we have over 3,000 Portuguese fishermen in port from 40 banking vessels and trawlers ... Although speaking a different language, the Portuguese are regarded here as friends.'[6] The editor's choice of words is significant – the Portuguese are 'foreigners' only 'in the strict sense of the word.'

The newspaper accounts of the Portuguese presence also suggest a popular local interest in, and knowledge of, things Portuguese. Newfoundland journalists would sometimes even be sent on assignment to Portugal to report on conditions of daily life in the homeland of the fishermen who arrived on these shores in their thousands every summer.[7] From St John's to Baccalieu the coast of Newfoundland bears the inscription of generations of early Portuguese navigators (Seary 1971, 1989), and there seems to have been a recurring interest by Newfoundland journalists in the theory that it was the Portuguese, not Cabot, who first discovered Newfoundland in the modern period.[8] Newspaper writers also display a close knowledge of the Portuguese fishermen themselves, noting how 'many of them are from Portugal's possession the Azores, [and] are trained in early youth for their arduous calling.'[9]

This sympathetic representation is evident even in the controversy over the barring of Portuguese fishermen from Canadian ports for alleged overfishing in the 1980s. Newspaper accounts note how the Portuguese 'incurred the wrath of federal officials,' yet 'City [of St John's] officials, including Mayor John Murphy ... expressed concern over ... the unofficial ban on the Portuguese vessels.'[10] Years later in an interview that I conducted with Murphy, the former mayor recalled how 'very, very reluctant' he had been to accept the ban.[11] He observed that the Portuguese fishermen, invariably 'extremely cordial' individuals, were always distinct from the fishing fleets of other nations in their appeal to Newfoundlanders. This representation of Newfoundlanders' view of the Portuguese recurs in earlier newspaper accounts of relations between the two peoples.[12] Newfoundlanders perceived the Portuguese not as they did the Russians or the Spanish, who also fished the Grand Banks and contributed to the economy of St John's, but much more intimately.

Mayor Murphy, whose family owned the Arcade store downtown, noted as well that only Portuguese fishermen traded with Newfoundlanders. They conducted this personal, under-the-counter trade largely in liquor from Portugal but also in handmade arts and crafts such as 'ornate lace tablecloths' and ship models, examples of which Murphy purchased and still possesses.[13] This entrepreneurship is one example of a gap in 'respectable' journalism on the relationship, which invariably mentioned only official trading ties. To rectify this lacuna a researcher must look to other sources, particularly regarding perhaps the two most prominent aspects of the non-economic relationship – soccer and sex.

Over the decades-long presence of the White Fleet on the Grand Banks there is not a single mention in Newfoundland papers of what remains perhaps the most defining characteristic of the Portuguese for the people of St John's: their love of soccer.[14] It is not until 1995, years after Canadian waters closed to Portuguese fishing vessels, that a newspaper article takes note of this passion. A flotilla of tall ships arrived in St John's harbour, and, although only the *Gazela* was of Portuguese origin, onlookers had memories only of the fishermen of the White Fleet. The headline reads, 'Tall Ships Evoke Memories of Soccer on the Waterfront,' and the article, consisting of interviews with members of the crowd, is dominated by their recollections of the Portuguese fishermen's love of the game. One man recalled, 'In the '40s when I was in school, when someone in your class said, "The white ships are in the harbour!" after school you'd run right down to see them.' Another observed, 'All the Portuguese wanted was a bit of music and a game of soccer ... They played soccer right out on the harbour front. I don't know who could kick a ball better.' Yet another recalled, 'They used to go up on the hill with us and play soccer ... The Portuguese were excellent soccer players. They'd all go up in the meadows and take off their shoes and it'd be a game of barefoot soccer.'[15]

This article is representative not only of my memory but of that of almost everyone over thirty whom I informally questioned. The first, primary association that people who lived in St John's during those years have of the Portuguese is their love for soccer.[16] The sight of sailing ships, most of which were not Portuguese, evoked memories of the White Fleet long after it had vanished from Newfoundland waters.

Note that this single recorded mention takes the form of a transcription of popular memories. We can only speculate why journalists of the 1940s, 1950s, and 1960s ignored the subject. Perhaps soccer was then regarded as a sport of the working classes and so not worthy of note? Perhaps personal contact between ordinary Portuguese and Newfoundlanders seemed less significant than the economic and political dimensions that dominate newspaper accounts.

A Play

The silence of the journalistic record on relationships between the fishermen of the White Fleet and the women of St John's is perhaps more understandable. Fortunately, the city's theatrical community fills that gap with the play *Terras de bacalhau* (Land of Cod), a 'collective' creation by eight artists of Newfoundland and Portuguese descent produced originally in 1980, when memories of the White Fleet were still fresh in the collective memory (see Anonsen et al. 1996). The play, a mingling of Portuguese songs and music with the wry social comedy characteristic of Newfoundland theatre, is set in the 1960s and is primarily the story of a Portuguese boy's coming of age when he makes his first voyage with his father on the White Fleet and of their bittersweet romantic and sexual relations with women in St John's. The sensitivity of this issue – given both the frankness and the sympathy with which it deals with the unhappiness of the wives whom the fishermen leave behind in Portugal, as well as adultery and clashes of cultures – suggests why there is sparse discussion in other media.

In the play's most poignant moment, the Newfoundland girl who is the love object of the young Portuguese sailor has a confrontation with her father:

CECIL. What do you think I'm runnin' here? A flop house for common whores who run around with Portuguese sailors?

KAY, *angry*. I am not a common whore and I don't run around with Portuguese sailors! I just happen to be going out with a guy from Portugal and (*emotional*) I, I think that I'm in love with him! (Act II, scene 5)

The memories of members of the Portuguese-Newfoundland community from this time support the notion that their sexual relations, like so many of their other types of relations, were more than just 'economic.' The Portuguese, both in literature and in memory, are represented as very attentive, romantic lovers. Indeed, often when Portuguese sailors went absent without leave and their ships returned to the Banks without them, Canadian immigration authorities found that a fisherman had done nothing more than sleep in after a 'long night with a Newfoundland girlfriend.'[17]

Terras de bacalhau makes effective comic use of the forms of confusion that inevitably accompany contacts between different cultures, without any trace of prejudice or resentment. Act I, scene 6, set in the

Arcade, opens with a passing reference to the cheap 'Portuguese sneakers' and details the attempts by several Portuguese fishermen to buy lingerie for their wives back home:

VOICEOVER. In our Arcade shoe department, downstairs, brandname sneakers. Out they go, while they last, at the incredibly low price of three for a dollar.

...

RITA. What size do you want? 34, 36, 38, 40? What size?

CARLOS. Wife size.

RITA. Is your wife a big woman or is she small like you?

CARLOS. Sim, sim, 93-56-93!

RITA. She must be deformed! You're going to have to go into yardgoods to get something to fit her.

CARLOS. Não, não, não, 93-56-93, like you, smaller. Like you.

RITA. Like me! Smaller! I don't have to take that from you ... And me after starving meself all day. Do you know what I had to eat all day? A piece of dry toast and a cup of weak tea, that's all.

KAY. Rita, I think he's talkin' in kilometres or something!

Indeed, the play often presents the Portuguese as confused spectators of Newfoundlanders' well-intentioned attempts to communicate. In Act I, scene 7, Kay takes her new Portuguese boyfriend, João, home to meet members of her family, who are engaged in a typical, argumentative card game:

RONNY. Dad, sure she just said he don't speak any English.

VANYA. What difference is it, b'y? Sure, cards are a universal language.

...

AGNES. Kay, where did you meet him?

KAY. At the Basilica.

AMBROSE. They goes up there all the time.

AGNES. The Basilica, the Basilica?

RONNY. Dad, he don't know what you're saying. Dad, Dad? He don't speak English.

CECIL. If you shut up, I can explain it to him.

Much as the scene in the Arcade reflects popular memory of Portuguese shopping habits, so this scene gives form to the memory of the frequent presence of the Portuguese in the basilica. Moreover, Kay's

father, Cecil, may be seen to embody the comic aspect of the play's representation of the relationship between the two peoples. Even when he
criticizes his daughter for dating a Portuguese man, he is angry more
out of concern for her than from any bigotry or cultural prejudice.

However, *Terras de bacalhau* also attempts to recreate the perspective
of the Portuguese fishermen. The songs they sing are often political,
critical of the dictatorship at home and of the Portuguese merchants
who exploit them. In Act I, scene 1, we hear Manuel singing 'Only a
Fisherman':

> I'm only a fisherman, and I do whatever I can,
> I don't like to take from my brothers and sisters,
> Who are just as poor as I am.
> ...
> Workin,' workin,' workin' for the rich man.
> Portugal was fascisto for years,
> People shed their tears for freedom,
> For a better way, they had their say,
> Like Mozambique, like Angola, they cried out.
> They said, 'No, no, no, to oppression.'
> Yes, I'm only a fisherman, and I do whatever I can,
> I don't like to take from my brothers and sisters,
> Who are just as poor as I am.

The poverty of so many of the fishermen, and their exploitation by
merchants back home, must have evoked their own plight for many
Newfoundlanders and made them identify so strongly with the Portuguese. However, this theatrical re-creation may also serve as a document of the forces that drove Portuguese emigration for much of this
century.

And in the End ...

In the introduction to the published edition of *Terras de Bacalhau*, the
editor contends that one of the play's main themes is the relation
between 'self and other' (Peters 1996). As this essay has shown,
however, the Portuguese were never really foreigners, never 'other' to
the people of St John's. Rather, in the context of their representation in
the memories and writings of Newfoundlanders, they seem to occupy
an ambiguous liminal space between self and other, indicative of the

shared cultural values of the two peoples and of a common experience of economic deprivation and life defined, to a great degree, by the ocean.

Clearly both the absence of substantial documentary evidence and the complexities of the relationship between Newfoundlanders and the Portuguese of the White Fleet necessitate an approach that supplements media with memory (in the forms of literature and interviews). It is an exercise imbued, for me as much as for the often-homesick fishermen whom I have been researching, with *saudade*. As Salman Rushdie writes, 'The past is a country from which we have all emigrated' (1991: 12).

In this sense, perhaps both Portuguese and Newfoundlanders are *saudosistas:* emigrants from a past that was materially poorer but culturally richer. This chapter, then, can be seen not only as part of the story of Portuguese fishermen in the New World but perhaps also as a reflection on a unique moment of cross-cultural exchange that has, sadly, been lost to everything save memory.

NOTES

1 Editorial, 'Welcome to the Portuguese,' *Evening Telegram* (St John's), 26 May 1955, 4.
2 The two key Portuguese words recurring in this chapter are usually translated in English as follows: '*saudade* (f.): longing, yearning; homesickness, nostalgia; heartache ... *saudosista* I. (a.) of or pertaining to one who yearns or longs for the past. *II.* (mf.) one who yearns or longs for the past, die-hard' (Houaiss and Avery 1967: 546–7).
3 G.A. Frecker, 'The Fleet's In: Portuguese Fishermen in St John's Follow Ancestors,' *Evening Telegram* (St John's) 11 Aug. 1953, 13.
4 Editorial, 'Welcome to the Portuguese,' *Evening Telegram* (St John's), 26 May 1955, 4.
5 Editorial, 'Reflections on Portuguese,' *Evening Telegram* (St John's), 1 June 1955, 4.
6 Editorial, 'Welcome to the Portuguese,' *Evening Telegram* (St John's), 26 May 1955, 4.
7 J. White, 'Portugal's Fishing Ties Reach Back to 1255: Fishermen May Have Been Here before Cabot,' *Daily News* (St John's), 1 Dec., 8.
8 Anon., 'Portugues [sic] Discovery Celebration Begins: New Hospital Steamer Arrives from Portugal,' *Daily News* (St John's), 27 May 1955.

9 Editorial, 'Reflections on Portuguese,' *Evening Telegram* (St John's), 30 May 1955, 1 June 1955.
10 Anon., 'Portuguese Vessels Are Barred from Entering Canadian Ports,' *Evening Telegram* (St John's), 6 May 1986, 3.
11 Mayor John Murphy, interview with the author, 2 Jan. 1997.
12 See Frecker, 'The Fleet's In.' 13; Editorial, 'Warm Welcome Extended Portuguese Ambassador,' *Daily News* (St John's), 11 June 1948, 4.
13 Mayor John Murphy, interview with the author, 2 Jan. 1997.
14 Here memory again serves to complement the documentary record. On the occasion of the annual meeting of the Canadian Association of Geographers in St John's in August 1997, I took a visiting Portuguese-Canadian academic on a tour of the city by cab. The taxi driver, on overhearing me recall the Portuguese and their love of soccer, began talking of how he had played with them himself in his youth; his recollections of their skill and sportsmanship had largely defined his high regard for them through the intervening years of Portuguese-Canadian quarrels over fishing rights.

   Certainly this perspective on the Portuguese passion for soccer is shared by almost every Newfoundlander of my acquaintance, which makes its almost complete absence from the newspaper record all the more puzzling.
15 J. Tompkins, 'Tall Ships Evoke Memories of Soccer on the Waterfront' *Evening Telegram* (St John's), 5 Aug. 1995, 3.
16 This informal survey consisted of responses in early August 1997 from ten people: three relatives or friends and the others chosen at random from the St John's population. I did this, without making any claims that these data would be significant, to satisfy my personal curiosity. Of those asked, everyone who lived in St John's during the period studied responded with wistful memories of the Portuguese and, of course, their passion for soccer.
17 António Duarte and Kathy Duarte, interview with the author, 28 Dec. 1996.

REFERENCES

Anonsen, K., R. Boland, J.E. Silva, J. Koop, J. Payne, J. Spence, G. Thomey, and M. Walsh. 1996. *Terras de Bacalhau* (Land of Cod). 1980. In *Stars in the Sky Morning: Collective Plays of Newfoundland and Labrador,* ed. H. Peters, 131–76. St John's: Killick Press.

Doel, P. 1992. *Port O'Call: Memories of the Portuguese White Fleet in St. John's, Newfoundland*. St John's: ISER Press.

Houaiss, A., and C.B. Avery 1967. *The New Appleton Dictionary of the English and Portuguese Languages*. New York : Appleton-Century-Crofts.

Peters, H. 1996. 'Introduction.' In *Stars in the Sky Morning: Collective Plays of Newfoundland and Labrador*, ed. H. Peters. St John's: Killick Press.

Rushdie, S. 1991. *Imaginary Homelands: Essays and Criticism 1981–1991*. London: Granta.

Seary, E.R. 1971. 'Some Portuguese, Spanish and Basque Place Names in Newfoundland.' Address to the Canadian Association of Hispanists, 26 May.

– 1989. 'The Portuguese Element in the Place Names of Newfoundland.' In *Vice-Almirate A. Teixeira da Mota: In memoriam*, vol. 2, 359–64. Lisbon: Academia de Marinha.

Teixeira, C., and G. Lavigne. 1998. *Os Portugueses no Canadá: Uma bibliografia (1953–1996)*. Lisbon: Direcção-Geral dos Assuntos Consulares e Comunidades Portuguesas.

PART TWO

Immigration from Portugal to Canada

6 Azorean Diaspora and Cultural Retention in Montreal and Toronto

MANUEL ARMANDO OLIVIERA

This chapter identifies some of the main factors that, in the day-to-day life of Azoreans and their descendants in the cities of Toronto and Montreal, influence their attitude with respect to cultural retention, i.e., the preservation of the language and culture that for many of them are their language and culture of origin, although for a growing number are those of their parents, of their ancestors.

I take the position that the hope of maintaining their culture and above all the Portuguese language is in all probability a lost cause, in particular for the descendants of Azorean immigrants. This is clearly suggested by the reality of Portuguese – but above all Azorean – immigrant communities abroad (Alpalhão and Da Rosa 1983; Neto and Gonçalves 1985; Leandro 1998; Da Rosa 1990; Santos 1995; Oliveira 2001; Oliveira and Teixeira 2004), and seems to be the case with other ethnic groups as well. That, in my opinion, should not be a cause for alarm, much less despair, because although language is the most important element of a culture, the latter includes a whole panoply of cultural elements, complexes, and patterns that constitute and typify the cultural heritage of a group. This cultural heritage may therefore be shared and transmitted even in the absence of knowledge of the language. Cultural retention in the sense just defined, namely by migrant groups and their descendants, is a fundamentally positive and thus desirable value, and in my opinion Azorean emigrants and their descendants should therefore strive to keep their culture. It is the objective of this chapter to offer a small contribution to that goal.

This chapter draws mostly from two sociological studies one of which I carried out singly and the other of which I co-authored. The first looked into emigration from an Azorean island to the city of

Toronto (Oliveira 1996), while the second dealt with the cultural and social relationships of young Portuguese and Portuguese descendants in Toronto and Montreal (Oliveira and Teixeira 2004).[1] The latter has shown that indicators of a lack of interest in cultural retention (in the sense above referred to and used throughout this chapter) manifest themselves much more intensely among Azoreans and their descendants than among the Portuguese from the mainland and their descendants.

The chapter also draws on data collected as a result of direct and participant observation that I have carried out over two decades in Toronto, and on a thorough review of the existing literature.

Cultural Retention and the Barriers It Faces

Numerous appeals from a variety of sources have been directed at Portuguese emigrants abroad and their descendants to commit themselves to retaining the Portuguese language and culture. Those appeals have gone largely unheeded. There is abundant evidence for this with respect to young Azoreans and Azorean descendants in Canada: most will answer in English (or in French in Quebec) even when addressed in Portuguese; the large majority have either a very poor command of the Portuguese language or none at all; only a relatively small percentage have been exposed to the language outside the family environment (Tables 6.1 and 6.2); by and large, those who attend Portuguese classes do so not of their own choosing but because they're forced by their parents (Table 6.3); even the relatively few who attend Portuguese courses at university level seem to do so, for the most part, not out of interest in or respect for the language and culture but because they hope to get good marks with comparatively little effort; most do not take part in any cultural events in the Azorean community, much less in the Portuguese community at large; and most will respond in English or French even if their parents insist on Portuguese being spoken at home exclusively. The day will come – it has, indeed, already arrived for many – when these parents will realize that the 'third death of the immigrant' is upon them, and will start, with increasing frequency, using one of those two languages when communicating with their children.[2]

Why, then, do the majority of Azorean and Azorean-descendant youth (just like the majority of Portuguese and Portuguese-descendant youth, although to a much larger degree), stay away from significant

Table 6.1
Frequency of Portuguese language usage at work, 2004

	Toronto		Montreal		Toronto and Montreal	
	N	%	N	%	N	%
Always	15	7.3	9	11.1	24	8.4
Frequently	35	17.1	7	8.6	42	14.7
Occasionally	34	16.6	15	18.5	49	17.1
Rarely	61	29.8	29	35.8	90	31.5
Never	60	29.3	21	25.9	81	28.3
Total	205	100.0	81	100.0	286	100.0

Source: Oliveira and Teixeira 2004, 173.

Table 6.2
Frequency of Portuguese language usage elsewhere, 2004

	Toronto		Montreal		Toronto and Montreal	
	N	%	N	%	N	%
Always	13	5.6	10	9.4	23	6.8
Frequently	52	22.4	26	24.5	78	23.1
Occasionally	54	23.3	35	33.0	89	26.3
Rarely	95	40.9	31	29.2	126	37.3
Never	18	7.8	4	3.8	22	6.5
Total	232	100.0	106	100.0	338	100.0

Source: Oliveira and Teixeira 2004, 174.

cultural events in their community, and show no interest in cultural retention?

When asked that question most young Azorean and Azorean-descendant youth tend to reply that they feel excluded from Portuguese institutions in general, namely clubs and associations, which in their opinion are controlled by old folks who seem always to define the terms of participation. In the words of one of those youth, 'Portuguese Associations are dominated by old dictatorial men who wish to talk of nothing but Portugal and Portuguese stuff, and to be sure, of

Table 6.3
Decision to attend Portuguese-language classes, 2004

Decision made by	Toronto (n = 132)		Montreal (n = 61)		Toronto and Montreal (n = 193)	
	N	%	N	%	N	%
Self	45	34.1	22	36.1	67	34.7
Parents	101	76.5	43	70.5	143	74.1
Other	8	6.1	2	3.3	10	5.2

Note: Number of responses exceeds number of respondents because some respondents answered in more than one category.
Source: Oliveira and Teixeira 2004, 171.

a Portugal that no longer exists. Moreover, all the talk must be done in Portuguese and Portuguese alone' (Oliveira and Teixeira 2004: 205). Another frequent explanation for the low enthusiasm for participation in cultural activities in the community is the claim that things Portuguese are 'boring.'

Although these statements are significant they do of course refer to only one factor in cultural retention: the lack of participation of the young Azoreans and Azorean descendants in activities that take place in Azorean institutions. The issue of linguistic and cultural preservation is a far broader and more complex one, however, encompassing a wide variety of factors. Among these the following seem to bear special importance:

1 Young people who make use of only English or French throughout the day, whether in school, at work, or with their friends have difficulty finding the motivation to switch to Portuguese at home, as it is a language they speak with increasing effort. The situation is aggravated by their knowledge that their parents can by now understand them well enough in English or French.
2 Anglo-American (and therefore Anglo-Canadian) culture and the English language enjoy unmatched prestige and popularity among young people all over the world. Young Azoreans and Azorean descendants are therefore naturally led to prefer identifying with the dominant culture, and above all speaking its language. Most Azorean youth who took part in the study we've been following

(Oliveira and Teixeira 2004) consider themselves Canadians first, and only then Azoreans or Portuguese.[3]

3 The so-called ethnic languages – which in Canada means every language but French and, above all, English – have a low status that was in some ways reinforced by the establishment of multiculturalism as official policy. The Canadian authorities decided that multiculturalism was to function within a bilingual framework. In other words all the languages but English and French were, from the outset of multiculturalism as public policy, destined to have an inferior status – officially recognized as such. And thus, while in Portugal, for instance, when someone is heard speaking a language other than Portuguese, it is generally taken as an indication of higher than average education, in Canada, when a person is heard speaking a language other than English (or French in Quebec) it tends to be taken as an indication of immigrant status: the speaker is regarded as an 'ethnic,' or 'a member of a multicultural group.' In these circumstances the language that one speaks becomes a differentiating factor between the dominant and the dominated segments of society and a clear motive for the latter to be accorded an inferior status. That knowledge drives many immigrants, and in particular their descendants, to feel ashamed of speaking their mother tongue in public. It also causes some of them who arrived in Canada as adults but who speak English or French with considerable fluency to make a conscious and noticeable effort to speak those languages 'with no accent,' in what could be interpreted as a clear attempt at 'passing.'[4]

4 The fact that many youth – and in fact many members of the first generation of immigrants as well – feel ashamed of publicly identifying themselves as Portuguese. Many still have a negative perception of Portugal and things Portuguese because of what they believe is the view shared by others that it is a backward and irrelevant country. As various scholars have observed this attitude is common among young Portuguese and Portuguese descendants living in various parts of the world. In France, for example, one author states that 'the relative prestige of cultures favors the French culture. The culture brought by their parents, being that of the immigrant group, is for that reason always belittled by the surrounding culture and *in many cases by the youth themselves*' (Leandro 1998: 210, emphasis added). The same author goes on to state that 'it is common to find Portuguese adolescents who do not

speak Portuguese outside the home so as to hide the fact that they are immigrants' (210).

It must also be said that many of the Azorean youth and Portuguese in general living in Canada seem to have a rather pragmatic and even utilitarian view of cultural retention: they might retain that culture and language if it brought them some real benefits and if it were not, a source of embarrassment to them.

The following letter sent to a Montreal newspaper by a young Azorean living in that Canadian city illustrates the point:

> Who will make up the Portuguese community of tomorrow? Will it not be today's youth? I'm sure that most Portuguese students (in Canada) profoundly dislike attending Portuguese classes, and yet no one seems to face up to this situation ... Unfortunately, I couldn't finish my secondary studies in the Portuguese school, because I couldn't stand it any more. The point is: What do we really learn by attending Portuguese school in Canada? We must understand that in reality, we live in Canada not in Portugal, and there is a huge difference between being a young Portuguese in Portugal and a young Portuguese descendant in Canada – above all, in that the latter is immersed in the Canadian and American cultures. Most Portuguese and Portuguese-descendant students in Canada certainly do not consider the Portuguese language as their first one, not even their second, but at best, their third. Their contact with the Portuguese culture, in the end, boils down to a few religious festivities and sports activities which they seem to appreciate. Taking all this into account, I, for one, think that to take courses in Portuguese, like History or Geography is not needed ... I remember reading Portuguese poems written God knows when – and dealing with God knows what, because as far as we were concerned, it all sounded like Japanese! ... I admit that I lost nothing by attending Portuguese classes – that they may even have given me a little knowledge of the language which then helped me in my Spanish studies. On the other hand, instead of making me appreciative of the Portuguese culture it made me hate it, because I was traumatized, and that led me to renounce my origins. My hatred toward the Portuguese culture was palpable – hence I used to tell my friends that I was Canadian and not Portuguese. Why are Portuguese and Portuguese-descendant youth in Canada not listened to? After all, they're the ones who know why they are attending Portuguese classes and why they don't like them. If that is so, then they should have most – if not all – the answers. (Fagundes 2000: 5)

My observations so far refer to young Portuguese and Portuguese descendants in general living in Toronto and Montreal, whether they have Azorean or Portuguese mainland origins. As previously stated, however, the various indicators testifying to the lack of cultural retention manifest themselves with considerably more intensity among the former than the latter (Oliveira and Teixeira 2004). Portuguese youth of Azorean origin have practically given up participating in the life of their community, as can be seen from their absence from all cultural events in Azorean clubs and *Casas dos Açores* (Azorean houses) in Toronto and Montreal. Anyone visiting a Portuguese class in one of those two cities and asking for a show of hands from youth of Azorean origin is certain to find that, after a moment of hesitation, one or two arms will be raised timidly from among twenty or so students. Many young people of Azorean origin behave as if they felt doubly ashamed: of their Portuguese origins, but even more so of their Azorean roots. Part of the reason – in particular with respect to retention of the Portuguese language – lies in internalized feelings of inferiority that were instilled in both the youth and their parents by mainlanders, above all for the way they speak Portuguese. Feeling diminished they then turn inward and prefer to distance themselves (Oliveira and Teixeira 2004).

It must be pointed out that much of what has been stated above with respect to young Azoreans and Azorean descendants might just as well be said with respect to their parents, even those – still the large majority – who are first-generation migrants. They evince the same lack of interest for most cultural events, the main exception being a few religious festivities. They have the same reluctance to publicly identify themselves as Portuguese and as Azoreans, and the same perception of the uselessness, for their children, of cultural retention. An Azorean immigrant woman in Toronto, when asked why her children, both of whom held degrees from Canadian universities, could not speak, indeed could hardly understand, the Portuguese language, she immediately responded,

> How selfish can one get?! In a way, our children were brought to this country not unlike the slaves of African origin were brought to North America – i.e., nobody cared to ask them whether they wanted to come, or stay. The same, obviously, happened to those who were born here – they had no choice! We all know that young Portuguese and Portuguese descendants in Canada face serious problems – problems having to do

with identity, with social adaptation to Canadian society, with academic achievement ... and we know, as well, that the consequences are bound to be serious indeed. And yet, instead of helping them – and helping ourselves in the process – as would be the case if we made a serious effort, right from the beginning, to learn English in order to be able to talk to our children in that language and, at the same time, increase our chances of integration into Canadian society and culture – instead of that, we insist that they must speak Portuguese. Not to their benefit – that is obvious enough – but for our own convenience! Forgetting – or not caring enough about it – that this is their country, English is their language, it is the one language they need to be proficient in, it is in the Canadian school they need to achieve good results. You know what? I'd like to have someone explain to me how it is that being able to memorize the Lusiadas from top to bottom, or to dance the Azorean *chamarrita* like a pro – how that would help a young Portuguese or Portuguese descendant to have a better life in Canada, to integrate into Canadian society and culture. (Oliveira and Teixeira 2004: 223)[5]

Her response raises the question of why Azoreans in general, and Azorean youth in particular, seem to have even less interest in preserving their culture and language of origin than do mainlanders.

Azoreans and Portuguese Mainlanders: The Two Solitudes

It is frequently said in both mainland Portugal and the Azores, and occasionally by some scholars, that unlike mainland Portuguese, who leave their country with a clear idea of some day returning once their objectives have been met, Azoreans leave the islands wishing never to return (cf Oliveira 1996). Despite the harsh realities of emigration, and despite the fact that the majority of emigrants harbour hope of returning to their homeland at some stage, there are still those who leave with no plans to return, except perhaps for a short visit (Neto 1981). Perhaps a case in point is emigration from the Madeira islands, and above all from the Azores.

Many mainland Portuguese have called our attention to the rather weak representation of Azorean and Azorean-descendant students in the Toronto schools where Portuguese is taught, a fact they interpret as a clear indicator of the different goals that Portuguese and Azoreans establish with respect to returning to their place of origin. Whereas the mainland Portuguese have a clear idea of returning and are therefore interested in their children attending Portuguese schools in Canada, Azoreans with no intention of returning might look at Portuguese school attendance by their children as an exercise in futility, a useless burden that would hinder their children's chances of doing well in the Canadian school system. Lopes (1986), for instance, states that 'in Winnipeg, there is, among the Azoreans, a greater acceptance of the Canadian way of life, than among the Portuguese from the mainland' a fact he interprets as proof that unlike the Portuguese, Azoreans do not intend to go back to the islands and therefore have no interest in their children speaking Portuguese.

The idea that Azoreans would leave their islands with a firm determination not to return needs to be treated with caution, though, for reasons I have explained elsewhere (Oliveira 1996). It cannot be applied sweepingly and without exception to the islanders as a group. This is not to deny the real differences between Azoreans and mainlanders with respect to cultural – and above all linguistic – retention. Conceivably broad attitudinal differences between mainlanders and Azoreans are somewhat influenced by different approaches to the idea of returning, but the topic needs further research.

Another factor that may help to explain the apparent lack of interest of young Azorean emigrants and their descendants in keeping their Portuguese culture and language is their emotional attachment to America and things American. One author calls our attention to how affectionately Azoreans in general look upon the United States, noting that 'politically, Azoreans are connected to Portugal, but all their interests as well as their hearts are with America' (Santos 1995: 110). Along the same lines I have referred to the contacts that Azoreans have, for centuries now, had with 'mother America,' and while those contacts have not been the only ones with the outside world, they have undoubtedly been the most significant materially and the most fulfilling emotionally for many Azoreans for a very long time (Oliveira 1996, 2001: 156). Furthermore many Azoreans have called our attention to a not too distant past when 'Americans' (Azorean immigrants in the United States) visiting the islands exhibited a hardly contained pride when telling the locals that their children could not – or could hardly – understand or speak the Portuguese language.

This affectionate inclination of Azoreans for things American might help explain a stronger predisposition of Azorean emigrants, and above all their descendants, to forsake the Portuguese language and culture, especially when they feel so attracted to this other culture which they so much admire and value. Granted, the examples above refer to the experience of Azoreans in the context of the United States, the main destination of Azorean emigration. But let us keep in mind that for Azorean emigrants and their descendants in Canada, there is no significant difference nowadays between this country and its neighbour to the south.

Other factors have certainly led Azoreans to show less interest in cultural retention, and one of the most significant is the nature of the relationship between Azoreans and mainland Portuguese living in Canada. Careful and prolonged observation of the nature of that relationship leads me to conclude that it causes Azoreans to feel looked down upon by the mainlanders, as if they are considered second-class Portuguese. Feeling unwelcome by the mainlanders, Azoreans tend to lose interest in things that are relevant to the Portuguese community as a whole and to avoid participation in the life of that community. Moreover, they seem to make no effort to achieve positions both within and outside of the community that they might otherwise aspire to as members of the most representative subgroup of the Portuguese in Canada.[6]

The Great Taboo

It is a topic of much talk among Portuguese immigrants of all stripes, and no student of Portuguese emigration to Canada is a stranger to it. Few are also unaware of how difficult it is to discuss openly and honestly: 'Understandably,' says one Portuguese scholar, 'this is a topic of great sensitivity, and as a Portuguese from the mainland, I soon learned how high that sensitivity can reach' (Marujo 1999: 19). With reference to a meeting she attended in Toronto, the same author remarked, 'As the meeting progressed, I made reference to my having noticed a certain level of hostility between Azoreans and Portuguese from the mainland. Later on, I was advised by various participants in that meeting never again to bring the subject up, or risk making a few enemies in the Portuguese community' (19). Similarly, when Carlos Teixeira and I were in the process of interviewing informants in Toronto for our study on young Portuguese and Portuguese descendants (Oliveira and Teixeira 2004), we were contacted by a community leader who vehemently criticized the fact that we dared deal with Azoreans and Portuguese separately with respect to some variables and then publicly discuss differences between those two groups. In his own words that was a racist attitude, no more no less ...

Why does such resentment and animosity exist between Azoreans and mainlanders, all of whom, after all, claim to be Portuguese, citizens of the same country, only born in different regions of that country?[7] First and foremost – as the members of both groups by and large agree and as students of Portuguese emigration to Canada have observed – the image that many mainland Portuguese have of Azoreans in general is not very favourable, to put it mildly. Why? In the 1940s, interrupting a centuries-old period of isolation during which most Azoreans and mainlanders ignored each other's existence, a large contingent of Portuguese servicemen were stationed in the Azores, many of whom established close contact with the local population. To this day in many villages and towns of mainland Portugal the locals can still remember the image that those military brought back with them about the Azoreans: the men backward and somewhat lazy; the women a little too tolerant of flirtation.

The large majority of mainland Portuguese immigrants in Canada, however, had their first contact with Azoreans only after arriving in that country. Before that the lack of knowledge was mutual and complete – although deeper among the mainlanders because Azoreans were taught about the Portuguese and Portugal in school. Thus many Portuguese mainlanders living in Toronto and Montreal today actually knew very little about the Azores and its people before immigrating to Canada. Some considered the Azores to be an overseas colony, not unlike Angola, Mozambique, and Cape Verde. From this point of view the Azores were regarded as a distant and mostly unknown land populated by a 'backward' people. In the words of one of our informants, 'Azoreans and mainlanders met as immigrants in a foreign land, and none of them seems to have appreciated much of what he was being introduced to' (Oliveira and Teixeira 2004: 142).

Table 6.4 shows the specific perceptions that mainland Portuguese hold about Azoreans: that they have little education, are a somewhat backward people, speak differently, and are of a different class and culture. As one author asserts, 'It is generally understood that mainlanders have a higher degree of education (therefore speak better Portuguese), have better jobs, and tend to take the leadership even in situations in which Azoreans are the majority' (Marujo 1999: 19). Few

Table 6.4
How mainland Portuguese perceive Azoreans, 2004

	Toronto		Montreal		Toronto and Montreal	
	N	%	N	%	N	%
Speak differently	35	57.4	11	52.4	46	56.1
Lower social class	5	8.2	1	4.8	6	7.3
Low education	2	3.3	0	0.0	2	2.4
Different culture	12	19.7	6	28.6	18	22.0
Other	7	11.5	3	14.3	10	12.2
Total	61	100.0	21	100.0	82	100.0

Source: Oliveira and Teixeira 2004, 154.

would dispute the notion that mainlanders tend to assume leadership roles.

Just as for Azoreans there is a 'Portuguese way' of speaking the language, so for mainlanders there is an 'Azorean way' of speaking it. Because Azoreans from the island of São Miguel form the majority of the archipelago population, it is not surprising that for the mainlanders, 'to speak Azorean' is to speak as Azoreans from São Miguel do.[8] Since the Portuguese spoken on São Miguel island, as on the other islands of the archipelago, is the same Portuguese as that spoken on the mainland, one gets the clear impression that the issue is primarily one of accent. Even Azoreans from the other islands find the Portuguese spoken on São Miguel somewhat ugly and unpleasant to the ear. This is clearly illustrated when, for instance, those responsible for the recording of public announcements go so far as to get them recorded on the mainland by native mainland speakers, especially from the Lisbon area, believed by some to be one of a couple of areas where the locals are privileged to speak 'standard Portuguese.'[9]

This attitude represents an undeniably important problem with potentially serious psychological and material consequences.[10] It causes many young Azoreans to feel diminished and to avoid speaking Portuguese in the presence of mainlanders – even get to the point of hiding their Azorean roots. I have witnessed the occurrence repeatedly, and it has occasionally been the object of reference in the local Canadian media.[11]

Table 6.5
How Azoreans perceive mainland Portuguese, 2004

	Toronto		Montreal		Toronto and Montreal	
	N	%	N	%	N	%
Arrogant	31	44.9	11	47.8	42	45.7
With higher education	10	14.5	0	0.0	10	10.9
Speak differently	15	21.7	9	39.1	24	26.1
Have different culture	4	5.8	2	8.7	6	6.5
Other	9	13.0	1	4.3	10	10.9
Total	69	100.0	23	100.0	92	100.0

Source: Oliveira and Teixeira 2004, 155.

Other attitudes and behaviours can be observed that at least implicitly put Azoreans and their culture in an inferior position with respect to mainlanders. When honorary titles handed out by the Portuguese government almost invariably go to mainlanders; when mainlanders take a leading role in practically all cultural events, including those in the Azorean community, but Azoreans rarely do; or when the Azorean community is for all intents and purposes banned from the local Portuguese media, most probably for 'speaking Azorean' – when all this happens in cities such as Toronto and Montreal, where Azoreans make up the large majority of Portuguese immigrants, then there is a clear message of marginalization, of devaluation, that is unequivocally captured by those on the receiving end.

The Vicious Circle of Marginalization

As could be expected, Azoreans feel considerable resentment that leads them to make generalizations about mainlanders in turn (Table 6.5). But the mainlander attitude toward Azoreans also triggers considerable anxiety in the latter, leading them to doubt fundamental aspects of their own culture and even to consider it somewhat inferior – in short, to turn inward and refuse to participate in important aspects of community life in which the mainlanders then predominate. And the vicious circle is completed as Azoreans are as a consequence again looked down upon by mainlanders, or simply ignored.

The analysis just presented illustrates my understanding of the reality of Azorean–mainlander relations in Canada specifically in Toronto and Montreal and how those relations influence the way that Azoreans feel and act with respect to cultural retention. Although the situation naturally affects first-generation Azoreans, it takes the biggest toll on the second generation. Many young Portuguese of mainland descent have described how their compatriots of Azorean descent avoid their company and in occasional and brief contact simply refuse to speak Portuguese. When asked to express their opinion about Azoreans many second-generation Canadians of Portuguese mainland descent made statements as negative as those of the first generation – if not more so:

'For the most part (of course there are exceptions) most Azoreans that I've met are terribly ignorant, uneducated, simply rude. The way they talk makes them almost impossible to understand.'

'I can't understand them when they talk – which is something they can't do ... '

'With respect to education, I don't think they take it as seriously as we do.'

'Azoreans are stupid and slow. In my opinion, there are reasons to feel proud of being Portuguese – if you're not an Azorean, that is.'

'Yes, Azoreans don't speak Portuguese well.'

'The Azores are to Portugal what Quebec is to Canada.' (Oliveira and Teixeira 2004: 156)

As for young Azoreans and Azorean descendants, their most common observations about mainlanders had to do with their arrogance and sense of superiority (Oliveira and Teixeira 2004: 157). When asked if they had ever experienced discrimination very few Portuguese youth from either the mainland or the Azores answered affirmatively, but all the Azoreans who did so responded without hesitation that the source of perceived discrimination was the mainland Portuguese.

It is also worth mentioning the observation made by some second-generation Azoreans about cultural retention and the contradictory issues it entails. 'On the one hand,' says one of those youth, everybody seems to be asking us not to forget the Portuguese language, to practise it in our daily lives, to feel proud of our language and our culture. And yet, as soon as we utter a word in Portuguese, we can be sure that we'll be laughed at, made to feel that our Portuguese [i.e., 'Azorean'] is not good enough' (Oliveira and Teixeira 2004: 159). Azorean youth in mainland Portugal occasionally face the same problem, but with an important difference. Those who live in Canada have a way out of the situation that their compatriots in mainland Portugal do not: they lose interest in the culture, ignore the language, and keep away from those who speak it.

Conclusion

This chapter has identified some of the main factors in the day-to-day life of Azoreans in Canada that influence their attitude toward cultural retention. We've seen that some of those factors are common to Portuguese immigrants in general, and to their descendants in particular, regardless of region of origin. It is difficult for anyone to be fluent in more than one language, under any circumstances, let alone those under which young Portuguese and Portuguese descendants are being asked to undertake the task. I Immigrants and their descendants also clearly perceive the majority language and culture as having a prestige that Portuguese language and culture cannot match. And an undeniable feeling of inferiority – rarely admitted to but easily noticeable – is the main reason for the known reluctance of many to identify as Portuguese.

Some other factors seem to affect only Azorean immigrants and their descendants. One, as we've seen, is the attitude toward return migration, which can influence the perception of and reaction to cultural retention. Another factor is the special emotional link resulting from the centuries-old contact that Azoreans have established with the United States, now being replicated with respect to Canada and Canadian culture, presumably with similar effects. Still another factor that affects Azorean attitudes toward cultural retention in a very strong way is the relationship between Azorean and Portuguese immigrants and their descendants. Too often it causes the former to feel rejected by the latter, somehow inferior to them, and finally to react with resentment, to distance themselves, and to avoid contact with their compatriots from the mainland.

This last set of factors, then, insofar as it fails to instil pride in the culture of origin, acts as a barrier to the preservation of that culture and language, causing Azorean immigrants, and above all their descendants, to lose interest in their culture – perhaps even to feel ashamed of it.

NOTES AND ACKNOWLEDGMENTS

I wish to thank the contribution made to this chapter by Carlos Teixeira by co-authoring *Jovens Portugueses e Luso-descendentes no Canadá*, on which the present paper draws heavily (Oliveira and Teixeira 2004).

1 Besides using direct and participant observation and interviewing 23 qualified informants in both cities, my co-author and I also collected data from a sample of 354 young Portuguese and Portuguese descendants, of whom 244 were in Toronto and 110 in Montreal. In both cities the sample took into account the Portuguese regional distribution of those interviewed (or of their parents) – Azores and mainland Portugal – as well as the distribution by sex, by age group and by education.

2 Taking into account young Portuguese and Portuguese descendants as a whole living in the cities of Toronto and Montreal, no more that 22.1 per cent participate in Portuguese clubs and associations (Oliveira and Teixeira 2004: 166).

   According to Selim Abou (1981) the 'third death of the immigrant' would happen when, confronted with the lack of interest, or even the revolt, of his children against their parents' culture, that immigrant would realize that his world – the world of his ancestors and his traditions – was finally coming to an end.

3 From among those who reported to feel Portuguese first, as many as 76.9 per cent are Portuguese or Portuguese descendants from mainland Portugal, and no more than 23.1 per cent are Azoreans or Azorean descendants. From among those who declared themselves Canadians first, only 21.3 per cent are from mainland Portugal whereas 78.4 per cent are from the Azores (Oliveira and Teixeira 2004: 85).

4 As Meintel and Fortin state, one's 'accent' constitutes a 'strong indicator of his or her "insider/outsider status," an inclusion and exclusion criterion' (2002: 3).

5 Os Lusíadas, or *The Lusiads*, is considered the masterpiece of Portuguese

epic literature. *Chamarrita* is a popular folk dance in the Azores.

6 It is estimated that of all the Portuguese and Portuguese descendants living in Canada, 60 to 65 per cent would be Azoreans or their descendants, whereas no more that 30 to 35 per cent would be mainlanders or their descendants (Higgs 1981; Anderson 1983; Teixeira 1999a, 1999b)

7 Illustrative of that attitude is the way in which many mainlanders sounded annoyed and how many of them reacted, when I provocatively asked what Azorean island they were from. 'Me, from the Azores?! ... What makes you think that I come from the Azores? Do I, by any means, talk like those people?' was a frequent reaction.

8 São Miguel is one of the nine islands of the Azores (see Figure 1.1, p. 5).

9 One can easily imagine what this practice does to the self-esteem of members of the local population, who thus see their representatives unequivocally consider their language (or at least the way in which they speak it) as not good enough to be heard in public.

10 As an example, during the Congress of Portuguese Communities a few years back, held in the Portuguese Parliament in Lisbon, an official responsible for hiring Portuguese teachers in the Portuguese embassy of a European capital told those in attendance how careful she always was when hiring teachers to work abroad. To illustrate her point she noted that she had just recently rejected a (fully qualified) applicant, because, being an Azorean, the applicant did not speak 'standard Portuguese.'

Another example of how those who speak 'Azorean' (and have had no opportunity for a process of 'language purification' on the mainland) can be materially harmed is that Azorean-accented Portuguese is not to be heard on the local radio or television from local politicians or others with highly visible occupations.

11 *Toronto Star,* 14 June 1992.

REFERENCES

Abou, S. 1981. *L'identité culturelle: Rélations inter-ethniques et problèmes d'acculturation*. Paris: Éditions Anthropos.

Alpalhão, J.A., and V.M.P. Da Rosa. 1983. *Da emigração à aculturação: Portugal continental e insular no Quebeque*. Angra do Heroísmo: Secretaria Regional da Educação e Cultura e Secretaria Regional dos Assuntos Sociais.

Anderson, G.M. 1983. 'Azoreans in Anglophone Canada.' *Canadian Ethnic Studies* 15, no. 1: 73–82.

Da Rosa, V.M.P. 1990. *Contribuição ao estudo da emigração nos Açores*. Angra do Heroísmo: Gabinete de Emigração e Apoio às Comunidades Açorianas.

Fagundes, L.C. 2000. 'A Escola Portuguesa é Traumatizante.' Letter to the editor. In *Jornal Voz de Portugal* (Montreal), 11 Oct., 5–12.

Higgs, D. 1981. 'Some Review Notes on a Decade of Portuguese-Canadian Studies.' *Canadian Ethnic Studies* 13, no. 2: 124–30.

Leandro, M.E. 1998. 'Jeunes portugais dans l'agglomeration parisienne – continuités et ruptures.' In *Présence portugaise en France*, ed. M.B. Roche-Trindade, 205–27. Lisbon: Colecção de Estudos Pós-Graduados, Universidade Aberta / Portuguese Open University.

Lopes, F. 1986. *The Portuguese Community in Winnipeg: An Overview*. Winnipeg: Privately printed.

Marujo, M. 1999. 'From the Margins to the Centre? A Case Study of the Integration of Culturally Diverse Student's First Language into the Mainstream Curriculum of an Elementary School.' PhD diss., University of Toronto.

Meintel D., and S. Fortin. 2002. 'Introduction.' *Canadian Ethnic Studies* 34, no. 3: 1–3.

Neto, J.B.N.P. 1981. 'O contributo do emigrante para o desenvolvimento regional – Uma perspectiva sociológica e antropológica.' *Separata da Revista 'Democracia e Liberdade,'* no. 19 (Apr.): 23–48.

Neto, F., and A. Gonçalves. 1985. 'Segunda Geração Portuguesa em França: Problemas de adaptação escolar.' *Jornal de Psicologia* 4 no. 2: 11–18.

Oliveira, A. 1996. 'Mito e realidade na emigração açoreana.' PhD diss., Technical University of Lisbon (ISCSP).

– 2001. *Pontas Negras: Memórias de uma aldeia açoreana*. Lisbon: Universidade Aberta / Portuguese Open University / Lajes do Pico, Câmara Municipal.

Oliveira, M., and C. Teixeira. 2004. *Jovens Portugueses e Luso-descendentes no Canadá*. Oeiras: Celta.

Santos, R. 1995. *Azoreans to California: A History of Migration and Settlement*. Denair, CA: Alley-Cass Publications.

Teixeira, C. 1999a. 'Portuguese.' In *Encyclopedia of Canada's Peoples*, ed. P.R. Magocsi, 1075–83. Toronto: University of Toronto Press.

– 1999b. *Portugueses em Toronto: Uma comunidade em Mudança*. Angra do Heroísmo: Gabinete de Emigração e Apoio às Comunidades Açoreanas.

7 Portuguese Women's Activism in Toronto's Building Cleaning Industry, 1975–1986

SUSANA P. MIRANDA

On 13 July 1984 striking cleaners at the First Canadian Place (FCP) tower in Toronto, almost all Portuguese immigrant women, learned that their strike was over. Their employer, Federated Building Maintenance (FBM), which was contracted to clean FCP by the owners of the building, Olympia and York Developments (O&Y), had agreed to a new contract with the union, the Food and Service Workers of Canada (FASWOC) Local 51. This contract saw the cleaners' wages rise by thirty-five cents an hour in the first year of their contract and another twenty-five cents in the second year.

This victory was the culmination of a six-week long strike in which these immigrant women raised picket signs for the first time in their lives, scuffled with police and strike breakers, and received much attention from the Canadian press. That night, the women congregated for a union meeting at St Christopher House, a social service agency located in a predominantly Portuguese neighbourhood. When the contract was accepted the cleaners embraced, cheered, and joined in impromptu dancing and singing of Portuguese folk songs as members of the press watched on. Emilia Silva, cleaner and president of the Local, stood on a table and shouted into a megaphone to be heard by the jubilant crowd, 'We have proven to everyone that we have the courage, we proved to Canada and Olympia and York, owners of the building, that we are women and we are immigrants but we can fight' (DiManno 1984).

Emilia Silva's statement alludes to the fact that many people – including employers, the labour movement, the press, and on occasion even the very women who were involved in the strike – had difficulty believing that a group of working-class immigrant women could wage and win such a struggle against major corporations. Part of this was the familiar gendered stereotype of immigrant women, and in particular southern European women, as passive and docile workers and wives. Additionally, the state had aligned with business interests against building cleaners and other contract workers, preventing significant improvement in wages and working conditions in the industry by failing to ensure 'successor rights' – the ability of contract workers to retain their union and collective agreement when contractors change – in labour law. As such this strike was very much a David-and-Goliath struggle, a metaphor favoured in the press.

Yet in addition to this successful strike much evidence points to the resistance of Portuguese immigrant women in the workplace generally, including in Toronto's building cleaning industry, which was dominated by this group for much of the 1960s, '70s, and '80s. This chapter examines how Portuguese immigrant women actively negotiated some power for themselves in the building cleaning workplace, and how their activism was shaped by their multiple identities as ethnic workers, migrants, women, wives, and mothers. These women who took on the state and big capital in 1970s and '80s Toronto had lived under a dictatorship in their homeland and had had no prior experience with unions.[1] They openly identified themselves as immigrant women who had a right to decent wages and basic security and respect in a country that had long declared itself to be an enlightened, liberal, immigrant-receiving nation.

Scholarship on Portuguese Immigrant Women

The experiences of immigrant women in Canada have received increasing attention from feminist historians (Parr 1990; Frager 1992; Iacovetta 1992; Gabaccia and Iacovetta 2002; Guard 2004a; Epp, Iacovetta, and Swyripa 2004). In particular, scholarship on the economic roles of immigrant women has stressed the importance of both their unpaid and their paid economic contribution to their families. Their multiple identities as wives and mothers, women, workers, and immigrants have structured their experiences in Canada, their treatment in the workplace, and their workplace activism. Indeed, one of the aims of recent historical feminist scholarship has been to challenge concepts and interpretations of working-class femininity, female respectability, family, and militancy that have been derived largely from studies of women who are members of the dominant Anglo-Celtic majority

(Iacovetta 2004). This chapter adds to the discussion on the complex identities of immigrant women by uncovering the history of a specific group of ethnic female militants, Portuguese immigrant building cleaners. There is a growing literature on the Portuguese in Canada, but there are still few historical studies of this group.[2] However, within the existing scholarship some attention has been paid to the roles of women. Like other immigrant women, Portuguese women have been crucial actors in maintaining the economic stability of their families, particularly through their paid labour activities. As Manuela Marujo and Ilda Januário have explained, Portuguese women's economic contributions to their families began in Portugal and intensified in the Canadian urban setting (Marujo and Januário 2000). Replacing the previous image of the Portuguese immigrant woman as housebound, fearful of her new surroundings, and docile in home and workplace is a more recent literature that stresses the complexities of her experience. She is now cast as sometimes a victim, sometimes an agent, but always as an important actor in the experience of Portuguese immigration to Canada (Anderson and Davis 1990; Marujo and Januário 2000; Giles 2002). As noted by Portuguese-Canadian scholars, the Portuguese immigrant woman as 'cleaning lady' is a familiar stereotype in Toronto. My aim is to move beyond that image to the complex history of migration, work, family strategies, and resistance.

Portuguese Immigrant Women in Toronto's Building Cleaning Industry

Large-scale migration from Portugal to Canada occurred in the 1960s and '70s, and by 1982, approximately 137,000 Portuguese had immigrated to Canada, the majority having settled in Toronto (Giles 2002). Toronto's postwar economy contrasted sharply with Portugal's; there, agricultural stagnation and minimal industrialization left few opportunities for Portuguese male and female workers. Due to their legal status as dependents, their low educational levels, and their inability to speak English, Portuguese women were confined to the lowest paid sectors of the female and ethnic job ghetto in Canada, which predominately included work in factories and cleaning hotels, private homes, and buildings.[3] As the size of government grew rapidly in the post–Second World War period Portuguese immigrant women found cleaning jobs in various municipal and provincial government buildings. Furthermore, Toronto's new position as Canada's most important

financial centre spurred construction of postwar skyscrapers in the
heart of downtown Toronto, including in 1975 the seventy-two-storey
First Canadian Place, home to the Bank of Montreal central offices. The
growth and centralization of Toronto's financial district and activity,
then, stimulated a parallel growth and centralization of cleaning jobs
for Portuguese and other immigrant women and men in these new
towers.[4] Alongside other groups of immigrant women, Portuguese
women were crucial workers in the expanding post–Second World
War service sector that so many 'Canadian' women shunned in favour
of white-collar jobs.

Although their job choices were confined, Portuguese immigrant
women made very calculated decisions about the kind of work they
would pursue in Canada. The case files from the International Institute
of Metropolitan Toronto, a social service agency that in addition to offering a variety of cultural, educational, and recreational activities aided
immigrants in such ways as applying for benefits, mediating family
crises, and finding them jobs, reveal the job strategies of Portuguese
families.[5] Portuguese immigrants were one of the largest groups of
clients of the institute for much of the 1960s until it closed in 1974, and
the institute's counsellors placed Portuguese immigrant women in
various jobs in these years. However, the women actively selected the
jobs they would pursue, and reject – moving between factory work,
hotel cleaning, domestic day cleaning, and building cleaning based on
factors such as past work experience, wages, ability to balance the work
with their family responsibilities, and ability to withstand the effects of
the work on their bodies. Although building cleaning was viewed as
physically demanding work, some women chose it because it fit specific
childcare and financial strategies. Since building cleaning is performed
at night a woman could care for her children during the day and her
husband could then take over watching the children when he returned
home from work in the early evening, when she left for her job. Furthermore, many Portuguese women laboured at two or more jobs at
once in the years that they settled and raised their families. A night job
was a complement to a day job in a factory or other cleaning work, and
allowed women to bring in more money to improve their family's standard of living. Thus, although they could choose from only a limited
range of jobs in a female immigrant job 'ghetto,' Portuguese immigrant
women actively selected work that would fit the demands they had as
wives, mothers, and migrants dedicated to the financial well-being of
their families in their new home.

Portuguese immigrant women faced very specific challenges in the building cleaning industry. The contracting out of cleaning functions within government departments and private enterprise began to become widespread in the 1970s, one of the consequences of the advent of neo-liberalism in Canada.[6] However, under the Ontario Labour Relations Act, cleaners and other workers employed through contractors received no protection for their unions; they have no 'successor rights.' This is still the case today. When cleaners organize they are threatened by their employer with the possibility that the cleaning contract will be terminated due to higher costs associated with wage increases and better benefits. Thus, most cleaners are not unionized, and when they are unionized any gains they make from collective bargaining are easily lost with the tendering of new contracts, a specific strategy used by employers to drive down the wages and benefits of the workers, including those being 're-hired' (Neal and Neale 1987; Aguiar 2000). Unionization is also limited by the nature of these workplaces, which tend to be small, to employ mostly female and immigrant workers, and to give them part-time hours. Employer resistance to unionization in this context is stiff. Compared to the collective bargaining model embedded in the postwar industrial relations regime that took the large factory as its model (permanent, full-time, and predominantly male employees), both the Ontario Labour Relations Act and the unions themselves were not set up for the work situations faced by cleaners. However, the hindrances to unionization of contract workers did fit with the larger effort of the Canadian neo-liberal state to undermine workers' collective power (Heron 1996). Ontario provincial governments, both Conservative and Liberal, have historically been unresponsive to calls for amendments to the Labour Relations Act that would ensure successor rights.

Private contractors rely on low wages and the intensification of work to maximize their profits and to beat their competition when bidding for a contract. It is immigrant women who bear the brunt of these cost-cutting measures. They are categorized as 'light duty' cleaners whereas men are categorized as 'heavy duty' cleaners, for which they earn a higher wage. Although 'light duty' and 'heavy duty' cleaners perform similar work employers have used these arbitrarily gendered distinctions to cut their costs by paying women less, and by hiring mostly immigrant women.[7] Immigrant women are thus extremely low-paid workers in a sector of the service industry that relies heavily on their labour. The fact that most contract cleaners are immigrant women and the state has limited their ability to unionize and retain their unions points to power relations that, contrary to multiculturalism rhetoric, serve to privilege white male Canadians at the expense of immigrants and, most of all, immigrant women (Das Gupta and Iacovetta 2000).

Queen's Park 1975–1976:
Portuguese Immigrant Women Struggle for Change

In early 1975 a group of female Portuguese cleaners at the Queen's Park complex, made up of five buildings at Bay and Wellesley streets, decided to unionize. These cleaners worked for Modern Building Cleaning (MBC), the contractor hired by the Ministry of Government Services to clean the complex. The contract cleaners were a particularly vulnerable workforce within the larger Queen's Park building network. Cleaners at other provincial buildings in Toronto were hired directly by the government, earned higher wages, and were members of the Civil Service Association of Ontario. The non-unionized female contract workers at the Bay and Wellesley complex earned minimum wage, $2.40 an hour and men $2.50 to $3.00 an hour, while female cleaners at the provincial legislature earned $3.74 an hour and male cleaners $4.62 an hour (Swenarchuk 1976). Unhappy with their wages, the non-unionized cleaners found their grievances exacerbated when MBC hired a female Portuguese supervisor whom they intensely disliked. When cleaners arrived at work even a few minutes late, she would dock time, and thus pay, from them. The cleaners were aware that this supervisor had left another building when the cleaners unionized there (Medeiros 1975). They thus decided that the only way to improve their wages and working conditions was to form a union, although none of them had had any experience with unions in the past. However, as mentioned, they were aware of unionization in other downtown buildings through networks of friends, families, and neighbourhoods. Furthermore, many of the women had husbands in construction trade unions, and the value of unionization was transmitted through these immigrant families into this workplace. Not knowing exactly where to begin the women started by asking their co-workers if they wanted to join a union, and if they agreed, to sign their names on a paper signalling their interest (Medeiros 1975). They took on the task of unionizing on their own, a difficult and even unusual task for women with little to no English skills, union experience, or political savvy. Yet they persisted despite these obstacles, as unionizing their workplace fit with the larger commitment of improving their families' financial well-being.

When an MBC official heard of the movement to unionize among the female cleaners he called one of the leaders, Leonilda Pimentel, to his office and fired her. Two male Portuguese-speaking company representatives then went to her home the next day, asking her for the list of names of those interested in forming a union. Leonilda had already ripped up the list into tiny pieces, essentially preventing them from knowing which cleaners they should fire. Instead, she insisted that she be the only one to face repercussions for union activity. At the workplace the next day all the cleaners were called to a meeting with MBC representatives and urged to sign another paper indicating that they did not want to join a union. Knowing that they would be fired if they did not sign almost all of the women did so. However, two adamantly refused and were fired as well. The leaders of the unionization drive then went from home to home collecting signatures from the cleaners who wanted to join a union (Medeiros 1975). MBC responded to the movement with a campaign of intimidation, including night-time visits to the women's homes, work speed-ups, transfers, threats on the job, and more firings. Despite these tactics on 29 April 1975 the Service Employees International Union (SEIU) Local 204 was certified as the bargaining agent for 106 workers in the complex (Swenarchuk 1976). At this time, the SEIU was the dominant union in the building cleaning industry representing cleaners at such workplaces as the Toronto-Dominion Centre and the University of Toronto.

A total of eight cleaners were fired for union activity, but these women refused to back down from their fight for justice. The cleaners contacted Services for Working People in downtown Toronto, an agency of the Ontario Human Rights Commission, which helped them complain to the Ontario Labour Relations Board (Medeiros 1975). At this point the cleaners came into contact with English-speaking supporters who would become important to them in their struggle for workplace justice. A Portuguese-Canadian worker at the Human Rights Commission sought out a legal advisor for the cleaners, and law student Michelle Swenarchuk joined the cleaners at the Labour Relations Board hearing. The SEIU lawyers urged the cleaners to take a settlement and give up their jobs, but Swenarchuk supported the cleaners' demands that they receive full compensation and their jobs. As Swenarchuk noted, it was illegal to fire workers for union activity when a union was certified and thus the women were legally entitled to their back wages and jobs. Their jobs were in fact reinstated by the board, and they were paid 100 per cent back wages from the date they were fired (Swenarchuk 2007).

The struggle of the female cleaners at the Queen's Park complex to unionize exemplifies the determination of female immigrant workers, who despite various obstacles were able to organize within a vulnerable sector of the service industry. Because male cleaners held a relatively privileged position in the workplace, earning higher wages than their female counterparts, they were not a dominant force in organizing. Despite their lack of knowledge of unions these women asserted their right to improve their wages and working lives and actively negotiated power for themselves in the workplace. Compared to Portugal, Canada allowed them some space to fight for their rights as workers, and they took full advantage of this opportunity.

Bargaining between the union and MBC began in July of the same year, and the female cleaners were intent on increasing their wages. However, MBC argued that it could not increase wages as it had received a stipulated contract price from the Ministry of Government Services and could pay higher wages only if it obtained a higher contract price. MBC thus decided to cancel its contract and the Ministry of Government Services opened bidding for the cleaning contract. On 5 September the cleaners received notices of termination from MBC, to become effective on 3 October, the date of the expiration of the contract (Swenarchuk 1976). Cancelling a cleaning contract when workers organized was a strategic move by employers in the building cleaning industry. Furthermore, the company taking bids, in this case the government of Ontario, refused to take a position as 'employer' and cast itself as a neutral player in negotiations although ultimately it had the power to retain the cleaners' jobs by hiring the same contractor.

The cleaners were aware that they would probably lose their jobs in the complex if they continued their campaign for higher wages, but they refused to budge and insisted that they would prefer to lose them than to settle for the minimum wage of $2.40 an hour again. The union called a vote on MBC's proposed new wage rates: $2.85 for light duty cleaners and $3.74 for heavy duty cleaners, the same wages paid to cleaners at the Toronto-Dominion Centre. The cleaners voted 45 to 29 against the proposal (McQuaig 1975a). Surely many voted in favour of the wage rates because they desperately needed their jobs, even if the raise was minimal. The women's wages were not merely supplementary to their husbands' income but crucial to the financial survival of the family. Many of the women were, in fact, the breadwinners of the family. One cleaner, Ana Maria Pacheco, who was pregnant and whose husband was unemployed, explained, 'If I didn't work, I don't know what we'd do for money' (Crawford 1975b). Like many other Portuguese immigrant women building cleaners she supplemented her income with a day job, working as a chambermaid at a hotel to make ends meet.

It is significant that many cleaners voted against the minimal wage increase and risked losing their jobs despite desperately needing their income at Queen's Park: they were willing to fight for a better standard of living for their families, the very reason they migrated to Canada and why they had unionized. They were acting as wives and mothers, dedicated to the well-being of their families. The small wage increase would make very little impact on their ability to support their families. As Ana Pacheco stated, 'It's just not enough' (Crawford 1975b). Furthermore, they asserted their rights as immigrant workers to decent wages as well as respect. The cleaners were acutely aware of the injustice of their low wages, when MBC had made more than $1 million in profit the previous year (Almeida-Medeiros 1975). Piedade Silva, a cleaner, told a reporter that she thought the company was trying to scare its employees into accepting a small wage increase by holding the threat of dismissal over their heads. Additionally, supervisory personnel had been harassing the workers on the job to accept MBC's offer (McQuaig 1975a). Many of the women rejected such intimidation and refused to be manipulated by MBC into backing down.

The 'Portuguese Cleaning Lady' as Public Symbol of a New Era

The contracting-out crisis at Queen's Park signalled the beginning of a larger awareness in the city of the plight of building cleaners in Toronto and contract workers in general. In this episode and in later ones the Portuguese cleaning woman became a symbol of the new era of neo-liberal assaults by big business and the state on the working class. Indeed, in press reports and political discussions about the contracting-out crisis Portuguese immigrant women were consistently identified as the main victims of these unfair labour practices.

Although Portuguese immigrant women were the impetus behind the fight for unionization and higher wages at Queen's Park, English-speaking intermediaries were crucially important in revealing their struggle to a larger audience. In addition to their legal advisor, Michelle Swenarchuk, the women received support from workers affiliated with St Christopher House such as Sidney Pratt, who acted as an advisor and interpreter for the women. These supporters, whom the cleaners had initially sought out, were able to build links to unions, women's and community groups, the press, and politicians and thus increase awareness of their plight. The supporters of the cleaners at Queen's Park made a calculated decision to involve the media by contacting journalists and holding press conferences, in order to pressure the government of Ontario to act in the cleaners' interest. In the middle of an election campaign the story had the potential to make very bad press for the Conservative government of Bill Davis.

The first press conference was called on 16 September, before the cleaners had received the new offer from MBC. They and their immediate supporters called on the government to hire the cleaners directly or to amend the bidding process to protect their jobs by stipulating in a new contract that the contractor hire these workers or by considering more factors than the size of the bid in awarding the contract (Swenarchuk 1976). Government Services Minister James Snow responded that it was government policy to accept the lowest bid when tenders were being called, thereby ignoring the role of government in setting wages for cleaners and casting the decision as one that would save taxpayers' money: a case of neo-liberal rhetoric. In this instance the state and the employer were one and the same, and the contradictory nature of two state practices that affected immigrants –multiculturalism and contracting out– was made very clear. For it was within the very realm of state space that immigrant labour was being exploited, in contrast to the state policy of multiculturalism introduced just four years earlier and espousing 'equal rights' for immigrants in the Canadian community.

On 18 September the cleaners informed MBC that they wanted $3.25 for light duty cleaning, and $4.14 for heavy duty cleaning. The next day bids were opened and the contract was awarded to Consolidated Maintenance Services Ltd, an American-based company whose bid was $70,000 lower than that of MBC on a two-year contract (Swenarchuk 1976). In effect the Ontario government had decided to put all of the cleaners out of work. Another press conference was held on 2 October, the day before the cleaners would lose their jobs, in the hope that the move could be averted. This press conference reflected a much larger support base for the cleaners, consisting of a loose coalition of various interest groups. It was held in the Queen's Park press gallery and was co-sponsored by the Ontario Committee on the Status of Women and the Civil Service Association of Ontario. A range of the cleaners' supporters spoke, such as representatives of the NDP, the Ontario Federation of Labour, and the municipal government. Cleaners, many with their children in tow because they could not afford babysitters, crowded into the room where the press conference was held (Crawford 1975a). The presence of the children was not strategic but was an important and visible reminder that these women had families to support, reinforcing the justice of their cause. Piedade Silva accused James Snow of not doing anything to help them, noting that the women had to support their children and would have difficulty finding other jobs because of their lack of English. Furthermore, most of the women had husbands in the construction industry who would soon be out of work for much of the winter (Almeida-Medeiros 1975). Another cleaner, Germana Travassos, explained that she had seven children, her husband had a poor salary, and she had to work to feed them, stating that she did not want to go on welfare (Crawford 1975a). James Snow, in attendance, simply reiterated that the contract bidding procedure would not be changed because it made 'good business sense' (Crawford 1975a). He offered no further help.

In their communications with the press these women directly challenged Canada's self-proclaimed liberal image as a benevolent 'nation of immigrants' that offered newcomers the opportunity not only to work but eventually to enjoy the status and entitlements that came with citizenship. They positioned themselves as immigrant women rather than as citizens, though many would in fact probably have acquired citizenship status. In their attempts to gain economic justice they appealed to the public's sense of human rights, positioning themselves as poor women unscrupulously exploited as cheap labour by rich businesses.

Increasing public pressure on Snow from various interest groups eventually moved him to respond to the issue. He announced that he would speak to a representative of Consolidated and ask it to hire the cleaners. Consolidated was also receiving telephone calls from the cleaners' supporters and the company vice-president arrived from New York to deal with the situation. He met Snow and also some of the cleaners, Swenarchuk, and Pratt. He agreed to hire all the workers if they would 'take what he gave them' (Swenarchuk

1976). He also agreed to recognize the union. This decision was not an entirely altruistic one. It was in the company's best interest to hire workers who knew the buildings and were already trained for the work within them (Swenarchuk 1976). Fearful of finding themselves out of work the cleaners accepted a new contract with Consolidated that would give them a base salary of $2.90 for light duty cleaning and $3.40 an hour for heavy duty cleaning. Increases would occur every six months; in the last stage of the contract, beginning April 1977, the base rate would be $3.25 an hour. This actually worked out to less than the increase offered to the cleaners' by MBC, which by January 1977 had offered a base rate of $3.46 an hour (*Globe and Mail* 1975). Both Snow and Consolidated were able to cast themselves in a benevolent role despite having kept the cleaners' wages low. The act was positioned as a half-way measure between saving taxpayers' money and securing the cleaners' livelihoods. However, failure to deal with the issue in law meant that similar contracting-out crises would keep recurring in Toronto's building cleaning industry.

Legacies of the Queen's Park Struggle

The contracting-out crisis did produce some positive outcomes. First, both MBC and Consolidated accepted that the cleaners should be making more than minimum wage, even though both companies offered only a slight improvement to it. Second, by October 1975 the Ontario government had agreed to implement regulations that would require firms receiving government contracts for cleaning, maintenance, and security to pay the going industry wage rate, as determined by the Ministry of Labour. That is, the government would no longer accept the lowest bid based on minimum wage (McQuaig 1975b). Furthermore, with the tendering of new contracts previous workers would have a right to retain their jobs under the new contractor (Almeida-Medeiros 1975). Thus the government introduced informal successor rights for government workers only. That the employer in this case was the provincial government did make a difference here; the government had a vested interest in how its own labour practices were viewed by the general public. Since the Ontario Labour Relations Act was not actually changed to provide successor rights for all contract workers, however, private companies that contracted out their cleaning had much more leeway about how they conducted their business and treated their works. Third, cleaners in downtown Toronto had become much more aware of the benefits of unionization. As one cleaner stated, 'It was good that we took this action. The use of newspapers and television opened many people's eyes. Many Portuguese women from other companies, when they travel with me on the streetcar, ask me how we did this, because they would like to do the same' (Medeiros 1975).

These outcomes were a result of the actions of the Portuguese immigrant women who cleaned at the Queen's Park complex and had unionized, and who complained to community agencies and to the press that they should be receiving more for their work. Without their activism and determination very early in the process, it is likely that the issue of contracting out labour and its impact on immigrant workers in the building cleaning industry would not have received the public attention it did, and continued to have in the following decade. The 'Portuguese cleaning lady' would appear again in the public sphere in her fight for economic security.

First Canadian Place 1979–1986:
Ongoing Battles of Portuguese Immigrant Women

In 1979 the Canadian Food and Associated Services Union, an affiliate of the Confederation of Canadian Unions (CCU), organized the mostly Portuguese building cleaners at First Canadian Place. As at Queen's Park a few years before it was Portuguese immigrant women who spearheaded the campaign for unionization. A Portuguese immigrant woman arrived at the union office one afternoon and asked Wendy Iler, an organizer, to visit her workplace, indicating that the cleaners wanted to unionize. When Iler arrived with union cards one night as the women got off work, she found that the cleaners had been waiting for her and she was able to sign almost all of them in one night (Iler, personal communication, 2006). Again, the cleaners had been aware of the benefits of unionization from their husbands' experience with construction unions, and were also aware of unionization among building cleaners in various downtown buildings through networks of families, neighbourhoods, and churches. Knowing that cleaners at such workplaces as Queen's Park and the Toronto-Dominion Centre had organized, the cleaners at FCP had some knowledge of the process and actively took steps to make sure their workplace saw the benefits of unionization.

Also as at Queen's Park, the cleaners' attempt to unionize met with resistance from their employer. Following normal practices copies of the Labour Board's Notice to Employees of Application for Certification and of Hearing was posted in various locations in the workplace, all in English (Ontario Labour Relations Board 1979). This notice indicated that a union was applying to represent employees at the workplace and that a vote would be held to determine whether they wished to be represented by the union in their employment relations with the employer. Federated Building Maintenance tried to block the union's certification, arguing that because most of the cleaners could not speak, write, or comprehend English, they could not understand the Labour Board notice posted in English. The company lawyer argued that the workers' right to petition against the union or to seek another union was denied because the notices were not posted in Portuguese (Deverell 1979). FBM insisted on bringing some of the cleaners before the board to prove they could not understand English. They were able to do so with one cleaner, who had to stand silently before the board as the lawyer for FBM asked her questions in English that she could not understand (Swenarchuk 2007). Representatives of FBM were effectively arguing that the workers could not possibly understand the collective action that was being undertaken, thus attempting to diminish the intellectual and political capabilities of this group of immigrant women. This view fit with the dominant gendered notions about southern European immigrant women as more passive and 'backward' than Canadian Anglo-Celtic women.

Even though most of the cleaners could not comprehend English and had little experience with the legal process of unionization, it is clear that they understood the action they were undertaking. For example, all employees were in attendance at the hearing on the board's premises, having been subpoenaed by the employer – in English. Clearly they understood they had to attend despite not being notified in Portuguese. Furthermore, not one of them came forward to support the employer's protest. They collectively took a stand against their employer at the hearing, and by unionizing. Of the 120 eligible, 96 cleaners had signed union cards, well above the 55 per cent required for automatic union certification. The Labour Board chair ruled that language had no bearing on the validity of the union's application arguing that the board 'does not presume that immigrant Canadian employees are less able than others to inform themselves and assert their rights under the Labour Relations Act' (Ontario Labour Relations Board 1979).

As in the Queen's Park case the union was certified despite employer tactics, and in October 1979 it began to represent the employees of FBM at the FCP.[8] That almost all of the Portuguese immigrant cleaners at FCP signed union cards indicates that these women were not only aware of their exploitation but were willing to fight for their rights despite the risk of losing the incomes that were so crucial to their families' well-being. Facing exploitation as ethnic immigrant women workers they actively unionized in an effort to attain the goals they had hoped for in migration, including ensuring a better life for their children.

In 1984 the union, which had been renamed the Food and Service Workers of Canada (FASWOC), was bargaining for the third time with FBM. Female cleaners at that point earned $5.83 an hour and men $6.97 an hour. The cleaners were demanding a wage increase from their employer of fifty cents per hour each year for two years retroactive to 13 April, the day the contract with the union expired. On 3 June the union local voted to reject a two-year contract offer that included a wage increase of thirty cents an hour effective from January 1985. The next day 250 cleaners, 90 per cent of whom were women, went on strike (Rosenfeld 1984).

In a period of heavy inflation the wage increase the employer had offered meant little to the workers. Like the Queen's Park cleaners in 1975 many of these women also held day jobs in factories or performed other cleaning work in order to make ends meet. FBM refused the union's demand of a greater wage increase on the grounds that since O&Y (a company with a net worth of approximately $3.5 billion) would not increase its contract price, FBM would lose its profit – a familiar argument (Ontario Labour Relations Board 1985). For most of the women this was their first strike, and they desperately wanted to fight for higher wages despite the risk of losing their jobs. Like the cleaners at Queen's Park they knew that any job action could result in the loss of their cleaning contract and their union, but they were determined to act anyway. In striking they made their own decision independent of their union leadership, which did not make any recommendation on whether to strike or not, knowing that the cleaners might not have jobs to come back to (Iler, personal communication, 2006). The cleaners voted 96 per cent in favour of a strike and actively pursued their own agenda (Crombie 1984). Once again the determination of the female Portuguese cleaners was at the heart of the struggle.[9]

Again the Portuguese cleaning woman emerged in the public realm to talk about her struggles, which further highlighted the position of Portuguese immigrant women in Canada. Most of the women were married with children. Like other working-class women, and the Portuguese immigrant women in the Queen's Park case, their activism was rooted in their everyday material realities and their responsibilities to their families. The real possibility of injury for Portuguese immigrant men performing dangerous jobs in construction meant that many of these women were the family breadwinners.[10] They included women such as Margarida Correia, who supported three small children because her injured husband had not worked for nearly four years (Goldenberg 1984). Some women cited their inability to buy and send clothes to their families in Portugal as an impetus to fight for higher wages (Harper 1984a). It was clear that as migrants they also had trans-Atlantic familial obligations. Migration provided not only new material hope for those migrating but important material aid to their impoverished families across the Atlantic. These women thus played a crucial breadwinner role for transnational family economies.

Furthermore, the striking cleaners were acutely aware of their vulnerable position as immigrant workers in the Canadian economy. In their coverage of the strike Toronto journalists noted the deep-seated sense of disappointment the women felt when, having come to Canada with visions of a better life and prepared to work hard, they found they were being exploited and ignored because they were immigrants and spoke little English. As Maria Cruz, a striking cleaner, explained to a reporter on the scene, 'I knew I had to work hard here, but I didn't know something like this would happen ... They are trying to exploit the immigrants, especially the immigrant women. Because we are women and we do not speak English, we have no rights' (Harper 1984a).

In taking to the streets and demanding better pay the women again challenged Canada's rhetoric of multiculturalism. In a letter to Albert Reichmann, president of O&Y, Emilia Silva, president of the local stated, 'Mr. Reichmann, surely you can understand our situation. We are immigrants to this country. We take pride in our work and we work hard. We are trying to make a better life for our families' (Silva 1984). They positioned themselves as immigrant women who were being exploited as cheap labour in a country that – despite rhetoric to the contrary – did not view them as citizens with equal rights to economic security.

On the Picket Line: Experiences and Representations
of Portuguese Immigrant Women

The picket line was marked by family and ethnic displays of solidarity, as well as physical altercations with police and strike breakers, and arrests. As in other strikes involving married women, children became very much part of the strike (Patrias 1990; Guard 2004b). The press noted that the children played tag around the buildings and that 'on most evenings, children strut along the sidewalk, carrying signs, slurping popsicles, shouting through a megaphone or generally annoying their mothers' (Goldenberg 1984). The presence of children on the picket line had much to do with the women's inability to pay babysitters at times when their husbands were at work and could not care for them, but it also served a strategic purpose. As at the Queen's Park press conference the children were visible reminders that the women had families to support. The union also encouraged husbands and children to join the picket line. The husbands' experience with construction unions led them to support their wives' activism; they shared the goal of attaining the financial security hoped for in migration and the desire for respect as immigrant workers in the Canadian economy.

As with other 'immigrant strikes' the ethnic identity of the strikers helped shape the character of the picket line. Cultural displays of picket-line behaviour and dissent reflected a blend of Portuguese rituals (including festive rituals and dances), worker solidarity, and even Catholicism. A booklet of songs sung on the picket line signalled the ethnic influence on working-class culture. In addition to English-language working-class songs the predominantly Roman Catholic women sang a Portuguese translation of 'We Shall Not Be Moved' as well as a Portuguese song to St John. Their religious faith was very much a part of their union activism. They also sang, and danced, a wedding and party favourite, the bird dance (FASWOC 1984). They appropriated and continually chanted a Latin American rallying cry in Portuguese, 'The people, united, will never be defeated' (McMonagle 1984). More than simply a way of gaining public attention, the ethnocultural expressions of militancy and solidarity so central to the strike offered a way of claiming a political identity. It defined the strikers in ways that distinguished them from Anglo-Canadian society even though the strike confirmed that the cleaners had much in common with other working-class women. For the Portuguese women who made up the majority of the cleaners on strike the overlapping bonds of ethnic, class, and gender solidarity served to reinforce the cohesiveness of the group, and a particular form of radicalism was borne of these multiple identities.

The solidarity of the group was challenged when a group of about ten workers who had been on strike were escorted across the picket line to return to work. Four strikers were taken to hospital for injuries and one person was arrested when a shoving match started between the two groups. Tensions mounted further when the police began helping 'scabs' cross the picket line. Many of them had been referred by the Canada Employment Centre for Students, a federally run agency. Picketers shouted at strike breakers who arrived in front of the building and attempted to block underground tunnels leading into the building. Maria Serafin stated, 'I'm angry. Tell them [the students] not to take my job because I have a family to feed' (Harper 1984b). One cleaner was arrested for hitting a male supervisor from FBM with her umbrella. The strikers were aware that they were fighting not only O&Y and FBM but also the government. Indeed, the women were particularly incensed over the state's role in recruiting strike breakers, and police efforts to protect these strike breakers.

Some Portuguese women did cross the picket line. According to a union representative who spoke with reporters these women had done so 'under pressure from husbands to give up the strike and return to the kitchen in the Portuguese tradition' (Harper 1984a). Yet the women were not 'returning to the kitchen' but to their jobs. The matter of engaging in paid employment was not the problem for these families. A wife's participation on a highly publicized and occasionally violent picket line might nevertheless have caused tensions at home for some couples. Some husbands might have also considered it an embarrassment to the family and the larger Portuguese community. However, it seems clear that a woman's decision to go back to work had less to do with her husband's notion of feminine respectability and far more to do with an immediate need for money. The loss of a regular pay cheque during the strike caused hardship to their families. The women also feared that, if they lost the strike, they would probably be fired.

Yet despite such fears being widespread the vast majority of the Portuguese women did not cross the picket line but stood firm. Their defiance is important in showing that so-called 'respectable' gender norms did not dampen the militancy of this group of ethnic female strikers, as has been noted for groups of Anglo-Saxon women workers in earlier periods (Parr 1990; Sugiman 1994; Sangster 1995). As in other strikes in which immigrant women predominated these women were not constrained by either dominant notions of femininity or working-class ones (Ventresca 1997; Guard 2004a) Indeed, activism and defiance were very much a part of the female Portuguese immigrant experience in Canada.

That said, the militancy of the strikers marked the strike as exceptional for this group of immigrant women who, as the press repeatedly noted, did not have any experience with unions in Portugal. One reporter declared that the 'strike has turned these docile women, keepers of home and hearth, into a bitter, vociferous group intent on fighting their employers' (Harper 1984a). In assuming that the women had been transformed into fighters the reporter was of course drawing on the all too familiar stereotype of immigrant women, including southern Europeans, as docile before husbands and employer alike. It is clear that for Canadian observers the women's militant behaviour on the picket line was in stark contrast to their expectation of how Portuguese women would act, which made them newsworthy. Most of all these otherwise ignored immigrant women emerged from their invisibility to publicly defy their economic exploitation right at the heart of Canada's most profitable financial district. This irony also helped draw attention to their cause in the Canadian press. In defiance of the stereotype that immigrant women workers were not 'typical' striking workers, the women themselves enlarged the definition of who could belong to an active and militant working class. In short they redefined the political and made themselves public, political, militant, female subjects.

As in the Queen's Park case a loose coalition of various interest groups came together to support the cleaners' cause. The striking workers received picket-line support from other cleaners, including those who worked at the Toronto-Dominion Centre and were now organized by the Canadian Union of Public Employees. Other unions and women's groups also supported them on the picket line, including other affiliates of the CCU, the United Auto Workers, Ontario Working Women, and the Canadian Congress of Women. Support from the Portuguese community came through the Portuguese-Canadian Democratic Organization and representatives from the Portuguese Pastoral Council. Much as in the Queen's Park case the coalition of different groups that supported the cleaners helped them to gain favourable media attention and increased pressure on FBM and O&Y to settle in the union's favour. Again the Portuguese cleaning woman became a symbol of the new era of neo-liberal assaults by big business and the state on the working class. And once again the cleaners' issues became explicitly political when their actions drew the attention of major politicians, particularly members of the New Democratic Party such as high-profile MPPs Bob Rae and Dan Heap, who joined the women on the picket line (Nettle 1984).

After six weeks the strike ended when the cleaners accepted FBM's new offer. It provided them with a thirty-five cent hourly increase retroactive to 13 April, when the old contract expired, and a further twenty-five cent increase in the second year of the agreement (DiManno 1984). Clearly these women accomplished an immense feat by winning a strike against a major corporation, a 'Goliath.' They also showed that female immigrants had a right to equality in Canadian society and could be strong and active union members, belying the notion that they were simply passive victims of an exploitative indus- trial-capitalist economy.

Aftermath at First Canadian Place: Old Struggles Continue

In the end the strike, for all its importance, did not secure long-term rights and security for immigrant cleaners. By February 1986 the 250 cleaners at the FCP were in danger of losing their jobs, their union, and their hard-won rights because O&Y was putting the cleaning contract up for tender precisely when the collective agreement was set to expire – a predictable situation for Toronto's cleaners. Wendy Iler suggested that the tendering process was all part of a scheme to force the union to water down its demands around wages and benefits during collec- tive bargaining (Contenta 1986). Liberal Premier David Peterson and Labour Minister Bill Wrye were facing ever-increasing pressure by cleaners, unions, municipal and NDP provincial politicians, and others to introduce successor rights legislation to prevent such instances from recurring.

Due to the public pressure the premier announced in the legislature that he had come to an agreement with O&Y in which it would write to each of the potential contractors specifying that as an additional term of tender, the contractor must offer first right of refusal on the job to current employees. However, he ensured only that jobs would be protected, not the union or the wages and benefits that the cleaners had fought so hard for (McMonagle 1986). The resolution and the rhetoric were the same as that put forth by Snow ten years before. Peterson emphasized the legal right of employers to tender contracts as a sensible business practice, refusing to see this issue, as the NDP did, as exploitation of immigrant labour, particularly of Portuguese women. Thus, like the Queen's Park case, the provincial government refused to alter labour law but took on a 'benevolent' role by helping the cleaners keep their jobs even if it was at sub-standard wages and conditions.

The cleaners at FCP accepted FBM's offer of a pay raise of just thirty-five cents in the first year, twenty-seven cents in the second year, an increased workload, and a half-hour reduction in their shift. They did so because it would allow their employer to remain competitive for gaining the contract with O&Y, which meant that they could keep their jobs and the collective agreement (*Globe and Mail* 1986). The cleaning contract was renewed. The cleaners were forced to give up many of the gains they had made during their six-week strike, and as is now clear, the contracting-out process worked in favour of employers and business interests.

Conclusion

Although FCP cleaners had to make concessions in order for FBM to retain the contract, the contracting crisis as a whole had one positive outcome. The loose coalition of unions, women's, and community groups that had supported cleaners' causes for a decade formally organized into a group committed to seeing legislative changes for contract cleaners, the Committee for Cleaners' Rights. By November 1986 the committee had gathered 10,000 signatures, mostly Portuguese, on a petition calling for the government to change labour law (Deverell 1986a). The issue was particularly important for the Portuguese community as it was still the largest source of building cleaners in downtown Toronto.

On 10 July 1986 NDP leader Bob Rae and member Bob Mackenzie introduced a private member's bill (Bill 132) in the provincial legislature in an attempt to tighten the successor rights portions of the Ontario Labour Relations Act. NDP members used the cleaners at the Queen's Park complex as an example of how the working lives of cleaners could be improved with such rights. Once the provincial gov-

ernment moved to a policy of requiring contractors performing government services to hire previous employees and to honour their collective agreement, the Service Employees International Union was
able to bargain the wages of light duty cleaners up to $8.08 an hour
and heavy duty cleaners to $8.96 by 1986 (Deverell 1986b). Thus
because of informal successor rights, government cleaners earned
higher wages than those hired by private corporations, such as the
cleaners at the FCP. The NDP argued that it was imperative to make
formal changes to the Ontario Labour Relations Act through Bill 132 so
that all cleaners had successor rights. When the bill went for a vote in
November 1986 cleaners congregated in the halls of Queen's Park
asking all parties to vote for it. It was defeated 41 to 23, however, with
all Liberal members voting against it and all NDP and three Conserv-
atives voting in favour. It was not until 1993 under the NDP provincial
government, through Bill 40, that successor rights for contract cleaners
were incorporated into changes to labour law. However, Bill 7, the first
major piece of legislation introduced by the Conservative Mike Harris
government in 1995, eliminated successor rights (Aguiar 2000). Immigrant women were once again denied the right to improve their wages
and working conditions.

The 'Portuguese cleaning lady' is a stereotype in Toronto but her
image belies a much more complex history of migration, working-
class family strategies, union organizing, resistance, and political
manoeuvring. Portuguese immigrant women were, and still are, dedicated to the financial well-being of their families in their new homeland. They therefore took on paid employment in the building cleaning industry, often in conjunction with other jobs, in order to meet
the family's financial and child-care needs. Indeed, Portuguese
women played a crucial role in the expansion of the post–Second
World War service sector by cleaning government and private offices.
They were confined to the female and ethnic job 'ghetto,' were low
paid, and toiled in inferior conditions. These conditions were supported by state laws that limited their ability to unionize and to
retain their unions throughout the contracting-out process, which
was lauded as good business practice by government and private
businesses. In fact the 'Portuguese cleaning lady' became one public
symbol of a new era of assaults by big business and the state on the
working class.

Yet despite rhetoric that positioned these southern European immigrant women as docile workers and wives, they were militant partici-

pants in the labour movement at a time when labour faced increasing limits on worker power. Despite their lack of English skills, union background, and political savvy these women were able to secure some power for themselves in the workplace by unionizing despite employer opposition, striking, and literally fighting to secure higher wages, and entering the public realm in order to challenge state laws on contracting out and the liberal rhetoric of multiculturalism. Their complex identities as ethnic workers, migrants, women, wives, and mothers structured their activism. Their desire to secure an improved standard of living for their families, as well as their desire for respect and dignity as female immigrant workers in the Canadian economy, was at the heart of their drive to improve their working lives.

Their determination focused the support of unions, women's and community groups, and politicians, leading to a wider resistance movement among cleaners in downtown Toronto through networks of family, friends, and neighbourhoods, policy changes in government labour practices, and ultimately, changes to labour law, however short lived. They made themselves public, militant, and political subjects in 1970s and '80s Toronto.

NOTES AND ACKNOWLEDGMENTS

My thanks to João Medeiros and Domingos Marques for allowing me access to their copies of *Comunidade* and for speaking with me about my larger project. I also wish to thank Michelle Swenarchuk and Wendy Iler for relating to me their experiences with Portuguese cleaners. My gratitude also goes to the editors of this collection, Carlos Teixeira and Victor M.P. Da Rosa, for including my work in the project. Portions of this article were first published in *Atlantis* 32 (1), www.msvu.ca/atlantis. Republished with permission.

1 A right-wing dictatorship in Portugal from 1933 to 1974 severely curtailed unionism and worker activism. The state enacted laws forbidding strikes, organizing, and collective bargaining.
2 Most scholarly work on the Portuguese in Canada has been produced by social scientists. See Noivo 1997 and Giles 2002. For historical works see Anderson and Higgs 1976 and Marques and Medeiros 1980.
3 Statistics from 1981 indicate that 86.96 per cent of Portuguese-born immigrant women in Canada worked for wages. Some 37.30 per cent were in

manufacturing, 8.70 per cent in accommodation and food services, and 13.46 per cent in 'other services,' which include cleaning (Giles 2002). However, the percentage of women in 'other services' was surely under-reported as many Portuguese immigrant women worked clandestinely in private domestic service.

4 A 1975 article cited 36,557 cleaners in Toronto, mostly immigrant women (Speirs 1975). A union organizer indicated that in Toronto most cleaners were Portuguese, though the Greek, Italian, Latin American, West Indian, and eastern European communities were also represented (Iler 1982).

5 Archives of Ontario, F884, International Institute of Metropolitan of Toronto fonds, case files MU 6510 to MU 6567. For secondary sources on the institute see Iacovetta 1998 and 2006.

6 In very simple terms neo-liberalism refers to a re-emergence of the influence of liberalism on economic policy during the 1970s and through the 1980s and '90s. It included, among other things, a move to less government control over the economy, privatization, allowing market forces to function more freely, and increased competition in business. In the building cleaning industry the move to contracting out cleaning fit with neo-liberal goals of cost cutting (and profit increasing) in the public and private sectors by unloading this service onto private contractors, who would have to compete for contracts, thereby driving down the wages of cleaners. For a more thorough analysis of the impact of neo-liberalism on cleaners in Canada see Aguiar 2006.

7 In the mid-1970s it was estimated that 80 per cent of all cleaners were women performing 'light duty' cleaning (Speirs 1975).

8 The first collective agreement was negotiated and came into effect on 13 April 1980. A second collective agreement with FBM was executed in 1982 for a two-year term (Ontario Labour Relations Board 1985).

9 For a lengthier discussion of this strike see Miranda 2007.

10 Franca Iacovetta discusses the participation of Italian men in dangerous construction trades in Toronto and how injury or death adversely affected the family economy (Iacovetta 1992).

REFERENCES

Aguiar, L.L.M. 2000. 'Restructuring and Employment Insecurities: The Case of Building Cleaners.' *Canadian Journal of Urban Research* 9, 1: 64–93.

– 2006. 'Janitors and Sweatshop Citizenship in Canada.' In *The Dirty Work of Neoliberalism: Cleaners in the Global Economy*, ed. L.L.M. Aguiar and A. Herod, 16–36. Malden: Blackwell.

Almeida-Medeiros, F. 1975. 'Governo nada fez pelas mulheres de limpeza.' *Comunidade* year 1, no. 4: 1, 7.

Anderson. G. and J.C. Davis. 1990. 'Portuguese Women in Canada.' In *Portuguese Migration in Global Perspective*, ed. D. Higgs, 136–44. Toronto: Multicultural History Society of Ontario.

Anderson, G., and D. Higgs. 1976. *A Future to Inherit: The Portuguese Communities of Canada*. Toronto: McClelland & Stewart.

Contenta, S. 1986. '250 skyscraper cleaners keep jobs and contract.' *Toronto Star*, 24 Feb., A6.

Crawford, T. 1975a. '97 Cleaners lose jobs tonight, government says hands are tied.' *Toronto Star*, 3 Oct., B01.

– 1975b. 'Trying to win their first contract cleaning women are facing layoffs.' *Toronto Star*, 17 Sept., A03.

Crombie, S. 1984. 'Cleaners on line,' *NOW* (Toronto), 21 June.

Das Gupta, T., and F. Iacovetta. 2000. 'Introduction: Whose Canada Is It? Immigrant Women, Women of Colour and Feminist Critiques of "Multiculturalism,"' *Atlantis* 24, no. 2: 1–4.

Deverell, J. 1979. 'Chars clean up – on the boss.' *Toronto Star*, 3 Oct., A3.

– 1986a. 'Cleaners lobby Queen's Park for job security.' *Toronto Star*, 20 Nov., B8.

– 1986b. 'NDP seeks more security for "vulnerable" cleaners.' *Toronto Star*, 11 July, A24.

DiManno, R. 1984. 'Strike wins women better deal.' *Toronto Star*, 14 July, A1.

Epp, M., F. Iacovetta, and F. Swyripa, eds. 2004. *Sisters or Strangers? Immigrant, Ethnic, and Racialized Women in Canadian History*. Toronto: University of Toronto Press.

Food and Service Workers of Canada (FASWOC). 1984. *Booklet of Songs, 1984.* CAW Local 40, FCP files, private holdings.

Frager, R. 1992. *Sweatshop Strife: Class, Ethnicity, and Gender in the Jewish Labour Movement of Toronto, 1900–1939*. Toronto: University of Toronto Press.

Gabaccia, D., and F. Iacovetta, eds. 2002. *Women, Gender, and Transnational Lives: Italian Workers of the World*. Toronto: University of Toronto Press.

Giles, W. 2002. *Portuguese Women in Toronto: Gender, Immigration and Nationalism*. Toronto: University of Toronto Press.

Globe and Mail. 1975. '97 dismissed cleaners hired by new company.' 7 Oct., 5.

– 1986. 'Cleaning jobs in jeopardy despite vote.' 17 Feb., A14.

Goldenberg, S. 1984. 'Cleaners vow they won't quit despite hardships of walkout.' *Globe and Mail,* 30 June, 19.

Guard, J. 2004a. 'Authenticity on the Line: Women Workers, Native "Scabs," and the Multi-Ethnic Politics of Identity in a Left-led Strike in Cold War Canada.' *Journal of Women's History* 15, no. 4: 117–40.

– 2004b. 'Canadian Citizens or Dangerous Foreign Women? Canada's Radical Consumer Movement, 1947–1950,' in *Sisters or Strangers? Immigrant, Ethnic, and Racialized Women in Canadian History,* ed. M. Epp, F. Iacovetta, F. Swyripa, 161–89. Toronto: University of Toronto Press.

Harper, T. 1984a. 'Cleaners' strike shakes dream of a better life.' *Toronto Star,* 11 July, A1.

– 1984b. 'Four arrested for trespassing at cleaners' picket line.' *Toronto Star,* 28 June, A3.

Heron, C. 1996. *The Canadian Labour Movement: A Brief History,* 2nd ed. Toronto: Lorimer.

Iacovetta, F. 1992. *Such Hardworking People: Italian Immigrants in Postwar Toronto.* Montreal and Kingston: McGill-Queen's University Press.

– 1998. 'Making "New Canadians": Social Workers, Women, and the Reshaping of Immigrant Families.' In *A Nation of Immigrants: Women, Workers, and Communities in Canadian History, 1840s–1960s,* ed. F. Iacovetta, P. Draper, R. Ventresca, 482–513. Toronto: University of Toronto Press.

– 2004. 'Feminist Transnational Labour History and Rethinking Women's Activism and Female Militancy in Canadian Contexts: Lessons from an International(ist) Project.' Paper presented at the 83rd annual meeting of the Canadian Historical Association, Winnipeg, 5 June.

– 2006. *Gatekeepers: Reshaping Immigrant Lives in Cold War Canada.* Toronto: Between the Lines.

Iler, W. 1982. 'A Look at the Cleaning Industry,' *Canadian Woman Studies* 4, no. 2: 70–1.

Marques, D. and Medeiros, J. 1980. *Portuguese Immigrants: 25 Years in Canada.* Toronto: Marquis Printers and Publishers.

Marujo, M., and I. Januário. 2000. 'Voices of Immigrant Women.' In *The Portuguese in Canada: From the Sea to the City,* ed. C. Teixeira and V.M.P. Da Rosa, 97–111. Toronto: University of Toronto Press.

McMonagle, D. 1984. '250 striking cleaners expect strike-breakers.' *Globe and Mail,* 9 June, 19.

– 1986. 'Firms must offer jobs to unionized cleaners.' *Globe and Mail,* 8 Feb., A16.

McQuaig, L. 1975a. 'Asked for higher pay, 97 cleaning workers get dismissal notices.' *Globe and Mail*, 17 Sept., 1–2.

– 1975b. 'Queen's Park to require going wage in cleaning contracts: No help to 97 who are losing jobs.' *Globe and Mail*, 3 Oct., 13.

Medeiros, J. 1975. 'Origem Da Luta Das Mulheres de Limpeza.' *Comunidade* year 1 no. 5: 1, 10.

Miranda, Susana. 2007. '"An Unlikely Collection of Union Militants": Portuguese Immigrant Cleaning Women Become Political Subjects in Postwar Toronto.' *Atlantis* 32, no. 1: 111–21. www.msvu.ca/atlantis.

Neal, R., and V. Neale. 1987. '"As Long as You Know How to do Housework": Portuguese-Canadian Women and the Office Cleaning Industry in Toronto.' *Resources for Feminist Research* 16, no. 1: 39–41.

Nettle, M.E. 1984. 'Immigrant Women Clean Up!' *Hysteria* 3, no. 3: 6–8.

Noivo, E. 1997. *Inside Ethnic Families: Three Generations of Portuguese-Canadians*. Montreal and Kingston: McGill-Queen's University Press.

Ontario Labour Relations Board. 1979. *Reports*. Canadian Food and Associated Services Union vs Federated Building Maintenance Company Limited. October Decisions.

– 1985. *Reports*. Food and Service Workers of Canada vs Federated Building Maintenance Company Limited and Olympia and York Developments Limited. November Decisions.

Parr, J. 1990. *The Gender of Breadwinners: Women, Men, and Change in Two Industrial Towns, 1880–1950*. Toronto: University of Toronto Press.

Patrias, C. 1990. *Relief Strike: Immigrant Workers and the Great Depression in Crowland, Ontario 1930–1935*. Toronto: New Hogtown Press.

Rosenfeld, Erika. 1984. 'Police accused of helping "scabs": Tension rises on cleaners' picket line.' *Globe and Mail*, 6 June, M4.

Sangster, J. 1995. *Earning Respect: The Lives of Wage-Earning Women in Small Town Ontario, 1920–60*. Toronto: University of Toronto Press.

Silva, E. 1984. Letter from the president of Local 51 FASWOC to Albert Reichmann, president of Olympia and York Developments Ltd., 30 June. CAW Local 40, FCP Files.

Speirs, R. 1975. 'Office cleaning: Big business or an "evil industry"?' *Toronto Star*, 27 Sept., B3.

Sugiman, P. 1994. *Labour's Dilemma: The Gender Politics of Auto Workers in Canada, 1937–1979*. Toronto: University of Toronto Press.

Swenarchuk, M. 1976. 'Portuguese Women Organize.' *The Law Union News* 3, no. 2: 1, 4–5.

Ventresca, R. 1997. 'Cowering Women, Combative Men?' Femininity, Masculinity and Ethnicity on Strike in Two Southern Ontario Towns 1964–1966,' *Labour/Le Travail* 39 (Spring): 125–58.

8 Portuguese Mobilization against Deportation: The Case of Hélder Marques

LUÍS L.M. AGUIAR

The role of deportation as an element of Canadian immigration policy recently dominated headlines in Canada when Laibar Singh, a paraplegic labourer from India, was ordered deported because he 'did not have sufficient ties to Canada' (Cross 2007). Only loud protest and organized demonstrations from the Indo-Canadian community of Vancouver, 'No One Is Illegal' activists, and other supporters – including at the airport itself – succeeded in getting him a temporary reprieve and a postponement of his return to India. It wasn't Canadian 'values' of compassion or humanitarianism that got Mr Singh a stay of deportation. Instead, 'safety and security reasons' brought a halt to the deportation order, so said an official with the Canada Border and Services Agency (Cross 2007).[1]

What exactly are these ties that the Canadian government deems necessary and without which Mr Singh cannot stay in Canada? When and how does one know when sufficient ties have been acquired to satisfy government officials and thus increase one's chance of remaining in Canada? Could it be that Mr Singh was not able to develop and nurture such ties because of his 'damaged' body? Are insufficient ties a façade used by the Canadian state to rid itself of a 'dis-abled' body in an increasingly fiscally conservative welfare state intent on promoting flexible, healthy, and self-enterprising bodies for the global economy (Creese, Dyck, and McLaren 2008)? This is not the first time the Canadian government has deported or attempted to deport migrants with physical and/or mental challenges (Menzies 1998; Kondro 2002). But Canada's immigration policy today is even more stringent than in the past (Simmons 1998) about screening for applicants with physically sound and rugged bodies for nation building (National Film Board

1989; Avery 1995; Abu-Laban and Gabriel 2002). I raise these questions because they remain relevant to contemporary discussions about belonging and inclusion and bear on the case study discussed below.

This chapter examines the case of Hélder Marques and the Canadian government's attempt to deport him to his birthplace of Portugal. At the time he received the deportation order, in 1996, Mr Marques had eighteen minor criminal convictions, and was suffering from AIDS and schizophrenia. He hardly presented a 'threat to the public' due to the advanced stage of the disease and his weakened immune system. And though he had no formal citizenship status in this country he had lived in Canada for twenty-seven of his thirty-three years; is it not safe to assume that along the way, Mr Marques had established 'significant ties' to this country?

I couch my discussion within a neo-liberal context of flexible and fit bodies for a new competitive Canadian regime (Simmons 1998; Creese, Dyck and McLaren 2008). A neo-liberal state seeks robust citizens capable of withstanding the competitive climate of the global economy in order to take on the business of globalization and succeed. Only strong, flexible, and able bodies can undertake this responsibility and lead Canada into the twenty-first century. Neither Mr Singh nor Mr Marques fit this scenario since they have 'damaged' and 'weak' bodies best returned to the 'old' countries of their birth. They can no longer benefit from government assistance to rehabilitate themselves since the welfare state is being downsized, downloaded, and contracted out to the private sector to enable the economy to compete better globally. Furthermore, the generosity of Canadians has worn thin due to immigrants' reluctance to play by the rules (Thobani 2007). This politico-economic climate has been heightened by the introduction of government legislation and joint task forces for the purpose of deporting residents who run afoul of the law – regardless of their 'ties' to the country. It is within this context that the Portuguese community in Toronto was encouraged to rally behind the campaign to keep Hélder Marques in Canada. And while Mr Marques had his own reasons for resisting the deportation order, many Portuguese saw his treatment and precarious position as potentially threatening to their own location in this country. This is not inconsequential given the Portuguese community's poor economic treatment and presumed questionable moral character, most recently captured in Franca Iacovetta's study of immigration settlement workers in Toronto (2006: 199).

Strong Bodies for a Robust Canada

Most of us today recognize signs of the economic restructuring Canada is undergoing and how it is undermining trade union rights, workers' rights, environmental protection legislation, and citizenship rights while exalting a new individualism based on pay incentive schemes actualized in consumer choices and product purchasing (McBride 2001). The state has not merely facilitated these processes but initiated its own re-engineering steps by reducing staff, cutting services, and legitimating the assault on the work ethic of the civil service (McElligott 2001). It has disciplined its 'clients' to accept a shift from redistributive features to an aggressive promotion of wealth-creating vehicles supported and protected by an increasingly vigilant and punitive state (Sears 1999; McBride 2001). These changes are evident in piecemeal reshaping of the welfare state (McBride and Shields 1997) and include the downloading of services to community groups, which are often inadequately prepared or have few resources to deal with them (Brown 1997). The state's attack on its most vulnerable citizens, often those on welfare or employment insurance, on the periphery of the labour market, or with uncertain status in the country, has been relentless (Sears 1999). No longer do we have a state defined in terms of its responsibilities towards its citizens. Rather, the state is increasingly shaped and responsive to the market, capital, and individualism.

The new Canada is for 'able bodies' who are also self-enterprising, self-motivated, and able to endure rigorous changes to the labour process and to take advantage of the many opportunities that a robust capitalism presents (Leslie and Butz 1998). Lesser than robust and flexible bodies are those 'weak', 'diseased,' and 'damaged' ones with little to contribute to an economy enmeshed in globalization and the competitiveness this entails for members of the nation-state. Weak bodies are not only uncompetitive but also burdens on the resources of the country; they stand in the way of providing the best financial support for the development of a robust Canadian capitalism. This neo-liberal discourse pervades most government social discourses, steering Canadians away from reliance on state programs to meet their needs and coaxing them to purchase services in the private sector or turn to a growing army of volunteers for relief. According to this view the 'nanny' state is insupportable because it interferes with a proper work ethic and the competitive advantage a nation seeks to erect.

This shift to a neo-liberal vision permeates government strategy by promoting competitiveness and rewarding inequality in a society for the 'strong' (Brodie 1995; Greenspon 2002). It is clear in immigration policies, issues, and the treatment of undocumented migrants, whether already in the economy or arriving off the coast of British Columbia in boats that have braved the treacherous waters of the Pacific (Gabriel 1999; Chan and Mirchandani 2002; McDonald 2007). According to Simmons (1999: 45) current immigration policies are 'entrepreneurial,' stressing the competitive skills of applicants in order to benefit Canada as it assumes a role as niche player in the global economy (see also Abu-Laban and Gabriel 2002). In addition family-class immigration has been reduced and 'cost recovery initiatives' have been put in place to discourage immigrants who might become 'welfare burdens' or 'unskilled' once in the country via this 'backdoor' entry (Simmons 1999: 45; see also Thobani 2007). This 'tends[s] to reinforce selection favouring individuals from wealthier families and countries who will not need settlement assistance' (Simmons 1999: 45). Not only is class a key criterion but so too is the physical status of the immigrant, who must be within the most productive age range (twenty-one to forty-nine years old) to be able to offer her skills as 'assets' to her new country (Satzewich and Liodakis 2007: 72, Table 3.3). Sunera Thobani (2007: 181) examined the federal government's review of its own immigration and social security model of the 1990s and found that immigrants have been made scapegoats for most of the nation's social and economic problems, seen as abusing Canadian generosity 'beyond the Nation's means.'

The neo-liberal discourse in Canada has reshaped citizenship (Aguiar 2006). In the postwar period the state enacted encompassing features of citizenship and responsibilities towards the well-being of its people. And though ethnic and visible minorities weren't always incorporated into its programs, the promise of an expanding welfare state held hope of inclusion (Gabriel 1999; Vosko 2000). However, neo-liberalism has reshaped our expectations of the state and its relation to civil society and citizenship (Herod and Aguiar 2006). In the current context we have learned that the state will no longer provide adequate services to meet the social needs of civil society. For instance, today British Columbia has the lowest unemployment rate in its history and yet carries the highest rate of child poverty in the country (Kines 2007).

The state has successfully disciplined us to be self-motivated, self-reliant, and entrepreneurial in order to make Canada prosper (Klein 2007). Greenspon makes this point clear in his evaluation of the Canadian performance at the Salt Lake Winter Olympics in 2002. He argues that the record number of medals won show how our athletes 'personify the spirit of an assertive, outward-looking, globally competitive Canada. They represent a new mood of excellence' (2002: A1). Previously, according to Greenspon, Canadian 'moods' centred on 'equity policies' of a welfare state, which stood in the way of a competitive, assertive Canadian identity. 'Finally [we] appear to be moving – slowly but inexorably – from policies based on equity to policies based on excellence.' He continues: 'Equity policies predicated on equalizing everyone – even if equalizing down – are giving way. No longer are we content as a society with coddling our losers. Rather, we seek to provide greater opportunity for individuals to turn themselves into winners' (quoted in Aguiar 2002: 12).[2] Had this assessment been made by an obscure critic publishing in a little-known source, one could dismiss it outright. But it was front-page news in the *Globe and Mail,* the country's newspaper of record, and it was authored by the then soon-to-be editor of that newspaper. 'Diseased' and 'damaged' bodies such as those of Mr Singh and Mr Marques are of little interest to policy shapers such as Greenspon and are irrelevant in the imagination of this new Canada.

Dominant Perceptions of the Immigrant Community

The Portuguese have been described as 'hardworking,' 'reliable,' and 'pliant' workers in Canadian workplaces. This perceived work ethic is something the community values and seeks to protect from disreputation (Giles 1993).[3] Doing so makes sense to a community that recognizes the increasing aggressiveness of capital and its ability to pit ethnic minority worker against ethnic minority worker (Anderson 1974; Alpalhão and Da Rosa 1980; Giles 1993; Giles and Preston 1996; Preston and Giles 1997; Aguiar 2000, 2001; Doel, this volume). This reputation is seen as worth preserving since it is one of the few advantages the Portuguese have in a restructuring labour market that is increasing their vulnerability (Preston and Giles 1997; Giles 2002). They consistently score among the poorest economic indicators in the country (Liodakis 2002; Aguiar 2006). They are also described as law abiding, though their civic participation has often been questioned (Alpalhão and Da Rosa 1980; but see Siemiatycki and Isin 1997).

In spite of their reputation and their economic 'invisibility,' the Portuguese have not been spared media scrutiny and controversy. In the mid-1980s the community in Toronto was caught in a web of bogus refugee claimants seeking asylum from persecution for their Jehovah's

Witness beliefs in their homeland of overwhelmingly dominant Catholic faith. Many were drawn by the booming construction industry in what was then known as the Greater Toronto Area. Pressure from community sources, labour unions, and construction capital tried to sway the government of the day to support their cause. A construction union hired a former Progressive Conservative cabinet minister, Dennis Timbrell, to persuade the federal government to grant amnesty to construction workers (10,000 of them Portuguese) or face a crisis in the house-building market where most worked and where the demand exceeded supply (Watson 1989). But the government 'refused to reward unfounded claimants by offering an amnesty [and] instead instituted a "fast-track" process which was supposed to clear the [refugee claimant] backlog within a year or so, but failed to do so' (Whitaker 1987: 23).

In the 1990s a series of articles in the media focusing on the Portuguese shocked the community. There was the front-page picture of John Terceira in the *Toronto Sun* when he was convicted of murdering a young girl in the apartment building he cleaned as a janitor. Dale Brazão from the *Toronto Star* reported on a child rapist who had escaped Canadian law by fleeting to the Azores until the reporter tracked him down (Brazão 1998a, 1998b). Brazão and McAndrew (1997) also literally brought a Portuguese-Canadian polluter to his knees after a chase at a job site in the City of York.[4] These vigilante reporters, rather than confine themselves to reporting the criminal acts of the suspect, took the law into their own hands by chasing and apprehending him. This too was front-page news. In these articles the suspects' immigrant background was made clear, fuelling the anti-immigrant sentiment of the time. This sentiment was palpable 'among leading politicians, media commentators, immigration experts, and ordinary Canadians across the country' (Thobani 2007: 180). It was a result of the rise of the Reform Party and its platform of criticisms of multiculturalism as a policy that undermined national identity while strengthening the political clout of 'special interest groups.' The latter appellation is often code for 'issues associated mainly with Black and other racialized groups' (Benjamin 2002: 187).

In this social climate the process of targeting landed immigrants for deportation was accelerated with Bill C-44 (Barnes 2002). In 1995 Sergio Marchi introduced the bill to target for deportation Canadian residents with criminal records but without citizenship. At the same time a joint RCMP–Immigration Canada task force was set up, quickly leading to the deportation of 497 foreign nationals in September 1995 alone (Barnes 2002: 194).

These developments followed on the heels of the killings of Todd Bayliss and Georgina (Vivi) Leimonis in Toronto. The former was a police officer and the latter a patron of Just Desserts café. Both were white, and two different black men did the shooting. These men had received deportation orders but had managed to remain in the country by living incognito in Toronto. In the case of Georgina Leimonis the killer had invaded 'white spaces' in the sense that the café (and crime) was located in a white middle-class section of the city. The other man killed a police officer. The mainstream media wrote of the randomness of these acts and of the prevalence of lawlessness in the city of Toronto. They also implied that whites were now more than ever at risk of violent injury from 'the other' (Ruddick 1996). Foster (1996) pointed out that the portrayal of these crimes in the media and the panic it fostered regarding race put every black man in Toronto under suspicion. No such concern or outrage, however, was shown toward the police who had shot or killed twelve black men in a span of sixteen years in Toronto. In all of these shootings only one police officer in total was convicted (Foster 1996: 214–15). Over 350 foreign-born criminals in Ontario alone were deported to their countries of birth between July 1995 and the summer of 1998. Among these were seventeen Portuguese nationals (Rickards 1998; Tyler 1998). But it was Jamaicans who were marked for special attention since almost 40 per cent of 'all persons declared a "danger to the public" and deported from Ontario' hailed from this Caribbean country (Barnes 2002: 194).

Not surprisingly several writers point to the toughening of Canadian immigration policy over the last two decades (Abu-Laban 1998; Bannerji 2000), as well as to its racism (Rickards 1998; Tyler 1998). The anti-immigrant sentiment at the time and the political climate of the 1990s blamed immigrants for taking advantage of the generosity of 'Canadians' since too many 'had become too accustomed to living off welfare ... With corporate downsizing and increasing economic uncertainty, and with Canadians being asked by governments to make sacrifices to reduce the debt, how could immigration be allowed to continue unchecked? The nation's compassion had to be measured; its excess had proved to be as detrimental as its lack' (Thobani 2007: 181–2). Today not only has immigrant screening become even tougher (Thobani 2007), but the Canadian Border Security Agency (CBSA) and the Greater Toronto Enforcement Centre (GTEC) do not hesitate in 'arresting, incarcerating, and deporting those persons deemed not acceptable within the national body politic' (MacDonald 2007: 129).

Hélder Marques: A Chronology of Events

In early November 1996 Hélder Marques received a deportation order for 8 November from Lucienne Robillard, then federal minister of citizenship and immigration (Da Silva 1996). In 1995 Mr Marques had turned himself in to the authorities and was being held at the West Toronto Detention Centre under the suspicion that he posed a danger to Canadian society. Now he faced deportation to Portugal for his eighteen criminal convictions as a landed immigrant with no formal Canadian citizenship status (Lopes-Teves 1996; Lopes-Teves et al. 1996). His sister Natalie then contacted the *Toronto Star* to try to publicize the circumstances surrounding his case in the hope of defeating the order.[5] Dias, a Portuguese-Canadian social worker in Toronto, read in disgust the *Toronto Star* article highlighting the Canadian government's deportation of a man dying from AIDS. He contacted the Marques family and offered to help.

From this moment the family, Hélder's lawyer, key community leaders, and José Dias plotted a strategy to get the Portuguese community, local politicians, social service agencies, AIDS activists, and community media to join forces to defeat the deportation order.[6] Within forty-eight hours a support group had convinced the minister that the file was incomplete and that key information on Marques's current mental state – and a recent assessment of the progression of his AIDS – were missing. The support group argued that the family should be granted an opportunity to complete the file to ensure that a decision was made with all the facts. Natalie argued that her brother would not survive a trip to Portugal because of his deteriorating health. And if he did, she warned that he would be unable to afford treatment for AIDS and schizophrenia. She also pointed out that Marques had left Portugal with his family when he was five years old and had been living in Canada for the last twenty-seven years. He no longer spoke Portuguese and had no one left in Portugal who could care for him (Lopes-Teves et al. 1996). In fact, he had 'insufficient ties' to Portugal. This campaign convinced the government to suspend the order temporarily so that the family could complete Marques's file. According to José Dias, this was a partial victory: 'So, the Minister tells us to produce the evidence. But the amazing thing is that she decides to go on holiday and gives us a deportation order with a specific date [13 Jan. 1997]. So we didn't have much time.'[7]

 The second round of campaigning to defeat a rescheduled deportation order was more intense and comprehensive. As in the first round it engaged the Portuguese community and its media, as well as local politicians and social agencies. More significantly, Marques's sister took centre stage in the campaign. Outside the detention centre where her brother was being held, and where he refused all treatment in protest, she announced a hunger strike.[8] The strike was Natalie Marques's way of showing solidarity with her brother and the circumstances he faced, but it was also a timely tactic to draw the media's attention to this case and at the same time use it to garner further support to defeat the order. The strategy had an impact. The *Toronto Sun* sympathized with the plight of the Marques family, and commended Natalie's efforts to keep her brother in Canada (Blatchford 1997; MacDonald 1997).[9]

In addition the support committee organized a protest march along University Avenue from the immigration office to Nathan Phillips Square on the Sunday prior to the deportation date. Many speeches were made and approximately 300 people braved a bitterly cold afternoon waving signs and shouting, 'Let him stay! Let him stay!' (Da Silva 1997; Josey 1997). On Monday, 13 January 1997, 'following an emergency motion before the Federal Court ... a temporary stay was granted in the deportation of Hélder Marques.'[10] In his news release Marques's lawyer pointed out that a federal court had granted the stay and not Minister Robillard. Meanwhile, hundreds of Portuguese supporters, not yet aware of the stay of the order, headed to the airport to disrupt the flow of traffic in an attempt to delay the scheduled departure of the plane designated to take Marques to Portugal.[11] But the KLM flight left without him since his lawyer announced the stay of the order at the airport. On hearing the news Natalie commented, 'I feel happy, but the war is not won' (Mascoli 1997b). A journalist pointed out the long process yet ahead for Hélder: 'If granted leave to appeal, he will then have to go through the appeal in Federal Court. Only if that is successful and the court quashes the deportation order will he be allowed to face a new panel of the Immigration and Refugee Appeal Board in an attempt to be allowed to stay' (Mascoli 1997a). With the deportation issue temporally resolved, the committee felt a sense of relief and accomplishment. Marques was eventually released to a drug addiction house run by an Italian priest.

The Portuguese could not believe the Canadian government's attitude toward them in its willingness to deport a Portuguese Canadian man with AIDS.[12] In a media release the Portuguese Canadian National Congress stated its repulsion toward the government, criticizing it for an immoral and inhumane approach in the case of Hélder Marques (PCNC n.d.). It called on the minister to rescind the deportation order on 'compassionate grounds.' The Portuguese Interagency Network (PIN) did likewise, soliciting support from politicians in Ottawa. In a letter to Bloc Québécois immigration critic Osvaldo Nunez, it stated that the minister ought to reconsider her decision on 'humanitarian and compassionate grounds.' PIN elicited Nunez's support with the following plea: '*Nothing has worked*. The inflexible, inhumane and cruel application of this new policy to deport legal residents of Canada who have broken the law, without any consideration for special circumstances, such as is the case with Hélder Marques, is a blatant slap in the face of Portuguese Canadians, to all immigrants, to mentally ill people, to AIDS victims, and [to] the human rights movement in this country' (PIN 1996, emphasis in original).

The treatment of Hélder Marques flew in the face of Canada's international humanitarian reputation, wrote his lawyer.[13] The 'compassion' discourse was repeated in letters of support from other politicians, labour leaders, and AIDS activists and addressed to the minister.[14] Even the media darling of the right wing, Christie Blatchford, wrote sympathetically about the case. She concluded one of her articles by saying that it did not warrant 'uncompromising harshness and rigidity' but rather 'mercy' and 'some of that much-vaunted Canadian tolerance' (Blatchford 1997). The perceived severity of the treatment towards Hélder Marques prompted one Portuguese letter writer to ask what kind of Canada we have: 'Are we, as a country, so inhumane that we would allow Hélder Marques to die alone, so far away from his home and family?' (Fernandes 1997). Does this discourse of compassion make sense in neo-liberal Canada? And does it make sense when the government was willing to deport a man under these circumstances? As I have argued above that discourse had been overtaken by a mean-spirited, anti-immigrant climate that blamed immigrants not only for their own problems but for most of the nation's as well.

Protests and demonstrations gained the public favour that led the government to stay the order. But one could argue that the government's goal – disciplining undocumented immigrants – had been achieved even if Hélder Marques hadn't been deported. The publicity of the order served as a disciplining tactic to all those positioned similarly to Marques. In other words, the tactic had an impact beyond the individuals specifically targeted. The Portuguese community had already suffered government deportation raids in its midst and considered this latest campaign as intimidating and potentially threatening to the entire community.

In the remainder of this chapter I want to examine the various discourses articulated and deployed within the Portuguese community, as well as the larger Canadian community, to organize resistance to deportation. The analysis reveals a two-pronged strategy: one within, and for, the benefit of the Portuguese community; the other for the community at large. Within this strategy two discourses are especially relevant: first an argument on 'rehabilitating the ethnic body,' and second the articulation of a 'dis-abled body' metaphor to gain support from the wider community.

Politicizing Hélder Marques

Given the economic position of the Portuguese it would be easy but inaccurate to assume that they are politically immature and passive in failing to respond to their position in the Canadian class structure. It would also be inaccurate to imply that they are partially responsible for their poor economic location. Some of these arguments have been made or hinted at (Anderson and Higgs 1976). Others suggest that intense internal community rivalries stand in the way of good old-fashioned political organizing (see Bloemraad 2006 for a summary). Without denying the validity of some of these points I would add that it is highly premature to designate the Portuguese as especially passive (or active) in the Canadian political scene. I make this point for the following reasons: (1) there is still little research on the Portuguese in Canada and especially on their political views and campaigns; (2) the definition of 'political' plays a role in designating the activism (or lack thereof) of a community, as does the scale of the investigation; (3) members of the Portuguese community are increasingly involved in official politics, and research will no doubt unearth more engagement in political parties and trade unions; (4) over the years the Canadian government has assaulted the Portuguese, and the latter has had to respond through visible political organizing such as the recent push to fight deportations of the Portuguese in the Toronto construction industry; and (5) such a position ignores politicization within the community itself with respect to issues that address both its internal dynamics and its positioning vis-à-vis the larger society. The case study herein presents a community that is much more politically conscious than has hitherto been acknowledged.

Esmeralda Carvalho, who organizes AIDS workshops in the community and was a member of Hélder's support group, explains how the connection between the community and Marques was forged: 'It was politicians ... people were moved by it and I think it is people's need to feel sorry, to feel pity for the less fortunate because they themselves feel less fortunate as a result of being on the low end of the totem pole in our society. But it was also very political. There were politicians on the radio, almost on a daily basis, talking about this case.'[15]

Tomás Ferreira, at the time president of the Portuguese Canadian National Congress, recognized the political efforts involved in forcing Hélder's issues on the Portuguese community:

> OK. First there was the social worker who worked very hard, the lawyer Farouk was very good on this thing, the sister worked very well, the PIN, the Congress and some of the important people in the community, like myself, who showed interest, the media, the politicians. But even so, and you know this better than I do, never mind what you do, if the community or the group doesn't want to be moved, it doesn't. So, I'm not saying Hélder was lucky to have all these things in his favour, but the ground was very fertile for the thing to grow. Because the Portuguese are obviously attracted to one suffering person. But seeing one suffering guy, particularly if he looks nice, he looks young; it is the best way to mobilize the Portuguese.[16]

Political organizing brought support and public attention to the case. This included politicizing Marques's plight within the community in order to establish a connection between the two. But this was not all. The interviews suggest that supporters drew on his symptoms to develop a discourse of empathy between Marques and the Portuguese community. But his symptoms could as easily have acted as a barrier to empathy due to misunderstanding or homophobia within the community. Therefore, his stigmatized body had to be explained and then reinscribed in order for the Portuguese community to assist in defeating the deportation order.

Rehabilitating the Diseased Body

In the 1990s people carrying HIV or infected with AIDS suffered from both the debilitating pace of the disease and the social stigma levied at them (Martin 1994; Brown 1997). Hélder's support committee was aware of both of these elements in mounting its campaign. It therefore sought to rehabilitate the ethnic body within the community to convince the Portuguese that supporting Marques would not further undermine an image already suspect in the Canadian media. It was important for the committee to allay fears that the case would characterize the community as morally corrupt or prone to illegal activities. The strategy was to explain clearly the key issues and to stress a discourse of empathy that emphasized 'Portugueseness,' including immigrant history, powerlessness in Canada, and socio-economic status. José Dias explains: 'A lot of people were concerned that this individual had 18 convictions; at this stage he doesn't have 18 convictions. It is also true that he didn't commit 18 crimes. Some of that is due to the fact that he did not appear when summoned by the courts. Every time he didn't show, another conviction was added to his name. So, we're trying to correct that [in the community].'[17]

Other interviews reveal the committee's concern to ensure that the 'stigmatized' body of Hélder Marques did not put off the community:

> The Portuguese community did not understand the fact that this man has schizophrenia. Once someone is diagnosed with schizophrenia, there is always [sic] a correlation between that and crime. My appeal to the community was to highlight that link and not to just see him as a criminal, to recognize him as a mentally ill man. We also know that when someone is diagnosed with schizophrenia, there is always the probability that person has been suffering from the illness for some time. So, there is a strong probability that the first conviction back in '83, he was already suffering from the illness. We also have documentation that he attempted suicide at the age of 17. So there are definitely a lot of things that the Portuguese community didn't know. My appeal to the Portuguese community is that he is mentally ill and deserves to be protected.'[18]

Ana Costa, from the Portuguese Interagency Network (PIN), corroborates: 'There was a lot of confusion around the issue. In terms of our own group it was important to clarify, demystify some of the myths that existed. Some people thought this man had not served his [prison] time. That was wrong. People could not understand that if he was schizophrenic, why wasn't that part of his assessment and why was he constantly being thrown back in jail if these were indeed medical conditions he had?'[19]

Other issues needed to be addressed and explained. As Ana Costa points out, 'People didn't realize this man was homeless on and off for a certain period in his life and also exposed to drugs. He also had a mental illness. These people fall through the cracks. Many times they are not diagnosed or assessed with the problem that they have and they will end up in jail with drug related problems.' The committee sought to explain this to the Portuguese since most were unfamiliar with the judicial system: 'They [the Portuguese] don't understand how the social and judicial system works. The strategy was to get clarity to our people, put pressure on politicians and get mainstream media on board like the *Star* and the *Sun*.' Once the issues were made clear, the community was encouraged to write, call, or fax, their federal representatives including, most importantly, Lucienne Robillard. Petitions were signed, and financial contributions solicited to help run the anti-deportation campaign.[20]

The second key component of this strategy rested on drawing on the common ethnic minority status between the victim and the Portuguese community at large. Ana Costa explains that ethnic minority status 'is important on every issue because it is one of the identifiers. This man was many things but he was also a Portuguese-Canadian. More Canadian than Portuguese. Ethnicity was downplayed a little in terms of strategy. It was played up in our own community and downplayed in the mainstream media.'[21] But ethnic identification was neither assumed to be unproblematic nor taken for granted. The committee repeated it at meetings, in community newspapers, in radio spots, and on Portuguese television programs.

Ethnicity took increasing relevance for two other reasons. First, the Canadian government expressed a primordial understanding of ethnicity in dealings with Marques. Since he was born in Portugal and did not acquire Canadian citizenship, for the federal government he was still Portuguese and the extent of his Canadian residency was irrelevant. Second, within the community ethnic minority status took greater importance as a result of the ease with which he was being deported. The Portuguese community supported Marques not only because he was Portuguese but also because the way he was handled exposed a common vulnerability in Canada. Perhaps they too were not yet 'completely Canadian' and occupied a 'probationary' (Muscio 2005) or 'black' position in Canada (Aguiar 2001).[22] For while the Portuguese recently celebrated fifty years of immigration to Canada, most remain at the economic and political margins of Canadian society and they share this unfortunate location with some Canadian visible minorities. Elsewhere I have argued that the making of their 'whiteness' is incomplete and probationary, as seen especially in public reaction to Portuguese transgressions (Aguiar 2001). This view made sense because the government confirmed it by deporting someone who was Canadian in that he was raised and socialized in this country. As Esmeralda Carvalho put it, deportation touched 'on their own fears of not being Canadian citizens for many of them who are still landed immigrants. And the whole fear of being thrown out of the country, a country that is not really theirs. And looking at the history of Angola, where most Portuguese were thrown out and forced back to Portugal, and so on. Maybe that touched this deep embedded fear in a lot of people.'[23]

Class is also a key signifier for the Portuguese in Canadian society (Liodakis 2002), and could not be ignored in this case. The Marques family lacked the financial resources to hire a top-notch lawyer to resolve the case sooner.

> Politically, things were difficult and other things were at play ... [the] social economic circumstances of his family ... If Hélder Marques could afford an expensive lawyer, quite possibly the case would not have gotten to what it was. Possibly a stay would have been granted earlier. He had a legal aid lawyer. When things got really bad, [his] family got another lawyer to try and salvage the situation. The major issue is [the] socio-economic circumstance of the family so this is not just an ethnic issue ... it is an issue of socio economic status ... it is an issue of power. First and foremost an issue of power ... who's got it and who doesn't have it. And we don't have it ... the Portuguese community doesn't have power.[24]

Like Hélder Marques the Portuguese community is often invisible and powerless in Canadian society. Lacking political clout the community could not harness its own political agents to intervene directly on his behalf:

> The Portuguese community doesn't have power. Power has to do with all the various factors at play: the social economic status, education, accessibility to jobs, good jobs, management positions, positions of power in agencies, boards and commissions. Accessibility to political levels ... with the bureaucracy or political level. Just about everything under the sun that has to do with empowering someone. Individually we don't have a lot of people who have attained power in terms of education or economic

capacity and as a group, we are still powerless because we have not as a group asserted ourselves ... as a group to say there are issues that need some attention paid to. I'm not suggesting that we are hopeless. I'm suggesting that we do not have power ... not that we won't have it. We are now gradually attaining, trying to have our place in the sun also ... The fact is this is not a game to see if the Portuguese can have more power than the Hispanics or the Blacks or whether the Jewish community is more powerful. It is an issue of equity and access. To have all this you have to be at level playing fields and our group is not.[25]

Some trace this lack of political weight to the Portuguese experience with fascism (Alpalhão and Da Rosa 1980), and some interviewees concur:

Our political background, as Portuguese has not prepared us for that. We have inherited this notion that you don't have to ask questions, should be humble, go in and do your job. We have tremendous work ethic, known for our work ethic and honesty. These are incredible attributes but they can become derogatory in some ways because that's all we are. 'Maria is so wonderful because she is a hard working housekeeper.' 'So and so is so hard working because he's been in construction for years.' And that is wonderful. We should be proud of these people. They have achieved tremendous things at tremendous odds. But number one we have allowed the communities established here to take advantage and exploit us to a certain degree and I think we have been victimized because not only the system has embraced us here in the way it has but of what we left behind. I think we are victims of what we inherited.[26]

Ana Costa has suggested that the Portuguese have been reluctant to integrate to mainstream society and have felt the consequences:

I think that because of the way we are here in Canada, especially in Toronto, people were able to cocoon themselves within these community-based organizations. People were able to live their lives without ever, ever, ever having to do any cross-cultural activities, not having to really immerse themselves in Canadian society, if there's such a thing. I mean they didn't have to, they had everything around them, they could cocoon themselves, they could protect themselves from all of that even in terms of getting their lives sorted out in terms of the needs they had; they could go to the travel agent who would fill out their employment forms, or would fill out whatever it was they needed. Personally, I believe that the Portuguese have lingered in that particular situation longer than other groups. Yes, I think they have. It's not hopeful; they are going to [have to] come out of it.[27]

Costa concludes that had the Portuguese managed to elect more politicians with clout, the nature of their resistance would have been different. Yet the Portuguese joined together and fought back from the grassroots. The implications of this may be important, especially with respect to the emergence of organic leaders within the community: 'If we had elected Portuguese politicians I don't think this [grassroots] approach would have been taken. What I think is that the community's emancipation and its ability to mobilize and its ability to assert itself, is what will result in people running for office and attaining certain positions. We've already seen some of that.'[28]

The rehabilitation of the ethnic Portuguese body was important for another reason. It sought to pre-empt community opposition to the Hélder Marques case. There was no organized opposition from the community, but enough criticism was heard in the media and community radio talk shows to warrant reinforcement of the rehabilitation of Portuguese identity: 'Response was good in the community. The Portuguese media were quite positive. Some thought it was an outrage that this man should be deported and others felt he should go. He was a criminal and someone we did not want here. There are those who saw him as just a criminal and others who saw him as a human being and someone who needed to at least have the dignity to live the rest of his short life.'[29]

Opponents of the anti-deportation campaign stated their position by invoking the need to 'protect' the fragile image of the community in larger society. Tomás Ferreira, who has a medical practice, often heard his patients' remarks: 'There is a large number of people in the community who are in favour of deportations. I heard it my practice: "They are sending him back? Good. They should send all of them back. They are not doing anything but sullying our reputation." In my practice and some people who work close to me said, "Let him go, he is involved in drugs, he has a criminal record, and the less we have of those guys the better."'[30]

Hélder Marques's 'body' was politicized and rehabilitated in order to build a community response to the deportation order. There was, then, an urgency to reinscribing his body, to make it worthy of support

considering how it stood in for the many Portuguese who felt neglected and harassed by the Canadian government (Iacovetta 2006).

The Dis-Abled Body

The strategy directed outside the community stressed the 'dis-abled
body' by focusing on Hélder Marques's diseases and underplaying his
ethnic minority status. He was described as Canadian, though born in
Portugal many years ago. Formal citizenship, argued his supporters,
ought not to be the determining factor in assigning someone a national
identity. José Dias explains: 'Hélder Marques has been in this country
since the age of 4 ½. So he has been socialized by Canadian society. He
is a Canadian individual whether he has a piece of paper saying he is
a Canadian citizen or not. If they don't take this into account, then it is
an insult to the intellectual capacity of this country, where time and
again studies have demonstrated that we are affected by our society,
by our peers, by our schools, and so on.'[31]
   For ethnic minorities formal citizenship has always been incomplete
in a nation-state in which Fordism did not extend political and social
rights to most and inconsistently addressed the citizenship needs of
immigrant workers in an industrial context (Bannerji 2000; Vosko
2000). Today, with globalization eroding the borders of the nation-
state, the politics of belonging and the idea of formal citizenship tied
to a fixed territorial location need to be rethought in order to make citizenship more, rather than less, inclusive (Castles and Davidson 2000;
Satzewich and Wong 2006). The government's attempt to 'fix' citizenship territorially by creating a partition between Portugal and Canada,
each with their own citizenship regimes, is increasingly inadequate
since it cannot deal with the global movement of populations or the
emerging transnational identity of contemporary migrants (Satzewich
and Wong 2006).
   The issue of deporting criminals to their country of birth has raised
many important political issues (Barnes 2002). Barnes paraphrases the
Jamaican minister of national security and justice, K.D. Knight, who
has 'questioned the ethical implications of deporting individuals who
have long severed their connections with their country of birth and
who are, in effect, products of the society to which they migrated' (2002:
196). In the Azores, and in particular on São Miguel, research on deportees indicates difficulties in reintegrating them into a society many left
as children. The difficulties often lead to social problems, which are

'resolved' by turning to crime. And though some of the deportees can carry on a conversation in Portuguese, this is insufficient for them to settle into their new surroundings (Rocha et al. 1999). Mário Faria, for example, was deported to São Miguel, an island he hadn't seen for twenty-five years since he left at age eight. Ten days after arriving he killed himself. According to his family he died from social isolation in a milieu no longer familiar to him (Açoriano Oriental 1999).

Conclusion

Though supporters were successful in highlighting the plight of Hélder Marques, and certainly partially responsible for keeping him in Canada, his case nonetheless illustrates the aggressiveness of the Canadian state in defining citizenship restrictively and on making a point that 'dis-abled' bodies are a drain on state resources that cannot be sustained. Such cases therefore need to be dealt with swiftly and completely, from the point of view of the state. In this case the option was to deport a man with AIDS to a country he barely knew, thus alleviating the government from the cost of treating his condition. This is not an insignificant point considering the fiscal frugality of the neo-liberal state (McQuaig 1995). But the Portuguese community would have none of it and fought to keep Marques in Canada in spite of the heightened anti-immigrant sentiment at the time.

The Portuguese community not only succeeded in defeating the deportation order but also asserted itself in the public domain. The most obvious example was the march along University Avenue to Nathan Phillips Square to denounce the government's treatment of Marques and to rally the community behind the campaign to let him stay. The support group and the Portuguese media often ended their discussions with the statement that the Portuguese community needed to fight back and remind the larger community that it was not a pushover but could organize politically to defend one of its own. The community's lack of political weight and influence was an issue, which was partially met by grassroots organizing that strengthened the campaign to defeat the deportation order. The campaign articulated different discourses within and without the Portuguese community, thus gaining the broadest support for its cause. The strategy also sought to situate Hélder Marques's issues within the community and to highlight the position of that community within the Canadian state, thereby making a statement about the political organizing of Portuguese Canadians in matters of national importance. It was also important to reinscribe Hélder's body with the values of a holistically sound, if fragile, body.

NOTES

1 Mr. Singh has now volunteered to return to India as he is exhausted by the struggle to stay and will receive better care from his family in India. He no longer has any hope of staying in Canada. www.canada.com/ story.html?id=904868.
2 This argument is quite revealing in that Greenspon chose the athletes at the Winter Olympics as representative of a 'new' Canada. It is commonly known that athletes at the winter games are almost exclusively white, whereas a large contingency of Canadian athletes at the summer games are black. Presumably, the latter cannot represent the 'new' Canada.
3 Ana Costa, interview with the author, 20 Oct. 1997.
4 Dale Brazão is a Portuguese Canadian working as a reporter for the *Toronto Star*. For a period it seemed that his stories were exclusively on 'digging up dirt' on the Portuguese community. He not only pursued and persuaded a polluter in the City of York to give himself up but also took several trips to Portugal and the Azores to track down ex-Canadian residents with criminal records residing there.
5 José Dias, interview with the author, 29 Mar. 1997.
6 José Dias, Tomás Ferreira, Ana Costa, and Esmeralda Carvalho were key members of this support committee. All four were interviewed for this chapter.
7 José Dias, interview with the author, 29 Mar. 1997.
8 Ibid.
9 This is evident in the title of one of the articles published by the *Toronto Sun*: 'Sis's loving plea for AIDS brother' (MacDonald 1997).
10 El-Farouk Khaki, media release, 14 Jan. 1997, author's files. Khaki was Hélder Marques' lawyer.
11 José Dias, interview with the author, 29 Mar. 1997; Ana Costa, interview with the author, 20 Oct. 1997.
12 Note the title of the following article: '300 call in debt from Ottawa as deport deadline looms' (Josey 1997, emphasis added)
13 El-Farouk Khaki, media release, 12 Jan. 1997, author's files.
14 Letters from Nunziata, 6 Nov. 1996, Fraser [UFCW], 13 Feb. 1997, and Rosenes, 7 Nov. 1996.
15 Esmeralda Carvalho, interview with the author, 19 June 1997.

16 Tomás Ferreira, interview with the author, 7 Aug. 1997.
17 José Dias, interview with the author, 29 Mar. 1997.
18 Ibid.
19 Ana Costa, interview with the author, 20 Oct. 1997.
20 Ibid.
21 Ibid.
22 In the preface to Inga Muscio's book Steven Flusty paraphrases her definition of 'probationary white' in the following way: 'Off-white, ethnic
   white, "probationary white" as one friend puts it – suffered to pass provided we've the good sense to keep our mouths shut' (2005: xi).
23 Esmeralda Carvalho, interview with the author, 19 June 1997.
24 Ana Costa, interview with the author, 20 Oct. 1997.
25 Ibid.
26 Ibid.
27 Ibid.
28 Ibid.
29 Ibid.
30 Tomás Ferreira, interview with the author, 7 Aug. 1997.
31 José Dias, interview with the author, 29 Mar. 1997.

REFERENCES

Abu-Laban, Yasmeen. 1998. 'Keeping 'em Out: Gender, Race, and Class
  Biases in Canadian Immigration Policy.' In *Painting the Maple: Essays on
  Race, Gender, and the Construction of Canada*, ed. Veronica Strong-Boag, Joan
  Anderson, Sherrill E. Grace, and Avigail Eisenberg, 69–82. Vancouver: UBC
  Press.
Abu-Laban, Yasmeen, and Christine Gabriel. 2002. *Selling Diversity: Immigra-
  tion, Multiculturalism, Employment Equity, and Globalization*. Peterborough,
  ON: Broadview Press.
Açoriano Oriental. 1999. 'Familia de repatriado encontrado morto atribui
  tragedia ao isolamento.' 18 Nov., www.acorianooriental.pt
Aguiar, Luís L.M. 2000. 'Restructuring and Employment Insecurities: The
  Case of Building Cleaners.' *Canadian Journal of Urban Research* 9, no. 1: 64–93.
– 2001. 'Whiteness in White Academia.' In *Talking about Identity: Encounters
  in Race, Ethnicity, and Language*, ed. Carl James and Adrienne Shadd,
  177–92. Toronto: Between the Lines.
– 2002. 'BC Liberal's Regressive "New" Era and Its Impact on Building
  Cleaners.' Paper presented at the Pacific Sociological Association Annual
  Meeting, Vancouver, 18–21 Apr.

– 2006. 'The New "In-Between" Peoples: Southern-European Transnational-ism.' In *Transnational Identities and Practices in Canada*, ed. Vic Satzewich and Lloyd Wong, 202–15. Vancouver: UBC Press.

Alpalhão, J.A., and V.M.P. Da Rosa. 1980. *A Minority in a Changing Society: The Portuguese Communities of Quebec*. Ottawa: University of Ottawa Press.

Anderson, Grace. 1974. *Networks of Contact: The Portuguese and Toronto*. Water-loo, ON: Wilfrid Laurier University.

Anderson, Grace, and David Higgs. 1976. *A Future to Inherit: Portuguese Com-munities in Canada*. Toronto: McClelland & Stewart.

Avery, Donald. 1995. *Reluctant Host: Canada's Response to Immigrant Workers, 1896–1994*. Toronto: McClelland & Stewart.

Bannerji, Himani. 2000. *The Dark Side of the Nation: Essays on Multiculturalism, Nationalism and Gender*. Toronto: Canadian Scholar's Press.

Barnes, Annmarie. 2002. 'Dangerous Duality: The "Net Effect" of Immigra-tion and Deportation on Jamaicans in Canada.' In *Crimes of Colour: Racial-ization and the Criminal Justice System in Canada*, ed. Wendy Chan and Kiran Mirchandani, 191–204. Peterborough, ON: Broadview Press.

Benjamin, Akua. 2002. 'The Social and Legal Banishment of Anti-Racism: A Black Perspective.' In *Crimes of Colour: Racialization and the Criminal Justice System in Canada*, ed. Wendy Chan and Kiran Mirchandani, 177–90. Peter-borough, ON: Broadview Press.

Blatchford, Christie. 1997. 'Marques case needs mercy and tolerance.' *Toronto Sun*, 14 Jan., 5.

Bloemraad, Irene. 2006. *Becoming a Citizen: Incorporating Immigrants and Refugees in the United States and Canada*. Berkeley: University of California Press.

Brand, Dionne. 2001. *A Map to the Door of No Return*. Toronto: Doubleday.

Brazão, Dale. 1998a. 'Child rapist urged to give up.' *Toronto Star*, 1 Mar., A3.

– 1998b. 'Fugitive child rapist tracked down.' *Toronto Star*, 28 Feb., A1.

Brazão, Dale, and Brian McAndrew. 1997. '"Dumping Bandit" now behind bars.' *Toronto Star*, 10 Nov., A1.

Brodie, Janine. 1995. *Politics on the Margins: Restructuring and the Canadian Women's Movement*. Halifax, NS: Fernwood.

Brown, Michael P. 1997. *RePlacing Citizenship: AIDS Activism and Radical Democracy*. New York: Guilford Press.

Castles, Stephen, and Alastair Davidson. 2000. *Citizenship and Migration: Glob-alization and the Politics of Belonging*. New York: Routledge.

Chan, Wendy, and Kiran Mirchandani, eds. 2002. *Crimes of Colour: Racializa-tion and the Criminal Justice System in Canada*. Peterborough, ON: Broad-view Press.

Creese, Gillian, Isabel Dyck, and Arlene Tigar McLaren. 2008. 'The "Flexible" Immigrant? Human Capital Discourse, the Family Household and Labour Market Strategies.' *Journal of International Migration & Integration* (forthcoming).

Cross, Allison. 2007. 'Deportation of paralyzed man delayed at 11th hour.' *Globe and Mail,* 11 Dec., S1.

Da Silva, Idalina. 1996. 'Português com sida deportado?' *Portuguese Star* (Toronto), 7 Nov., n.p.

– 1997. 'Hélder Marques fica no Canadá ... até revisão total do seu caso.' *Portuguese Star* (Toronto), 16 Jan., 11.

Fernandes, Celia. 1997. 'To All Metro Toronto Cabinet Ministers and Members of Parliament.' Letter, 14 Jan.

Flusty, Steven. 2005. 'Foreword: Conceptions of a Pale-Skinned Savage.' In Inga Muscio, *Autobiography of a Blue-eyed Devil,* vii–xiii. Emeryville, CA: Seal Press.

Foster, Cecil. 1996. *A Place Called Heaven: The Meaning of Being Black in Canada.* Toronto: HarperCollins.

Gabriel, Christina. 1999. 'Restructuring at the Margins: Women of Colour and the Changing Economy.' In *Scratching the Surface: Canadian Anti-Racist Feminist Thought,* ed. Enakshi Dua and Angela Robertson, 127–64. Toronto: Women's Press.

Giles, Wenona. 1993. 'Clean Jobs, Dirty Jobs: Ethnicity, Social Reproduction and Gendered Identity.' *Culture* 13, no. 2: 37–44.

– 2002. *Portuguese Women in Toronto: Gender, Immigration and Nationalism.* Toronto: University of Toronto Press.

Giles, Wenona, and Valerie Preston. 1996. 'The Domestication of Women's Work: A Comparison of Chinese and Portuguese Immigrant Women Homeworkers.' *Studies in Political Economy* 51 (Autumn): 147–81.

Greenspon, Edward. 2002. 'A new and assertive national mood.' *Globe and Mail,* 26 Feb., A1.

Herod, Andrew, and Luís L.M. Aguiar. 2006. 'Introduction: Cleaners and the Dirty Work of Neoliberalism.' In *The Dirty Work of Neoliberalism,* ed. Luís L.M. Aguiar and Andrew Herod, 1–10. Malden: Blackwell.

Iacovetta, Franca. 2006. *Gatekeepers: Reshaping Immigrant Lives in Cold War Canada.* Toronto: Between the Lines.

Josey, Stan. 1997. '300 call in debt from Ottawa as deport deadline looms.' *Toronto Star,* 7 Jan.

Kines, Lindsay. 2007. 'B.C. has highest child poverty rate in Canada.' *Times Colonist,* 26 Nov., www.canada.com/victoriatimescolonist/news

Klein, Naomi. 2007. *The Shock Doctrine: The Rise of Disaster Capitalism.* Toronto: Alfred A. Knopf.

Kondro, Wayne. 2002. 'Canadian Prohibition against Immigrants with Disabilities Is Challenged.' *Lancet,* 19 Jan., 1–2.

Leslie, Deborah, and David Butz. 1998. '"GM Suicide": Flexibility, Space, and the Injured Body.' *Economic Geography* 74, no. 4: 360–78.

Liodakis, Nick. 2002. 'The Vertical Mosaic Within: Class, Gender and Nativity within Ethnicity.' PhD diss., McMaster University.

Lopes-Teves, Helena. 1996. 'Situacao de Hélder Marques continua por resolver.' *Sol Portugues* (Toronto), 15 Nov., 1.

Lopes-Teves, Helena, Antonio Perinu, and Vasco Oswaldo Santos. 1996. 'Comunidade unida contra a deportação de Português com doença fatal.' *Sol Português* (Toronto), 8 Nov.

MacDonald, Moira. 1997. 'Sis's loving plea for AIDS brother.' *Sun* (Toronto), 18 Jan., 16.

Martin, Emily. 1994. *Flexible Bodies: The Role of Immunity in American Culture from the Days of Polio to the Age of Aids.* Boston: Beacon.

Mascoli, Philip. 1997a. 'Deportation order stayed for man dying from Aids.' *Toronto Star,* 16 Jan., A7.

– 1997b. 'Man told at airport deportation on hold.' *Toronto Star,* 14 Jan., A4.

McBride, Stephen. 2001. *Paradigm Shift: Globalization and the Canadian State.* Halifax, NS: Fernwood.

McBride, Stephen, and John Shields. 1997. *Dismantling a Nation: The Transition to Corporate Rule in Canada.* Halifax, NS: Fernwood.

McDonald, Jean. 2007. 'Citizenship, Illegality, and Sanctuary.' In *Interrogating Race and Racism,* ed. Vijay Agnew, 112–34. Toronto: University of Toronto Press.

McElligott, Greg. 2001. *Beyond Service: State Workers, Public Policy and the Prospects for Democratic Administration.* Toronto: University of Toronto Press.

McQuaig, Linda. 1995. *Shooting the Hippo: Death by Deficit and Other Canadian Myths.* Toronto: Penguin.

Menzies, Robert. 1998. 'Governing Mentalities: The Deportation of "Insane" and "Feebleminded" Immigrants out of British Columbia from Confederation to World War II.' *Canadian Journal of Law and Society* 13, no. 2: 135–76.

Muscio, Inga. 2005. *Autobiography of a Blue-eyed Devil.* Emeryville, CA: Seal Press.

National Film Board. 1989. *Who Gets In?* Directed by Barry Greenwald. Montreal: NFB.

Portuguese-Canadian National Congress (PCNC). n.d. 'Communicado.' Press release.

Portuguese Interagency Network (PIN). 1996. Letter to Osvaldo Nunes, M.P. 20 Jan.

Preston, Valerie, and Wenona Giles. 1997. 'Ethnicity, Gender and Labour Markets in Canada: A Case Study of Immigrant Women in Toronto.' *Canadian Journal of Urban Research* 6, no. 2: 135–59.

Rickards, Colin. 1998. 'Bill C-44 Condemned as "Anti-Jamaican."' *Pride* (Toronto) 5–11 Nov., 3.

Roberts, Barbara. 1998. *Whence They Came: Deportation from Canada, 1900–1935.* Ottawa: University of Ottawa Press.

Rocha, Gilberta P.N., Octávio H.R. de Medeiros, Fernando J.A. Diogo, and Licino M.V. Tomás. 1999. 'Repatriados e Integração Social na Ilha de S. Miguel.' *População e Sociedade* 5: 221–51.

Ruddick, Susan. 1996. 'Constructing Difference in Public Spaces: Race, Class and Gender as Interlocking Systems.' *Urban Geography* 17, no. 2: 132–51.

Satzewich, Vic, and Nick Liodakis. 2007. *'Race' and Ethnicity in Canada.* Toronto: Oxford University Press.

Satzewich, Vic, and Lloyd Wong, eds. 2006. *Transnational Identities and Practices in Canada.* Vancouver: UBC Press.

Sears, Alan. 1999. 'The "Lean" State and Capitalist Restructuring: Towards a Theoretical Account.' *Studies in Political Economy* 59 (Summer): 91–114.

Siemiatycki, Myer, and Engin Isin. 1997. 'Immigration, Diversity and Urban Citizenship in Toronto.' *Canadian Journal of Regional Science* 20, nos. 1, 2: 73–102.

Simmons, Alan. 1998. 'Racism and Immigration Policy.' In *Racism and Social Inequality in Canada,* ed. Vic Satzewich, 87–114. Toronto: Thompson Educational Publishing.

– 1999. 'Immigration Policy: Imagined Futures.' In *Immigrant Canada: Demographic, Economic, and Social Challenges,* ed. Shiva S. Halli and Leo Driedger, 21–50. Toronto: University of Toronto Press.

Thobani, Sunera. 2007. *Exalted Subjects: Studies in the Making of Race and Nation in Canada.* Toronto: University of Toronto Press.

Tyler, Tracey. 1998. 'Deportation law "targets" Jamaicans.' *Toronto Star,* 19 Aug., B5.

Vosko, Leah F. 2000. *Temporary Work: The Gendered Rise of a Precarious Employment Relationship.* Toronto: University of Toronto Press.

Walcott, Rinaldo. 2003. *Black Like Who? Writing Black Canada.* Toronto: Insomniac Press.

Watson, Paul. 1989. 'Union hires Timbrell to help Portuguese facing deportation.' *Toronto Star,* 28 June, A10.

Whitaker, Reg. 1987. *Double Standard: The Secret History of Canadian Immigration Policy.* Toronto: Lester & Orpen Dennys.

9 Invisible No More? Citizenship and Politics among Portuguese Canadians

IRENE BLOEMRAAD

Despite its size in Ontario and other areas in Canada the Portuguese community is consistently described as politically 'invisible' in Canadian politics. Strikingly, the same description is also used in discussions of Portuguese immigrants' citizenship and political engagement in the United States, suggesting that there is a common problem of civic and political participation among Portuguese migrants to North America. Indeed, Onésimo Almeida argues in this book (pp. 255–68) that a common cultural legacy appears to undermine Portuguese immigrants' ability to support political candidates or engage in sustained civic and political projects – whether in France, the United States, or Canada – once the initial emotions over a particular problem die down.

Explanations for this perceived political invisibility vary. Political apathy is variously attributed to low levels of education among these migrants, socialization under a dictatorship that actively discouraged civic and political participation, factionalism within the community, the liability of newness or immigrant origins for effective political voice, or ingrained cultural traits that discourage political involvement. All these explanations presume that the problem of Portuguese immigrants' lack of political voice lies with the immigrants themselves.

This chapter argues that while such obstacles are significant, accounts of Portuguese political invisibility have failed to consider how the political institutions and policies of the new home affect citizenship and electoral success. Portuguese immigrants in Canada, and especially in the metropolitan Toronto area, are much more visible than their compatriots in the United States. Portuguese immigrants in

Canada are more likely to hold citizenship than are those in the United States (Bloemraad 2002). Between 1980 and 2005 dozens of Portuguese Canadians ran for office at all levels of government in greater Toronto, and a number of them met with success. At least seven Portuguese Canadians won seats on local school boards, two sat in municipal government, two sat as members of the provincial Parliament and, in 2004, Toronto residents elected the first Portuguese-born member of federal Parliament.[1] In contrast, over this same period, only one Portuguese American woman held elected office in the metropolitan Boston area, as a school board member, and no Portuguese American held city, state, or national office (Bloemraad 2006). At least in the Toronto region, and perhaps elsewhere in Canada, it might be more accurate to ask whether Portuguese Canadians are invisible no more.[2]

Why are those of Portuguese origin having greater success integrating into Canadian politics in the Toronto area? I argue that in Canada greater government funding of community organizations, an ideology and rhetoric of multiculturalism and integration, and the intersection of the Canadian political system with a unique group of left-wing Portuguese migrants living in Toronto has helped to foster greater engagement and success in politics. In comparison the lack of U.S. government funding, the prevalence of a race-based discourse about diversity, and the relative weaknesses of social democratic politics has contributed to Portuguese Americans' greater invisibility.

I make these arguments based on a large-scale study of immigrant political incorporation in Canada and the United States. Here I bring together evidence based on census statistics, in-depth interviews with sixty-two Portuguese community members in the Toronto and Boston areas, an additional twenty interviews with government officials and community activists who work with Portuguese immigrants, and documentary data gathered from governments and community-based organizations.[3]

This chapter is divided into three parts. In the first section I outline the rationale – in many ways legitimate – that academics and community advocates provide to explain Portuguese political invisibility. In the second I show that despite the many commonalities between the Portuguese immigrant communities in greater Toronto and Boston, those living in Toronto enjoy higher levels of citizenship and greater success in electoral politics. The final section sketches out the reasons for the difference, focusing on government policies that provide resources to local community groups, the discourse of multicultural-ism, legal practice, and the intersection between the political system and selective elite migration.

Portuguese Immigrants' Political Invisibility

Though insufficiently studied in North America, Portuguese immigra-tion to Canada and the United States has been substantial and long-standing. In Canada most Portuguese immigrants settled in urban centres such as Toronto and Montreal (Teixeira and Lavigne 1992; Teix-eira and Da Rosa 2000), while in the United States they live largely in north-eastern states such as Massachusetts, Rhode Island, and New Jersey or in the west, in particular in California (Allen and Turner 1988; Williams 2005). This study of political engagement focuses on Ontario and Massachusetts because both contain large Portuguese communi-ties. According to the 2001 Canadian census (Statistics Canada 2002), Portuguese immigrants were the eighth-largest immigrant group in the province of Ontario (112,510 individuals, or 3.6 per cent of all foreign-born residents) and in metropolitan Toronto (3.8 per cent of all foreign-born residents). In Massachusetts the 2000 U.S. Census counted 66,627 Portuguese-born individuals, the largest immigrant group in the state (8.6 per cent of the total foreign-born population) and the eighth-largest group in metropolitan Boston (3.9 per cent of all foreign-born residents).[4]

The movement of people from Portugal, especially from the Azores, to the United States began in the nineteenth century (Pap 1981; Williams 1982, 2005), while substantial Portuguese migration to Canada began only in the 1950s (Anderson and Higgs 1976; Marques and Marujo 1993). In the post–Second World War period, however, the flows of people crossing the Atlantic Ocean to North America were very similar. Teixeira and Lavigne (1992: 5) estimate that in the late 1960s over 10,000 Portuguese migrated to the United States every year, while Canada – with a tenth of the U.S. population – welcomed approximately 6,000 per year, about two-thirds to three-quarters of whom hail from the Azores. Most of the remainder came from main-land Portugal, often from the Lisbon area or northern Portugal, and smaller groups hail from Madeira or Portugal's former African colonies. Anderson (1983) confirms this pattern of predominantly Azorean migration for Toronto, while Ito-Alder (1980) does the same for Cambridge and Somerville, the two most heavily Portuguese suburbs of the Boston metropolitan area. Crucially, the bulk of Portuguese migrated to North America before Portugal's transition to democracy in the mid-1970s.

Overall the Portuguese immigrant populations of Ontario and Massachusetts look largely the same (Bloemraad 2002, 2006). Age and gender profiles, marital status, and business ownership patterns are nearly identical. Portuguese immigrants are largely ethnically homogeneous and almost all are Roman Catholic.[5] Before moving to North America the majority of migrants engaged in subsistence farming, fishing, or manual labour (Williams 2005). Portuguese workforce participation rates in North America resemble those of native-born residents, with many Portuguese employed in manual and semi-skilled jobs such as cleaning, factory work, and construction. The only demographic or socio-economic difference that stands out is Portuguese Canadians' somewhat higher median income as compared to those living in the United States, a difference that might be in part attributable to higher rates of unionization in Canada (Reitz 1998). In Toronto, many Portuguese men have found employment in construction, often in unionized positions, generating a decent income despite low levels of education. In the United States fewer Portuguese work in non-residential construction and they appear less likely to be members of a union. The difference in income probably drives, in part, slightly higher levels of home ownership in Canada.

Portuguese immigrants are noteworthy as one of the most residentially concentrated immigrant groups in both Canada and the United States (Balakrishnan and Kralt 1987; Allen and Turner 1988). Normally geographic concentration facilitates political voice and electoral success (Pelletier 1991). Yet the Portuguese community is consistently described as politically 'invisible' in the United States (Taft [1923] 1969; Smith 1974; Pap 1981; Valdés 1995; Almeida 1999) and in Canada (Anderson and Higgs 1976; Alpalhão and Da Rosa 1980; Almeida 2000). As noted above, Portuguese political apathy is variously attributed to low levels of education (Pap 1981), socialization under a dictatorship that actively discouraged civic and political participation (Anderson and Higgs 1976), factionalism in the community (Wolforth 1978), the liabilities of immigration and 'newness' in a country, or ingrained cultural traits that discourage political involvement (Almeida 1999). Let's consider each in turn.[6]

Education and English-Language Ability

A long history of political science scholarship shows that low levels of education depress electoral participation (Rosenstone and Hansen 1993; Verba, Schlozman and Brady 1995; Miller and Shanks 1996). Education generates political interest, information, and skills, all of which correlate to political involvement. Education indirectly affects voting and campaign activity by increasing income, chances for recruitment, and civic skills (Verba, Schlozman, and Brady 1995: 433–6). Familiarity with the host society's predominant language – English in both countries and French in certain parts of Canada – also facilitates citizenship acquisition and voting (Cho 1999; Bloemraad 2002).

An important reason for Portuguese immigrants' political invisibility consequently rests in relatively low levels of educational achievement and English-language skills. In Toronto the Portuguese have by far the lowest levels of educational attainment of any ethnoracial group. In 1996 over 51 per cent of Portuguese between the ages of twenty-four and sixty-four had only primary schooling or none at all, and almost 70 per cent had not completed high school, more than double the 31 per cent among all Toronto residents (Ornstein 2000: 38). At the other end of the educational ladder fewer than 4 per cent held a university degree. Portuguese are also three and a half times more likely than other Toronto residents to report an inability to carry out a conversation in English or French (Ornstein 2000: 30). Numbers in the United States are similar: in 2000, 45 per cent of Portuguese immigrants in Massachusetts had never attended high school; only 37 per cent held a high school diploma; and less than 6 per cent held a university degree.[7] These numbers compare to 6 per cent, 85 per cent, and 33 per cent, respectively, within the general population in the state. In addition, more than half of Portuguese immigrants in the United States cannot speak English well, although many have lived in the country for over thirty years.

Those with limited schooling express fear of the political system and blame a lack of knowledge for their reluctance to become involved. Maria, a Portuguese American who migrated in the 1960s, is typical of many, whether living in the United States or Canada. In the Azores Maria completed four years of schooling and helped on the family farm. In North America she works as a cleaner and found time to attend evening classes and achieve a high school equivalency diploma.

But despite decades in Boston she has never voted: 'I'm afraid to vote for the wrong person; I am not confident in myself ... I always feel that I am going to do a mistake or something.'[8] Political activists recognize the difficulty of mobilizing a community with limited education and English-language skills, although lack of schooling can be a very sensitive, if not taboo, topic in the Portuguese community. For example, former Toronto councillor Martin Silva, who immigrated to Canada as a youth, attributes his failure to win re-election in part due to comments he made on Portuguese-language radio describing illiteracy as a significant problem for the community.

Previous Political Socialization

Most activists within the Portuguese community feel that homeland experiences feed into political silence in the adopted country. One Portuguese-Canadian leader explained, 'In the Portugal that they knew, you fended for yourself. You didn't expect anything from the state, except for the expectation that Salazar was going to take more and more away from you. You were not to trust the state, you were not to get involved. The further away you are, the farther removed, the better off.' Another person elaborated, 'Not only were they not allowed to vote, but they were not supposed to participate either. They are not used to using the vote to get into the decision-making circles.' On several occasions ordinary Portuguese immigrants would dismiss my questions about political participation with a wave of the hand. In interviews adjectives such as 'dirty' or phrases such as 'can't be trusted' cropped up frequently in reference to politics: 'A politician has to be a self-centred individual that will sacrifice friends, will sacrifice anything for the sake of achieving that end.' Being in office makes elected officials 'dilute the things they stand for.' As one person put it, 'Politics for a lot of Azoreans was considered what is called the "realm of the witches."'

To a certain degree Portuguese attitudes mirror the feelings of native-born Canadians and Americans, but the Portuguese appear to hold more reservations about politics than other groups do. Surveys of ethnic groups in Toronto find that Portuguese respondents express relatively little faith in the use of organized action or political parties to resolve problems, and while they are on average quite satisfied with life in Toronto, they are less likely than most other groups to feel that they have access to local politicians (Breton et al. 1990).[9] Although

North America is poles apart from pre-1974 Portugal, it takes significant convincing to change a lifetime of distrust and disinterest.

Internal Divisions and Community Solidarity

Community leaders consistently cite internal divisions as a major reason for lack of political success. This refrain focuses particularly on regional prejudices, especially between mainlanders and Azoreans but also between Azorean islands or between people from different villages on the same island. Such divisions, which revolve around perceptions of superiority and relative backwardness, divide Portuguese immigrants into distinct social networks and organizations.

While they do at times recognize their views as stereotypes, those from the mainland often characterize Azoreans as overly religious, conservative, and provincial. For their part islanders see those from the continent as morally loose, always looking to exploit the islands, and arrogant. One Portuguese immigrant in Toronto, born in São Miguel but married to a mainlander, remembers that when she got married, 'All the people from my side [were] against the other side. My parents, they did not like it ... Noooo, no, no. Because ... [mainlanders] do lots of bad things to the young Azorean girls.' Those who have run for office regularly mentioned that one's hometown can influence a candidate's level of support within the Portuguese community.

Class differences provide a second line of internal tension, although the influence is often latent rather than explicit. Ordinary immigrants allude to the gap between their own issues and the activities of prominent community members by using a shrug of the shoulder and a reference to 'those guys.' In most cases difference in class, income, and education do not produce outright clashes but rather detachment between community subcultures organized around different occupational paths and social organizations.[10] For some, however, lingering resentment over class inequalities in the homeland colour perceptions of compatriots in the receiving society. As one Portuguese American, a man of modest background who was able to work his way up into a white-collar occupation in the United States, explained in talking about a local elite, '[He] looks up to himself. He cares about everybody else, but appearances are also very important ... If you have a problem communicating with people, and you only have your eyes focused to high level type of society ... [you can] forget. He or they cannot forget that the global community, the people themselves, are very important ... And when I say "the people" I mean the average people.'

Prominent first-generation Portuguese often had access to education that was denied to the vast majority of their compatriots. The education gap between the community leaders I interviewed and the average Portuguese immigrant is striking. The North American environment equalizes such differences somewhat – working-class Portuguese buy houses and purchase the material possessions of the middle class – but divisions remain.

The Liability of 'Newness' and the Immigrant Experience

Finally, the liability of being an immigrant and not having multigenerational roots – and political contacts – crops up repeatedly as an obstacle to political participation. Research on native-born citizens finds that those who move to a new town or neighbourhood are less likely to participate politically than those with long-standing ties to their community since 'new arrivals face the many demands of relocation ... They must reestablish themselves politically ... [and] they must wait for new channels of political information and encouragement to develop' (Rosenstone and Hansen 1993: 157). The number of years of residence an immigrant has in his or her adopted country correlates strongly with electoral participation and naturalization (Jones-Correa 2001; Lien 2001; Ramakrishnan and Espenshade 2001).

Even though most Portuguese immigrants migrated more than thirty years ago, liabilities of newness continue to affect the community. Ordinary immigrants sometimes still believe that they understand politics less well than those born in North America. Among would-be politicians an immigrant background is clearly seen as an obstacle. One Portuguese-born woman in Toronto who is active in politics observed,

> It's difficult because, no matter how you look at it, you don't always have the same connections. Even myself, who has been in different jobs, in different interactions with different people at different levels. I mean, I'm not in their circle. I don't play golf with them on weekends. I can't compete with their incomes, or with their power, or with who they know. I may have worked with them. I may call upon them to make a donation, but ... I don't rub shoulders with these people ... I'm not part of that circle. I never have been, you know. I take a step in, I say hello, and I step out again.

A Portuguese-American political candidate in Massachusetts made a similar observation, explaining, 'Because I came at 14, I didn't have the school buddies, the friends from elementary school that would be your natural supporters.' In contrast, other candidates have deep roots into the native-born community.

Visible or Invisible? Portuguese Canadians' Greater Political Incorporation

All of these reasons for political invisibility – lack of education and language skills, prior socialization, internal divisions, and immigrant 'newness' – should affect Portuguese communities in Canada and the United States equally. Indeed, among the more than 100 migrant groups that have moved to North America, Portuguese immigrants appear among the most similar on either side of the forty-ninth parallel. If political invisibility were only a function of immigrants' characteristics we should find the same levels of citizenship and elected representation in Toronto and Boston.[11] Yet we find evidence for greater political incorporation among Portuguese immigrants in Canada.

Citizenship and Naturalization

Citizenship acquisition is an important indicator of political incorporation. Citizenship denotes legal and symbolic membership in a country and is a necessary prerequisite for voting almost everywhere in North America. To become a citizen an immigrant must prove a certain number of years of residence (three in Canada, generally five in the United States), demonstrate basic knowledge of civics and English (or French in Canada), swear (or affirm) an oath of allegiance, and show 'good moral character' such as the absence of a criminal record. These requirements are largely the same in Canada and the United States. The benefits of citizenship are higher in the United States: U.S. citizenship makes it easier to sponsor relatives and provides guaranteed access to social welfare benefits, while Canadian law makes no such distinctions between Canadian citizens and foreign-born permanent residents.

Given the higher benefits of citizenship in the United States, it is surprising to see that whereas 67 per cent of Canadian residents born in Portugal held Canadian citizenship in 1996, only 59 per cent of Portuguese-born residents in the United States were American citizens in 2000. Moreover, these figures understate the extent of the naturalization difference because Portuguese migration to the U.S. Northeast is of slightly older origin than to Ontario. Since citizenship is strongly correlated with length of residence we need to compare immigrants who entered North America at the same time. Doing so for Portuguese immigrants in Ontario and Massachusetts, we find that among those with eleven to fifteen years of residence citizenship levels in Ontario are double those in Massachusetts, 52 per cent and 26 per cent respectively.[12] The gap diminishes for older cohorts, but even after thirty years of residence Portuguese men and women living in Massachusetts are still less likely to be naturalized than compatriots in Ontario.

We can use statistical controls to further compare a Portuguese immigrant's probability of being a citizen in Ontario and Massachusetts. By using statistical modelling we can artificially compare people with the same individual characteristics in terms of language ability, length of residence, income, gender, and a host of other attributes to test whether individual differences among Portuguese immigrants in North America drive the citizenship gap between the two countries.

I report on the detailed statistical modelling elsewhere (Bloemraad 2002, 2006), but the upshot of the analysis is that even when we take into account all the things that might differentiate Portuguese immigrants in the two countries – such as Portuguese Ontarians' somewhat higher income – the probability that a Portuguese immigrant will hold citizenship is higher in Ontario. We can use a statistical model to imagine the 'typical' Portuguese immigrant: a person who migrated to North America in 1970 or 1971 at the age of twenty-four, who speaks English but has completed only elementary school, and who earns the median income of any Portuguese immigrant. Statistical simulation predicts that there is about a 68 per cent chance that this immigrant has acquired Canadian citizenship. The likelihood that the same person, living in Massachusetts, possesses American citizenship is 46 per cent. In sum while personal characteristics affect citizenship status, where an immigrant lives matters a great deal in predicting odds of citizenship.

Electoral Success: Winning Office

An alternative measure of Portuguese immigrants' political presence is their ability to win elected office at all levels of government, from school boards to national legislature. Election to political office is, compared to naturalization, a much more elite level of political participation, but it can reflect the political strength of a community if that community throws its support behind an ethnic candidate. My interviews clearly suggest that many immigrants value political representation from their community for its symbolism, for the potential access it gives them to power brokers, and for the possible representation of substantive interests. As one Portuguese-Canadian activist argued, 'I feel that other politicians cannot take our cause equally well ... It's the sense of belonging to a particular group. It has nothing to do with it being a Portuguese-Canadian group. It could be the group of the fifty year olds that make quilts ... It's the identification with a particular group, knowing the history, knowing some of the challenges and the issues and so on. Really having the interests of that group at heart. And that's what makes the difference.' Yet despite strong interest in ethnic representation most Portuguese lament what they see as their community's lack of political presence on municipal, state/provincial, and national decision-making bodies.

Importantly, these complaints seem more founded in the Boston area than in metropolitan Toronto. As listed in Table 9.1 at least ten Portuguese Canadians have held elected to office in the Toronto area, from serving on local school boards to the 2004 election of Canada's first Portuguese-born member of federal Parliament, Mario Silva.[13] Also strikingly all but one of these individuals is a first-generation immigrant, someone born in Portugal. Portuguese-Canadian advocates have some grounds for complaint regarding their political presence: in the 1990s, Portuguese representation on Toronto municipal council, at just under 2 per cent of all seats, was only half of the community's proportion in the city. But at the same time, we see a clear trend to increasing electoral participation and, especially, electoral success.

In Boston and its immediate suburbs Teresa Cardoso, a U.S.-born Portuguese American, is the only person of this ethnic origin elected in the last twenty-five years. Given that Portuguese Americans accounted for almost 4.5 per cent of the population in Cambridge and over 8 per cent in Somerville in 1990, the lack of political representation is striking. The Portuguese community has had somewhat more success in politics in parts of New Jersey and California, but especially in the Californian case these individuals tend to be the third- or fourth-generation descendants of Portuguese immigrants who came to the

Table 9.1

Portuguese-origin elected representatives, Metro Toronto and Boston, 1980–2005

Politician	Place elected	Area represented	Tenure in office	Party affiliation[1]	Generation[2]
Toronto					
Carl DeFaria	Provincial legislature	Mississauga	1995–2003	Conservative	1
Domingos Marques	Separate school board	Downtown Toronto	1991–4	NDP	1
Christine Ferreira	Public school board	Downtown Toronto	1997–2003	NDP	2
Peter Fonseca	Provincial legislature	Mississauga	2003–present	Liberal	1.5
Tony Letra	Separate school board	Downtown Toronto	1982–4, 1994–7	Liberal	1
Nellie Pedro	Public school board	Downtown Toronto	2000–3	Liberal	1
Maria Rodrigues	Public school board	Downtown Toronto	2003–present	NDP	1.5
Vasco Santos	French public school board	Downtown Toronto	1985–7	NDP	1
Mario Silva	City council	Downtown Toronto	1994–2003	Liberal	1.5
	Federal House of Commons	Downtown Toronto	2004–present		
Martin Silva	Metro Toronto council	Downtown Toronto	1988–97	NDP	1.5
	Separate school trustee to public school board	Downtown Toronto	1985–6		
Boston					
Teresa Cardoso	Public school board	Somerville	1991–present	Democrat	2

1 Toronto city and school board elections are nonpartisan, but some candidates run campaigns with explicit reference to their party affiliation, even though this is not indicated on the ballot. Party affiliation is included to provide information on the political leanings of elected Portuguese Canadians.

2 People who migrated as adults are listed as first generation (1); those who migrated as children are listed as 1.5; and those born in North America are listed as second generation (2).

Source: Author's interviews and published electoral returns.

United States in the early twentieth century. Their immigration experience has become so distant that comparisons to Canada's largely immigrant and second-generation Portuguese population become highly problematic.[14]

How Does the Context of Reception Matter?
Explaining (In)Visibility

What explains Portuguese Canadians' relative political visibility compared to Portuguese Americans? I highlight three factors, all of which underscore the role played by receiving societies in immigrants' political incorporation.

Government Support and Organizations

First, we need to consider the role of government in facilitating the creation and maintenance of ethnic or immigrant community organizations. Civic associations, sports clubs, religious bodies, social service agencies, and a host of other organizations provide material and human resources, as well as physical spaces, from which to mobilize people, even if the organization's primary mission is not at all political. For example, organizations can facilitate citizenship, especially for immigrants who face significant language or education barriers, by filling in forms, teaching civics and English, providing counselling and more generally by offering encouragement to go through with the citizenship process (Alvarez 1987; Bloemraad 2006). Having numerous organizations in an ethnic community, or certain large, strong organizations, also facilitates participation in the formal electoral system. Politicians see such groups as an easy and efficient way to reach large numbers of potential voters (Parenti 1967; Marwell 2004).

In Canada governments provide more support to immigrants and local community organizations than do those in the United States, especially in connection with immigrant integration such as job counselling, language instruction, and translation and interpretation assistance (Bloemraad 2006). For example, over the 2003–4 fiscal year Citizenship and Immigration Canada allocated $100 million to English-language instruction to immigrant newcomers. Combined with other programmes that amounted to federal spending of about $1,500 per new immigrant admitted (Canada 2003: 2, 6). No similar programmes exist in the United States for immigrants such as the Portuguese, and while local ·or state governments offer some assistance, funding tends to be meagre. In 2002 the Office of New Bostonians in Boston City Hall estimated that an immigrant faced a two-year wait for public ESL classes, with a somewhat reduced wait for priority clients such as those who have children in the city's public schools.[15] The Canadian government's official policy of multiculturalism, as well as comparable provincial and municipal policies, also provides financial and symbolic support to ethnic associations ranging from advocacy organizations to folklore groups. In the United States governments favour more distant, neutral relations with immigrants, ethnic organizations, and community advocates. Only legally recognized refugees and asylum seekers can access government-funded programmes for resettlement. While the United States holds a strong ideology as a country of immigrants, its policy on community building has been largely laissez-faire.

Portuguese Canadians in Toronto enjoy a relatively richer organizational infrastructure than in the Boston area (Bloemraad 2005, 2006), and the groundwork for political mobilization is thus stronger. Although the numbers of ethnic Portuguese in Toronto and the Boston area are roughly similar – approximately 87,200 in Toronto and 78,500 in metropolitan Boston – there appear to be about six times more organizations in downtown Toronto than in the Cambridge/ Somerville area of Boston. As Table 9.2 suggests, the degree of difference between the Canadian and American cities changes depending on the type of organization considered, but we find many more political and professional associations, ethnic media, social services, and advocacy groups in Toronto, even though Portuguese migration to Massachusetts has a longer history and has had more time to develop an organizational infrastructure.

It is worth noting that one of the biggest imbalances is in media organizations. Part of the difference reflects the relative importance of the two areas as the focus for the larger provincial or state Portuguese community. Toronto is a centre for Portuguese activities in Ontario, but in Massachusetts, larger and older Portuguese communities in New Bedford and Fall River produce newspapers and some radio programming that is consumed in the Boston area. However, greater regulatory support for multicultural radio and television programming in Canada also plays a role. In Toronto two local TV stations are dedicated to the city's linguistic minorities, and various radio stations offer a multicultural selection of programming. Although in some cases the Portuguese are granted only a few hours per day or per week on these

Table 9.2
Portuguese community organizations, Toronto and
metropolitan Boston, 1999

Type of organization	Boston	Toronto
Advocacy	0	7
Catholic churches	1	4
Social	8	37
Media	2	28
Political	0	2
Professional	1	4
Social service	4	16
Total	16	98

multiethnic channels, the Toronto ethnic media has been a particularly fertile ground for community advocates and politicians. One former member of municipal government had a regular radio show before being elected, a former school trustee worked as a newspaper journalist, and at least two elected school board members have regular programmes on Portuguese-language television.

Without a clear policy in favour of multicultural broadcasting at the national or state level, ethnic communities such as the Portuguese in the Boston area are dependent on local authorities and the volunteer energies of community members. City governments in metropolitan Boston require cable companies to provide community television channels in return for distribution contracts. A few Portuguese Americans have produced shows for these local stations. However, those active in ethnic media complain that distribution of the shows tends to be very localized because of complicated cable agreements; as well their efforts are largely amateur and require sustained community support that often fails to materialize. Lacking a local, professional ethnic media many Portuguese immigrants in the Boston area watch RTPi, the international Portuguese broadcast station. There is some local content on RTPi – mostly focused on south-eastern Massachusetts – but the lack of sustained local input makes it a poor vehicle for political mobilization.

Government policies in Canada toward immigrant integration, the funding of community organizations, and regulation of multicultural media thus facilitate participatory citizenship in Toronto, while the lack of similar efforts in the United States aggravates Portuguese political invisibility.

The Party System and Ideological Congruence

A second reason for the greater political visibility of Portuguese immigrants in Toronto lies in the relationship between local political structures and community elites. In Toronto a stronger and more competitive party system, greater ideological diversity between parties, and more localized nomination procedures lower barriers to running for office and make elections appear more meaningful than in heavily Democratic Boston. Especially noteworthy is the activism of a small but vocal group of left-wing Portuguese Canadians in Toronto, an advocacy presence missing in Boston.

Portuguese migrating to North America largely did so for economic reasons, usually setting their sights on the United States, but a small minority of elite Portuguese immigrants moved to Canada for political reasons. Most are from the mainland and were involved in the Communist party and its efforts to overthrow the dictatorship. In some cases these individuals embraced the Communist party and its ideology. Others, a larger proportion, participated in networks or joined in events organized by Communists because there was no other organized, viable opposition to the dictatorship. Some of these individuals moved to Canada because of prior family ties, but others consciously avoided the United States because of Americans' perceived anti-Communism; Canada was seen as a relatively more welcoming country.[16] These people brought a leftist mind-set to Canada that found a home in the New Democratic Party (NDP) and, for some, became reinforced by the Canadian union movement.

For example, José Manuel left Portugal in the late 1960s for political reasons. In his words, 'The political police were after me. I thought I'd like to go there [to Canada]. I don't fit in with the American mentality. I had a friend who had escaped from the compulsory military service and he offered to take me to Canada.' After entering Canada on a tourist visa he confirmed his vague, positive notions about the country and decided to stay, regularizing his situation in 1972. He soon found a political home in the left-wing Portuguese Canadian Democratic Association and, through friends at the association and other political activities, he became heavily involved with the NDP, including a brief stint in elected office.

The individuals who chose Canada for political reasons influenced a larger group of future community advocates. Some current Portuguese-Canadian community leaders trace their political beliefs and activism to people like José Manuel. The left-wing group also generated political opposition in the community by those with more conservative views. Such ideological cleavages split the Toronto Portuguese community, but from the viewpoint of political participation this competition has been positive: it spurred other Portuguese to run for office in opposition to the left-wing group. The left-leaning elite do not represent the political ideology of the majority of the community, which probably supports the Liberal Party for the most part, yet five of the ten Portuguese Canadians elected to office have been affiliated with the NDP, and their activism has spurred others to participate.

Similar dynamics are largely absent in Boston. Certainly some individuals involved in the anti-Salazar opposition in Portugal migrated to Massachusetts, but these people did not find a similar home in the Democratic Party or the union movement of the Boston area, at least not to the point of standing for office. Often the most active Portuguese leaders in Cambridge and Somerville separate their community-based activism from mainstream politics. Armando, for example, is widely recognized for his leadership in community events, but for him community participation is personal while his political activities are 'at a different level.' Strong local Democratic 'machines' – party structures with loyalties to particular people – also make it difficult for the Portuguese to break into politics in places such as Somerville, which are often dominated by Irish and Italian Americans.

Multiculturalism, Immigration, and Race

Third, and finally, languages of race and ethnicity operate differently in Canada and the United States, and these discourses impede Portuguese immigrants' political visibility more in Boston than in Toronto. In Canada the predominant language of multiculturalism is oriented to ethnicity, allowing Portuguese Canadians equal standing to Chinese Canadians, Italian Canadians, or Vietnamese Canadians. In the United States political multiculturalism tends to be understood in terms of broad racial groupings. In this context the Portuguese are grouped with other white ethnic groups in Boston. This is problematic because these other 'white ethnics' – notably the Irish and the Italians – have more distant immigrant pasts. Almost all the Irish and Italian political elites in Boston are American born. In their everyday lives Portuguese immigrants face linguistic, cultural, and socio-economic barriers similar to visible minority immigrants, but when local advocates try to forge immigrant coalitions the Portuguese are sometimes excluded because immigration in the United States is often equated with racial minority status.

Although the Portuguese are a European group their status as 'white' in American racial classifications was not a foregone conclusion.[17] In Massachusetts the presence of darker skinned Cape Verdeans led some Americans to consider all Portuguese as 'black,' an experience recalled by some of my older respondents. When Congress debated the inclusion of Latinos and Hispanics into federal minority programmes in the 1960s and '70s many in the community thought that Portuguese immigrants should be included. One researcher who surveyed the Portuguese populations of Cambridge and Somerville in the 1970s summed up the general attitude when he argued, 'Whatever the national political logic of this position, it [the Hispanic category] is conceptual nonsense in terms of defining minorities as far as this local area is concerned. If speaking a different language, sharing a foreign cultural background, or being an immigrant population is sufficient reason to be considered a minority in the case of non-black Hispanics, then the Portuguese are definitely a minority' (Ito-Alder 1980: 25).

However, certain Portuguese elites opposed the designation, arguing for the distinctiveness of Portuguese culture vis-à-vis that of Hispanics. A letter stating such objections was sent to Congress and read into the Congressional record. In subsequent legislation the Portuguese were excluded from the Hispanic/Latino designation, while another European group, immigrants from Spain, was included.

Portuguese 'whiteness' has had significant political consequences, notably in the lack of Portuguese linguistic assistance under the Voting Rights Act. The act, passed by Congress in 1965, aimed to assure African American access to the ballot box. Renewed in 1970 and again in 1975, the second renewal extended its guarantees to linguistic minorities. Asian, Hispanic, and Native American groups successfully lobbied Congress to include provisions guaranteeing linguistic minorities' access to ballots, instructions, and voter information pamphlets written in their own language, as well as to multilingual poll workers. Under the act a political jurisdiction contains a linguistic minority if 10,000 people or 5 per cent of the population speaks a language other than English and reports limited English competency as measured by the census. In addition the group must show a level of illiteracy above the national average. In Massachusetts various Portuguese immigrant communities satisfy these provisions, but the act limits its coverage to 'persons who are American Indian, Asian American, Alaskan Natives, or of Spanish heritage'.[18] In 2002 a total of 296 municipalities and counties across the United States were required to make special linguistic accommodations (Kong 2002). In Massachusetts the cites of Lawrence, Holyoke, Springfield, Boston, and Chelsea had to provide Spanish-language services to electors during the 1990s, but Portuguese speakers received no special assistance.[19]

In contrast Canadian multiculturalism is primarily ethnic. Groups are recognized based on national origin or, more rarely, by subnational ethnicities if the group is relatively large and cohesive. A major advantage of such public rhetoric is that it accords well with most immigrants' self-perceptions. A Portuguese-Canadian woman who migrated from the Azores as a young girl still considers herself first and foremost Portuguese, rather than Canadian or Portuguese-Canadian. She nonetheless speaks approvingly of Canadian multiculturalism: 'What it means to me is different nations of people, different, all types of people gathered ... It shows that everybody can get along together. It's not discrimination against anybody. We all feel that in some way we are important to each other. That this person is not better than [a] Portuguese person, not better than the next person. To me it's VERY important.' In both recognizing and legitimizing immigrants' difference, multiculturalism helps this immigrant and others feel that they have grounds to make claims on government and fellow citizens, and that they may do so despite their origins.

The emphasis on ethnicity combined with the relatively universal nature of many Canadian settlement programmes creates two contradictory impulses for community leaders: a sense of integration and welcome, along with fear of political isolation through ethnic 'ghettoization.' One Portuguese Canadian told me, 'I think official multiculturalism ... is used to pander down, to buy votes and to kind of ghettoize a little bit. This whole ethnic thing also bothers me ... Because I think that's another way in which the immigrant communities are kind of marginalized and ghettoized.' Noteworthy in this assessment is the respondent's belief that politicians seek to 'buy votes' through such programmes, a process of inclusion rather than exclusion. Fear of ghettoization leads community leaders in Toronto to encourage fellow immigrants to embrace Canadian citizenship.

In addition, when organizations receive money and legitimacy from government departments or programmes called Multiculturalism or Citizenship, community advocates make an implicit link between government, inclusion, and participation. From the point of view of many Portuguese-Canadian leaders the state welcome newcomers, and while it clearly could do more, a certain loyalty emerges:

> I know that a lot of people resent the multiculturalism policy; they feel that it ghettoizes us, and puts us into separate little communities, and it prevents us from fully integrating and so on. There is a bit of truth to that ... Having said that, however, on another level we have fought and we have gained, and other organizations have fought for services, social services, health care services ... A system that has had a lot of faults – that's why we're still lobbying and advocating for a lot of things – but a system that gives us, from what we hear from other jurisdictions and other countries, [something] that I think has been incredibly good to newcomers in terms of trying to address a lot of the different needs.

Such sentiments encourage community leaders to mobilize in favour of citizenship and political participation in Toronto.

Conclusion

The comparison of Portuguese immigrants' political 'invisibility' in the Boston area to that of their compatriots in Toronto teaches us two important things. First, Portuguese political invisibility is not inevitable. By a number of measures Portuguese immigrants in Toronto have achieved significant political voice and political visibility. A large majority of the community holds Canadian citizenship and thus can access important political rights. While the acquisition of citizenship among Portuguese immigrants is lower than among many other groups in Canada, it is significantly higher than in the United States, and it has had a bigger effect on political outcomes, propelling at least nine Portuguese-born Canadians into elected office from the metropolitan area and one Canadian-born woman of Portuguese origin. There is no reason to believe that political invisibility is the necessary lot of Portuguese migrants around the world.

However, this chapter has also demonstrated a second important point: government policy, the local political system, and interpretations of multiculturalism have provided more fertile ground for political growth to Portuguese in the Toronto area. Whereas past accounts of Portuguese invisibility blame, or explain, Portuguese immigrants' lack of political engagement on their lack of interest, skills, and resources, the experience of the Toronto Portuguese-Canadian community shows that the social and political context in which immigrants find themselves exerts a powerful influence on voice and visibility. Portuguese immigrants in Canada face significant hurdles in gaining political voice: limited English-language ability, low levels of schooling, distrust of politics, and a lack of long-standing political networks. However, if the second generation can build on the advances of the first, we may well see significant political visibility among Portuguese Canadians in the future.

NOTES AND ACKNOWLEDGMENTS

An earlier version of this chapter was presented at the Portuguese Studies Program, Institute of European Studies, University of California, Berkeley, 23 April 2004 and then published in *Fashioning Ethnic Culture: Portuguese-American Communities along the Eastern Seaboard*, edited by Kimberly DaCosta Holton and Andrea Klimt (2008). A more Canadian-centred version of the chapter is revised and reprinted here with permission. This research benefited from the financial support of the National Science Foundation (SES-0000310), the Canadian Social Science and Humanities Research Council, the Quebec Fonds FCAR, the Social Science Research Council, and Statistics Canada (Division of Housing, Family and Social Statistics).

1   Mario Silva is the first Portuguese-born person to serve in the federal Canadian Parliament. Some members of the Portuguese-Canadian community point to John Rodriguez, an MP from 1972 to 1980 and 1984 to 1993 in the riding of Nickel Belt, Ontario, as the first MP of Portuguese ethnicity. Rodriguez was born in Georgetown, Guyana.

2   The research reported here centres on the metropolitan Toronto and Boston areas. In the Boston area Portuguese immigrants have historically settled primarily in the cities of Cambridge and Somerville, municipalities immediately adjacent to the city of Boston. With time some Portuguese immigrants and their children have moved to other communities in the cities of Arlington, Belmont, and Medford. I use the terms 'metro Boston,' 'greater Boston,' 'the metropolitan Boston area,' or 'the Boston area' to refer to the city of Boston and these immediate inner-ring cities

encircling it. In Toronto the historical heart of the Portuguese-Canadian community lies just west of the downtown core, south of College Street and west of Spadina Avenue. With time some Portuguese immigrants and their children have moved to the surrounding suburbs, especially the city of Mississauga. I use the term 'Toronto' when I refer to the city of Toronto, and 'metro Toronto,' 'greater Toronto,' or 'the Toronto area' when I include Portuguese-origin communities in suburbs beyond the city.

3 This chapter draws from and synthesizes results reported in Bloemraad 2002, 2005, and 2006. The fieldwork was conducted between 1996 and 2001, largely in the downtown core of the city of Toronto and in Cambridge and Somerville, cities directly adjacent to Boston. These areas are historical sites of first settlement for post–Second World War Portuguese immigrants and continue to have high proportions of Portuguese in their population. The sixty-two Portuguese-origin individuals interviewed fell into two groups: community leaders (eighteen in Toronto, thirteen in the Boston area); and ordinary immigrants (fifteen in Toronto, sixteen in the Boston area). For further information about the research design and methods see Bloemraad 2006 and 2007.

4 In Massachusetts the historical centres of Portuguese-American settlement are the cities of Fall River and New Bedford in the south-eastern part of the state. According to the 2000 U.S. census 47 per cent and 39 per cent of town residents, respectively, report some Portuguese ancestry, compared to 7.5 per cent for Somerville and 3.1 per cent for Cambridge, Massachusetts (United States Census Bureau 2002). I discuss some of the implications of the large community in south-eastern Massachusetts later in the chapter, notably with respect to Portuguese media. It is worth emphasizing that while Fall River and New Bedford have produced more Portuguese-American politicians – usually of native, not immigrant, birth – than has the Boston area, Portuguese Americans are far from dominating local politics, a somewhat surprising situation given their overwhelming numerical presence in the area. Portuguese-American politicians have also been elected in New Jersey and California; most, however, were born in the United States, not in Portugal.

5 According to the 1991 Canadian census (20 per cent sample) 96 per cent of Portuguese-born adults in Ontario reported being Catholic (Statistics Canada 1995). The United States Census Bureau does not ask question about religious affiliation, but a survey conducted in south-eastern Massachusetts in 1999–2000 found that 95 per cent of Portuguese-American respondents reported being Roman Catholic (Barrow 2002).

6 The first four explanations probably do help to explain differences between the Portuguese and other ethnic groups, and I consider them in depth. The fifth carries a cultural determinism that seems suspect. Almeida suggests that the political failings of the Portuguese probably stem from a general mind-set characterized by 'a high degree of emotion [sic] life strongly connected to and affecting their intellectual domain' (1999: 237). He believes that Portuguese share such a cultural orientation with other Mediterranean cultures, but such an explanation flies in the face of Italian over-representation in Toronto politics at all levels of government (Siemiatycki and Isin 1997). Almeida (this volume) also argues that Portuguese immigrants in New England and Ontario share the Portuguese psyche, yet we find important cross-national differences in electoral success.

7 The Ornstein data (2000) are based on reported Portuguese ethnicity, and thus include some Canadian-born Portuguese, while the U.S. data are only for immigrants. The Canadian data consequently understate the extent of the skill gap among Portuguese immigrants.

8 This quotation and all others in the text come from in-depth interviews I conducted with members of the Portuguese community in the Toronto and Boston areas. See Bloemraad 2006, 2007 and the current chapter for details on the methodology and profiles of those interviewed. Pseudonyms have been used to protect the confidentiality of interviewees.

9 To my knowledge no surveys exist that measure the political attitudes of Portuguese Americans in the Boston area. A study of Portuguese Americans in south-eastern Massachusetts found relatively low levels of political interest in affairs outside the local community, but the small number of people sampled means that these results should be treated with caution.

10 There is a clear educational gap between individuals who are identified as community leaders or who hold formal positions of authority in community organizations, and the rest of the community. Many community leaders have a university education or some postsecondary training, while the majority of Portuguese immigrants have a Grade 8 education or less. This probably feeds into a 'brokerage' system of political engagement, in which community leaders speak for the community to the mainstream press and politicians. Some do this for political gain, while others do it for economic standing or to enhance prestige in the community (see also Brettell [1977] 2003).

11 We can consider the similarities of Portuguese migration to be akin to a laboratory experiment. Although ethical and practical considerations

mean that immigrants cannot be randomly assigned to move to Canada or the United States, Portuguese migration offers a quasi-experiment of how the political and policy environment might matter.

12 These data are from the 1990 U.S. and 1991 Canadian censuses (Ruggles et al. 2004; Statistics Canada 1995). Because of the strong effect of length of residence and the lack of contemporary Portuguese migration, these differences become somewhat attenuated by 2000.

13 This count is based on interviews and published electoral returns, and it is meant to be exhaustive for the period covered, 1980–2005. It is possible that it misses some elected Portuguese Canadians, especially at the school board level. Because of Canada's historic compromise between English Protestants and French Catholics in the nineteenth century, there are four Toronto school boards: the 'public' English and French ones (which were historically influenced by Protestantism) and the Catholic English and French school boards, which are supported through public taxes. Since 2005 an additional second-generation Portuguese Canadian was elected to the provincial legislative assembly from Mississauga South, Charles Sousa, in 2007.

14 Immigration researchers call those who are foreign born and who physically migrate the first generation. The native-born children of these immigrants are the second generation, and the native-born grandchildren of the original immigrants are third generation. In some cases researchers talk about the 1.5 generation, people born in another country but who migrated as children and who were largely educated and socialized in the country of residence.

15 Telephone conversation with Office of New Bostonians, 17 Dec. 2002.

16 This perception has some basis in reality. In the United States an individual must formally declare past Communist affiliation on the citizenship application. Past membership in the Communist party constitutes grounds upon which U.S. Citizenship and Immigration Services can refuse American citizenship. There is no similar question on Canadian citizenship forms.

17 In Hawaiian ethnoracial hierarchies the Portuguese were historically considered somewhere between the local non-white population and the European-origin 'Haole' community, a distinction reflected in Hawaiian census reports that differentiated between 'Portuguese' and 'other Caucasians' from 1853 to 1930 (Geschwender, Carroll-Seguin, and Brill 1988).

18 Voting Rights Act, sections 14(c)(3) and 203(e). These provisions were renewed in 1982, 1992, and 2006.

19 This includes the burgeoning Brazilian population in the state as well.

The presence of a significant Brazilian community, a group from Latin America that is not Hispanic, adds further complexity to the classification of minority communities.

REFERENCES

Allen, J.P., and E.J. Turner. 1988. *We the People: An Atlas of America's Diversity.* New York: Macmillan.

Almeida, O.T. 1999. 'The Portuguese-American Communities and Politics: A Look at the Cultural Roots of a Distant Relationship.' *Gávea-Brown: A Bilingual Journal of Portuguese-American Letters and Studies* 19–20: 229–43.

– 2000. 'Value Conflicts and Cultural Adjustments in North America.' In *The Portuguese in Canada: From the Sea to the City,* ed. Carlos Teixeira and Victor M.P. Da Rosa, 112–24. Toronto: University of Toronto.

Alpalhão, J.A., and V.M.P. Da Rosa. 1980. *A Minority in a Changing Society: The Portuguese Communities of Quebec.* Ottawa: University of Ottawa Press.

Alvarez, R.R. 1987. 'A Profile of the Citizenship Process among Hispanics in the United States.' *International Migration Review* 21, no. 2: 327–51.

Anderson, G.M. 1983. 'Azoreans in Anglophone Canada.' *Canadian Ethnic Studies* 15, no. 1: 73–82.

Anderson, G.M., and D. Higgs. 1976. *A Future to Inherit: The Portuguese Communities of Canada.* Toronto: McClelland & Stewart.

Balakrishnan T.R., and J. Kralt. 1987. 'Segregation of Visible Minorities in Montreal, Toronto and Vancouver.' *Ethnic Canada: Identities and Inequalities,* ed. Leo Driedger, 138–57. Toronto: Copp Clark Pitman.

Barrow, C.W., ed. 2002. *Portuguese-Americans and Contemporary Civic Culture in Massachusetts.* North Dartmouth, MA: Center for Portuguese Studies and Culture and the Center for Policy Analysis, University of Massachusetts – Dartmouth.

Bloemraad, I. 2002. 'The North American Naturalization Gap: An Institutional Approach to Citizenship Acquisition in the United States and Canada.' *International Migration Review* 36, no. 1: 193–228.

– 2005. 'The Limits of Tocqueville: How Government Facilitates Organisational Capacity in Newcomer Communities.' *Journal of Ethnic and Migration Studies* 31, no. 5: 865–87.

– 2006. *Becoming a Citizen: Incorporating Immigrants and Refugees in the United States and Canada.* Berkeley, CA: University of California Press.

– 2007. 'Of Puzzles and Serendipity: Doing Research with Cross-National Comparisons and Mixed Methods.' In *Researching Migration: Stories from the*

Field, ed. Sherrie Kossoudji, Louis DeSipio, and Manuel Garcia y Griego, 35–49. New York: Social Science Research Council.

Breton, R., W.W. Isajiw, W.E. Kalbach, and J.G. Reitz. 1990. *Ethnic Identity and Equality: Varieties of Experience in a Canadian City.* Toronto: University of Toronto Press.

Brettell, C. [1977] 2003. 'Ethnicity and Entrepreneurs: Portuguese Immigrants in a Canadian City.' In *Anthropology and Migration: Essays on Transnationalism, Ethnicity, and Identity,* by C. Brettell, 127–38. Walnut Creek, CA: AltaMira Press.

Canada. House of Commons. 2003. *Settlement and Integration: A Sense of Belonging, 'Feeling at Home.'* Report of the Standing Committee on Citizenship and Immigration. Ottawa: Communication Canada.

Cho, W.K. Tam. 1999. 'Naturalization, Socialization, Participation: Immigrants and (Non-)Voting.' *Journal of Politics* 61, no. 4: 1140–55.

Geschwender, J. A., R. Carroll-Seguin, and H. Brill. 1988. 'The Portuguese and Haoles of Hawaii: Implications for the Origin of Ethnicity.' *American Sociological Review* 53, no. 4: 515–27.

Ito-Alder, J.P. 1980. *The Portuguese in Cambridge and Somerville.* Combined ed. Cambridge, MA: Cambridge Department of Community Development.

Jones-Correa, M. 2001. 'Institutional and Contextual Factors in Immigrant Naturalization and Voting.' *Citizenship Studies* 5, no. 1: 41–56.

Kong, D. 2002. '30 states have multilingual ballots.' *Washington Post,* 25 Sept., A1.

Lien, P. 2003. 'Ethnicity and Political Adaptation: Comparing Filipinos, Koreans, and the Vietnamese in Southern California.' In *Asian Pacific Americans and American Politics: Participation and Policy,* ed. Don Nakanishi and James Lai, 193–210. Lanham, MD: Rowman and Littlefield.

Marques, D., and M. Marujo. 1993. *With Hardened Hands: A Pictorial History of Portuguese Immigrants to Canada in the 1950s.* Etobicoke, ON: New Leaf.

Marwell, N.P. 2004. 'Privatizing the Welfare State: Nonprofit Community Organizations.' *American Sociological Journal* 69, no. 2: 265–91.

Miller, W.E., and J.M. Shanks. 1996. *The New American Voter.* Cambridge, MA: Harvard University Press.

Ornstein, M. 2000. *Ethno-Racial Inequality in the City of Toronto: An Analysis of the 1996 Census.* Report prepared for the Access and Equity Unit, City of Toronto. Toronto: City of Toronto.

Pap, L. 1981. *The Portuguese-Americans.* Boston: Twayne Publishers.

Parenti, M. 1967. 'Ethnic Politics and the Persistence of Ethnic Identification.' *American Political Science Review* 61, no. 3: 717–26.

Pelletier, A. 1991. 'Politics and Ethnicity: Representation of Ethnic and Visible-Minority Groups in the House of Commons.' In *Ethno-Cultural Groups and Visible Minorities in Canadian Politics: The Question of Access*, vol. 7, ed. Kathy Megyery, 101–59. Research Studies, Royal Commission on Electoral Reform and Party Financing. Toronto: Dundurn Press.

Ramakrishnan, S.K., and T.J. Espenshade. 2001. 'Immigrant Incorporation and Political Participation in the United States.' *International Migration Review* 35, no. 3: 870–907.

Reitz, J.G. 1998. *Warmth of the Welcome: The Social Causes of Economic Success for Immigrants in Different Nations and Cities*. Boulder, CO: Westview Press.

Rosenstone, S.J., and J.M. Hansen. 1993. *Mobilization, Participation, and Democracy in America*. New York: Macmillan.

Ruggles, Steven et al. 2004. Integrated Public Use Microdata Series: 3.0. Machine-readable database. Minneapolis: Minnesota Population Center.

Siemiatycki, M., and E. Isin. 1997. 'Immigration, Diversity and Urban Citizenship in Toronto.' *Canadian Journal of Regional Sciences* 20, nos. 1–2: 73–102.

Smith, E.M. 1974. 'Portuguese Enclaves: The Invisible Minority.' In *Social and Cultural Identity: Problems of Persistence and Change*, ed. T.K. Fitzgerald. Southern Anthropological Society Proceedings. Athens: University of Georgia.

Statistics Canada. 1995. 1991 Census Public Use Microfile. Computer file. Ottawa: Statistics Canada.

– 2002. 2001 Census of Canada. Population and dwelling counts, 93F0051XIE. www12.statcan.ca

Taft, D.R. [1923] 1969. *Two Portuguese Communities in New England, 1910–1920*. New York: Arno Press and the New York Times.

Teixeira, C., and G. Lavigne. 1992. *The Portuguese in Canada: A Bibliography*. Toronto: Institute for Social Research, York University.

Teixeira, C., and V.M.P. Da Rosa, eds. 2000. *The Portuguese in Canada: From the Sea to the City*. Toronto: University of Toronto Press.

United States Census Bureau. 2002. 2000 Census of Population and Housing. Summary file 3 (SF 3), sample data. http://factfinder.census.gov.

Valdés, A. 1995. 'Proclaiming their presence: In Mass. potential clout.' *Boston Globe*, 20 Apr., 61, 64–5.

Verba, S., K. Lehman Schlozman, and H.E. Brady. 1995. *Voice and Equality: Civic Voluntarism in American Politics*. Cambridge, MA: Harvard University Press.

Williams, J.R. 1982. *And Yet They Come: Portuguese Immigration from the Azores to the United States*. New York: Center for Migration Studies.

– 2005. *In Pursuit of Their Dreams: A History of Azorean Immigration to the United States*. Dartmouth, MA: Center for Portuguese Studies and Culture, University of Massachusetts – Dartmouth.

Wolforth, S. 1978. *The Portuguese in America*. San Francisco: R. & E. Research Associates.

PART THREE

Portuguese Communities
and 'Little Portugals'

10 On the Move:
The Portuguese in Toronto

CARLOS TEIXEIRA AND ROBERT A. MURDIE

In the postwar period Canada's large metropolitan areas, especially Montreal, Toronto, and Vancouver, have become increasingly cosmopolitan (Li 2003; Murdie and Teixeira 2006). By 2006 some 46 per cent of Toronto's population, 40 per cent of Vancouver's, and 21 per cent of Montreal's was born outside of Canada (Statistics Canada 2007a). A multitude of cultures, races, and religions has transformed the urban landscapes of these three cities – first in central city immigrant reception areas such as Kensington in Toronto and more recently in the suburbs. The Portuguese, who first settled in Canadian cities in the 1950s and continued to arrive in large numbers in the 1960s and '70s, have played an important role in this transformation.

Since the early 1950s the number of Portuguese immigrants choosing Canada, and particularly the province of Ontario, has grown considerably. The 2006 census (Statistics Canada 2008) indicates 189,405 people of Portuguese ethnic origin (single origin) in Ontario, accounting for 72 per cent of Canada's Portuguese population. According to recent census figures, the overwhelming majority (69 per cent) resided in the Toronto Census Metropolitan Area (CMA) (see Figure 1.3, p. 9). Other important centres of Portuguese settlement in Ontario include Kitchener (7.3 per cent), Hamilton (6.4 per cent), and London (4.1 per cent).

The purpose of this chapter is to show how and where the Portuguese have settled in the Toronto region. We look mainly at their settlement patterns, residential mobility, and housing choices. We also contrast their current demographic and socio-economic characteristics in the central city and the suburbs. Initially, we consider their early settlement in the Kensington area followed by westward spatial expansion, particularly into Portugal Village, the core of the Portuguese community shown in Figure 10.1, and finally their more recent dispersal to Toronto's western suburbs, especially Mississauga. We conclude with an overview of Portuguese demographic and socio-economic characteristics in central Toronto and suburban Mississauga. Information for the study was obtained from interviews with leaders of the Portuguese communities in Toronto and Mississauga and two surveys of a sample of Portuguese home owners in Mississauga, the first conducted in 1990 and a follow-up in 2003 of a subset of the original respondents. Other sources included statistical data from the Canadian census, written documents, the Portuguese ethnic press, and participant observation.[1]

Early Settlement in Kensington, Toronto's Initial 'Port of Entry'

On arrival in Toronto in the 1950s and '60s the Portuguese first settled within the heart of the city in two well-defined neighbourhoods: Kensington Market and Alexandra Park (the initial area of settlement in Figure 10.1). These were poor working-class districts, with older, badly maintained housing, and were already ports of entry for other immigrant groups such as Hungarians, Italians, Jews, Poles, and Ukrainians (Murdie 1969; Lemon 1985).

The Kensington area (bounded to the north by College Street, to the east by Spadina Avenue, to the west by Bathurst Street, and to the south by Dundas Street) was the site of Toronto's, and probably Canada's, first Portuguese-owned business, a restaurant on Nassau Street (Figure 10.1).[2] This was one of the first meeting places for the Portuguese. On the same street the First Portuguese Canadian Club was established, one of the oldest and most important Portuguese cultural institutions in Canada (Ribeiro 1990). Other Portuguese businesses began during the same period on Augusta Avenue and surrounding streets. Gradually the Portuguese transformed what was known as a 'Jewish market' into a 'Portuguese market' (Brettell 1977). Augusta became a very popular commercial artery for Portuguese immigrants and was soon known as the 'street of Portuguese' (*A rua dos Portugueses*).

From the late 1950s to the early '70s Kensington was Toronto's major commercial area for the Portuguese and housed a notable concentration of Portuguese families. It had affordable housing for sale or rent and was close to job sites and transportation – determining

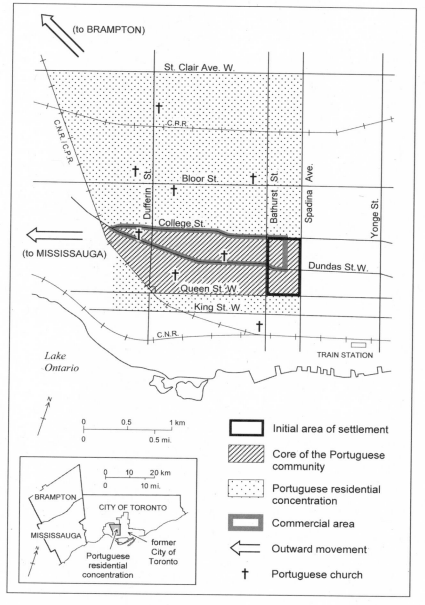

Figure 10.1. Portuguese in Toronto, 2007

factors in residential choice. Moreover, for sponsored immigrants during the 1960s and '70s the choice was often made for them; newly arrived Portuguese commonly lived with their sponsors or in housing belonging to their sponsors (Anderson 1974; Anderson and Higgs 1976).

Most Portuguese started out as renters and roomers. Apartments were often overcrowded, with two or three families sharing the same house or apartment (Marques and Medeiros 1989). Most of these immigrants came from rural areas of Portugal and arrived with little money, no English, and limited education. Their residential location was determined by these disadvantages, together with the Portuguese propensity to settle near friends and relatives and the availability of inexpensive housing, jobs, and transportation. Boarding houses became a transitional phase for Portuguese newcomers, who aspired to become home owners at a later stage, as well as for Portuguese families who owned houses and wanted to pay off their mortgages as soon as they could. Relatively inexpensive rental housing enabled newcomers to save for home ownership, and as a result Portuguese home ownership increased considerably during the late 1960s and '70s in the Kensington area and surrounding neighbourhoods.

The Portuguese left their imprint on Kensington, especially through their businesses and colourful houses, with front yards filled with flowers, vegetables, and grape vines. The *Toronto Star* observed, 'The Portuguese, like the equally charming Newfoundlanders, like to paint their houses bright colours, scarlet being the favourite. They will even occasionally paint the mortar between the bricks white. They often grow cabbages and other vegetables in their front yards unless the yard contains a shrine to Our Lady of Fátima, in which case flowers are preferred' (Turner 1973: A3). Saints and religious figures were also depicted on *azulejos* (Portuguese glazed tiles) and placed beside the main door of the house.[3] Immigrants brought the *azulejos* representing religious figures such as Our Lady of Fátima, St Anthony, Christ of Miracles, and popular saints from regions or islands of Portugal. On their frequent trips to Portugal they also brought seeds for flowers and vegetables in an attempt to recreate the rural atmosphere of their homeland in their relatively small back and front yards. For some this type of 'urban farming' was a way to put into practice the agricultural skills they had perfected in their homeland.

The legacy of the Portuguese may be seen to this day in Kensington, where some Portuguese businesses and colourful houses remain as markers of this chapter of the neighbourhood's remarkable history. In 2003 Kensington was nominated by Carlos Teixeira to become a national historic site of Canada, and in November 2006 it was officially designated as such by the minister of environment, primarily due to its role as a major reception area for immigrants from various parts of the world who have settled in this colourful area of Toronto (Whyte 2003).

Westward Expansion: The 1960s On

During the late 1960s and early '70s, the Portuguese began to move westward from the Kensington area, creating Portugal Village as the core of the Portuguese community (see Figure 10.1). Overcrowding in Kensington, the increase in Portuguese immigration to Toronto, and the desire to purchase a better house in a better neighbourhood contributed to this movement into adjacent neighbourhoods west of Bathurst Street. The area bounded mainly by College Street to the north, Bathurst Street to the east, King Street West to the south, and Dufferin Street to the west was the principal destination, with College and Dundas Streets gradually becoming Portuguese commercial strips. As more families arrived in Toronto in the 1970s and '80s the Portuguese increasingly moved into older areas of the city north-west of Portugal Village, replacing the Italians.

This continual flow of immigrants resulted largely from chain migration, a point confirmed by responses to the 1990 survey of a sample of Portuguese who had recently purchased housing in suburban Mississauga but had lived in the City of Toronto when they first migrated to Canada. Seventy-two per cent of the respondents indicated that a member of their nuclear or extended family sponsored them. More than 70 per cent of the respondents indicated that friends and relatives were 'very important' or 'important' in helping them find a job and housing, as well as in selecting a city and neighbourhood (Teixeira 1993).

Propensity for home ownership was among the most important cultural traits that the Portuguese transplanted from Portugal (Anderson and Higgs 1976; Alpalhão and Da Rosa 1980; Lavigne 1987). Many bought houses in Kensington, and particularly in Portugal Village, at relatively low prices. They then undertook extensive renovations including new plumbing, new wiring, finishing the basement, building a wine cellar, constructing an additional kitchen and/or bathroom, painting the exterior façade with bright colours, and subdividing the house into one or two more apartments to accommodate additional families and thereby provide extra income. Some of the new home owners worked in construction, often with Italian immigrants, and acquired skills and knowledge about house building. Most renovated their houses with the help of family members and friends, receiving little or no financial assistance from the government. Indeed, mutual help and support were very common among Canada's Portuguese immigrants (Krohn, Fleming, and Manzer 1977).

The majority of Portuguese immigrants see home ownership as both a secure economic investment and the realization of a dream. In response to the 1990 survey more than 90 per cent of the respondents indicated 'very important' or 'important' to the following motivations for home ownership: 'to have something of my "own"'; 'as a symbol of security to the family'; 'home ownership as an investment'; 'it brings greater privacy to the family'; 'brings a feeling of having succeeded in this country (Canada)'; and 'accomplishment of a "dream."' For these Portuguese immigrants a house is more than a commodity, a physical structure, or an investment. The importance they attach to home ownership reflects the immigrant dream of settling down in one place and acquiring security, privacy, and a home of one's own.

The Portuguese community in Portugal Village and environs is self-contained and self-sufficient. In the last four decades the Portuguese have constructed a thriving, complex community, setting up organizations, businesses, and communication-information services in their own language. The high degree of institutional completeness (Breton 1964) is well demonstrated by the appreciable number of ethnic businesses including grocery stores, bakeries, travel agencies, real estate agencies, furniture stores and restaurants. The Catholic church also plays a significant role in the lives of many Portuguese families. As shown in Figure 10.1 eight Portuguese Catholic churches are located in and around the core of the Portuguese community. Clusters of Portuguese immigrants, mainly first generation, live near the churches, which provide religious services daily in their mother tongue. The church as a 'pole of attraction,' has been a major force in shaping Portuguese settlement patterns in Toronto.[4]

Suburbanization: The Move to Mississauga

Mississauga is both a bedroom suburb of Toronto and an area of commercial and industrial growth. Population growth has been rapid since the early 1970s, increasing from 156,070 in 1971 to 665,655 in 2006 (Statistics Canada 1973, 2007b). Mississauga has also become an important area of immigrant settlement in the Toronto CMA, and by 2006 just over half of Mississauga's population was foreign born (Statistics Canada 2007a). The Portuguese are an important part of the immigrant influx to Mississauga. Beginning in the 1970s many Portuguese families moved from Portugal Village and other parts of the City of Toronto to Mississauga, and the Portuguese community there expanded from 1,415 (mother tongue) in 1971 to 24,700 (single ethnic origin) in 2006 (Statistics Canada 1973, 2008).[5]

In the 1990 survey of recent Portuguese home buyers in Mississauga referred to earlier 35.1 per cent of the respondents mentioned size of the house and/or lot as the most important reason for choosing their residence; 19.3 per cent chose area/neighbourhood; 15.8 per cent chose price of house/good investment; 14 per cent chose type of housing; and 6.1 per cent mentioned 'proximity to relatives and/or friends.' The desire to acquire a modern 'dream' house – preferably a single-family dwelling with amenities such as a basement, back yard, front garden, garage, modern kitchen, and location in a quiet place with pleasant surroundings and good schools – represents the ultimate goal for Portuguese families relocating to Mississauga.

A subset of these respondents (39 of 110) was re-interviewed in 2003 to determine their satisfaction with the move to Mississauga, their continued links to Portugal Village, and their participation in Mississauga's Portuguese community. Almost all expressed high levels of satisfaction with their present dwelling and neighbourhood (Teixeira 2007). Twenty-nine of the thirty-nine returned regularly to Portugal Village or other Portuguese areas in Toronto to visit relatives (65.5 per cent) or friends (37.9 per cent) or to shop (24.1 per cent).

Regardless of close connections with the Portuguese community in central Toronto, the vast majority of respondents indicated that they also maintain close contact with the Portuguese community in Mississauga, whether visiting family members (74.3 per cent), going to Portuguese religious services (62.9), or shopping at Portuguese businesses (54.3 per cent). Furthermore, almost two-thirds (61.5 per cent) mentioned that the majority of their friends were Portuguese. Clearly, there is an important network of contacts, including friendship and kinship ties that have been transplanted from Toronto and flourish among Portuguese immigrants in Mississauga. The lack of strong contacts with non-Portuguese friends and with members of other ethnic communities in Mississauga may be the result of language barriers, a cultural preference for socializing only with other Portuguese, or even the lack of a driver's licence, and thus lack of mobility in a car-oriented suburb.

Although the Portuguese community in Mississauga constructed two new Catholic churches in 1979 and 1995, the community has not been able to build a vibrant business enclave similar to Portugal Village. Respondents to the questionnaire thought that given the large number of Portuguese people in Mississauga, the city should have a more institutionally complete Portuguese community, with a larger and more diverse commercial structure to satisfy the needs and preferences of Portuguese living in the city. However, by demonstrating a preference for businesses in Toronto's Portugal Village, respondents may be preventing the expansion of Portuguese businesses in Mississauga. These continuing links with the Portuguese enclave in Toronto help explain the vitality of the businesses, institutions, and community organizations that remain in Portugal Village. In contrast to other immigrant groups in Canada – for example, the Chinese in Toronto and Vancouver, whose suburbanization in the last two decades has led to the relative decline of inner-city Chinatowns (Lo and Wang 1997) – the exodus of Portuguese to the suburbs has not yet led to the decline of Portugal Village. Further evidence of the respondents' satisfaction with their move to Mississauga is indicated by their plans for the future. Eighty-five per cent said they had no plans to move in the next five years. Of those who planned to move most wanted to buy a smaller house or apartment in Mississauga. Thus for these respondents Mississauga remains the place they want to be, the place where they have attained the 'Canadian dream' and where they want to stay. The 7.7 per cent of respondents who plan to leave the city after ten years or more are those who want to return permanently to Portugal when they retire.

Toronto's Portuguese Community in the Early Twenty-First Century

Toronto's Portuguese community has expanded since its original settlement in Kensington and Portugal Village in the 1960s and '70s. Two patterns emerged: first, a north-west movement in the traditional immigrant corridor, where the Portuguese are replacing Italians; and second, a shift to the suburbs, especially Mississauga (Figure 10.2). Yet while the 2001 census shows a community dispersing, the core in Toronto remains, albeit in a diminished form. In 1971 people of Portuguese ethnic background accounted for about 28 per cent of the pop-

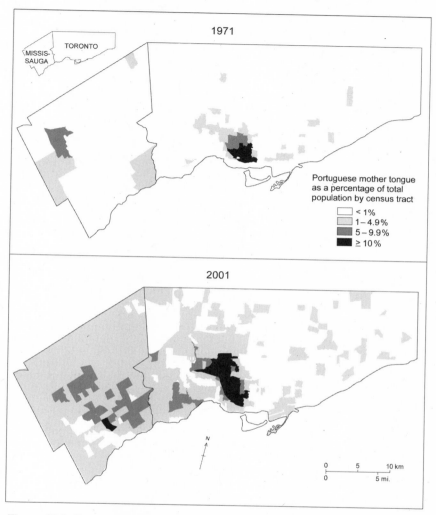

Figure 10.2. Portuguese mother tongue as percentage of population,
Metropolitan Toronto and Mississauga, 1971 and 2001
Source: Data from Statistics Canada, 1971 and 2001 Censuses.

Table 10.1
Portuguese vs total population, Toronto CMA and selected sub-areas, 1971–2006

Area	1971[1]	1981[2]	1991[2]	2001[2]	2006[2]
Portugal Village[3]					
Total population	44,590	35,140	33,050	30,940	28,085
Portuguese	12,285	19,655	15,945	11,220	9,040
% Portuguese	27.6	55.9	48.2	36.7	32.2
West Central Toronto[4]					
Total population	124,355	103,110	106,276	108,190	91,765
Portuguese	18,235	31,645	27,125	19,660	14,985
% Portuguese	14.7	30.7	25.5	18.2	16.3
Mississauga					
Total population	162,920	299,115	471,013	629,875	665,655
Portuguese	1,415	8,655	21,175	25,280	24,700
% Portuguese	0.009	2.9	4.5	4.0	3.7
Toronto CMA[5]					
Total population	2,628,125	2,998,947	3,893,046	4,647,955	5,072,075
Portuguese	39,550	127,635	124,330	129,280	130,865
% Portuguese	1.5	4.3	3.2	2.8	2.6

Notes:
1 Portuguese mother tongue.
2 Portuguese single ethnic origin.
3 Portugal Village = Census tracts 40, 41, 42, 43, 44, 45, 46. Also identified as City of Toronto neighbourhoods Little Portugal and Trinity Bellwoods. Note that Portugal Village is embedded within West Central Toronto.
4 West Central Toronto = Census tracts 4, 5, 7.01, 7.02, 8, 10, 40, 41, 42, 43, 44, 45, 46, 47.01, 47.02, 48, 52, 53, 54, 55, 56, 57, 58. Also identified as City of Toronto neighbourhoods South Parkdale, Liberty Exhibition, Niagara, Trinity Bellwoods, Little Portugal, Roncesvalles, Dufferin Grove, Palmerston–Little Italy.
5 Toronto CMA = Toronto Census Metropolitan Area, which is roughly the Greater Toronto Area.
Sources: CHASS Data Centre, University of Toronto; Canada Census Profiles, 1971, 1981, 1991, 2001, 2006 (Census tract level).

ulation in Portugal Village (Table 10.1). With increased immigration to Canada the Portuguese population in Portugal Village increased to 56 per cent of the total in 1981 but declined thereafter to 48 per cent in 1991, 37 per cent in 2001, and 32 per cent in 2006. In 2006 about 9,000 Portuguese continued to live in Portugal Village and almost 15,000 in

Table 10.2
Portuguese population distribution, selected sub-areas of the Toronto CMA,
1971–2006

	Portuguese population as percentage of total Toronto CMA Portuguese population		
	Portugal Village[3] (%)	West Central Toronto (%)	Mississauga (%)
1971[1]	31.1	46.1	3.6
1981[2]	16.4	24.8	6.8
1991[2]	12.8	21.8	17.0
2001[2]	8.7	15.2	19.6
2006[2]	6.9	11.5	18.9

Notes:
1 Portuguese mother tongue.
2 Portuguese single ethnic origin.
3 Note that Portugal Village is embedded within West Central Toronto.
Sources: CHASS Data Centre, University of Toronto; Canada Census Profiles, 1971,
1981, 1991, 2001, 2006 (Census tract level).

the more broadly defined West Central Toronto area, which corresponds roughly to the area of Portuguese residential concentration south of Bloor Street and west of Bathurst Street in Figure 10.1. However, the Portuguese in Portugal Village represented a rapidly diminishing proportion of Portuguese in the Toronto CMA, declining from 31 per cent of Toronto's Portuguese population in 1971 to not quite 7 per cent in 2006 (Table 10.2).

In the meantime the Portuguese population in Mississauga continued to increase: from 1,415 in 1971 to 8,655 in 1981, 21,175 in 1991, 25,280 in 2001, and declining slightly to 24,700 in 2006 (Table 10.1). Mississauga's Portuguese population as a proportion of Portuguese in the Toronto CMA also increased dramatically, from 3.6 per cent in 1971 to 6.8 per cent in 1981, 17.0 per cent in 1991, and 19.6 per cent in 2001, before declining slightly to 18.9 per cent in 2006 (Table 10.2). By 1991 more Portuguese were living in Mississauga than in Portugal Village, and by 2001 the Portuguese population of Mississauga exceeded the broader West Central Toronto area.

There are also similarities and differences in the social and demographic characteristics of the Portuguese who have remained in Portugal Village and environs and those who have relocated to Mississauga. And

Table 10.3
Characteristics of Portuguese vs total population, Toronto CMA and selected sub-areas, 2001

	Portuguese, West Central Toronto[2] (%)	Portuguese, Mississauga (%)	Total population, Toronto CMA (%)
Immigrant population[1]			
Born outside Canada	69.5	59.0	45.2
Year of arrival:			
1961–70	25.8	33.0	12.4
1971–80	37.8	38.4	16.9
1981–90	22.1	15.2	20.8
Age and household structure			
Younger than 15	12.0	16.4	19.8
15–24	15.6	15.9	13.1
25–44	29.2	34.4	33.3
45–64	26.7	23.9	23.0
65 and over	16.5	9.4	10.8
One-family household	72.8	84.1	69.8
Education			
Less than Grade 9	47.1	26.7	9.2
Grades 9 to 13	27.8	37.0	27.0
Some college/university	20.5	30.2	38.9
University degree	4.6	6.0	24.9
Occupation[3]			
Management	5.8	9.8	12.6
Professionals (skill level A)	5.8	6.5	18.5
Supervisors, etc. (skill level B)	31.1	30.8	26.1
Clerical workers, etc. (skill level C)	28.6	34.9	31.6
Sales and service, other manual (skill level D)	28.7	18.1	11.3
Average household income	$59,995	$80,210	$76,454
Housing			
Owned	66.4	88.5	63.1
Rented	33.6	11.5	36.9
Constructed before 1946	60.4	1.8	13.1

Table 10.3 (*continued*)

	Portuguese, West Central Toronto[2] (%)	Portuguese, Mississauga (%)	Total population, Toronto CMA (%)
Constructed 1946–80	30.2	45.8	36.9
Constructed 1981–2001	9.4	52.4	34.6
Single detached	15.4	53.2	45.1
Semi–detached and row housing	53.0	30.7	16.7
Low- and high-rise apartments	31.7	16.0	38.0
Condition of dwelling: regular maintenance only	70.5	78.7	68.3

Notes:
1 Portuguese = Portuguese single ethnic origin with/without Canadian ethnic origin.
2 West Central Toronto = Census tracts 4, 5, 7.01, 7.02, 8, 10, 40, 41, 42, 43, 44, 45, 46, 47.01, 47.02, 48, 52, 53, 54, 55, 56, 57, 58, City of Toronto neighbourhoods (South Parkdale, Liberty Exhibition, Niagara, Trinity Bellwoods, Little Portugal, Roncesvalles, Dufferin Grove, Palmerston–Little Italy).
3 Skill level A occupations usually require university education; skill level B occupations usually require college education or apprenticeship training and include supervisors, skilled crafts, semi- professionals, and technicians; skill level C occupations usually require secondary school and/or occupation specific training and include clerical workers and semi-skilled manual workers; skill level D occupations usually require on-the-job training.
Source: Adapted from Statistics Canada 2007c.

there are differences between the Portuguese in these two areas and Toronto's population as a whole. Table 10.3 illustrates the similarities and differences between the two groups in 2001. The older central area is identified in the table as West Central Toronto. Corresponding figures for the total population in the Toronto CMA are given for comparison.

In both the central and suburban areas the majority of the Portuguese population was born outside Canada, although more so for West Central Toronto than Mississauga, thereby confirming the larger proportion of second-generation Portuguese in Mississauga. Both areas also reflect the large-scale immigration of Portuguese to Canada during the 1960s and '70s. The Portuguese who have relocated to Mississauga are somewhat younger than those who have remained in

West Central Toronto. This is reflected particularly in the proportion of population under fifteen (12 per cent in the central area; 16.4 per cent in Mississauga) and over sixty-five years old (16.5 per cent in the central area; 9.4 per cent in Mississauga). The presence of a younger adult population in Mississauga, where 34.4 per cent of the population is between twenty-five and forty-four years of age compared to 29.2 per cent in the central area, further confirms the central city/suburban distinction. Overall the household structure of the Portuguese is predominantly single family, especially in Mississauga where 84.1 per cent of Portuguese households are single family. Compared to Toronto's population as a whole Portuguese households have a high propensity to live in single-family households.

Considerable differences in educational achievement exist between the Portuguese in West Central Toronto and Mississauga, as well as between the Portuguese and Toronto's population overall. The Portuguese who have remained in West Central Toronto have a substantially lower level of educational achievement than those in Mississauga. Almost half of Portuguese in the central area have less than Grade 9 education, compared to about a quarter of Portuguese in Mississauga. Correspondingly, the Portuguese in Mississauga have higher levels of education, both high school and some college or university. In both areas, however, very few Portuguese have a university degree compared to the general Toronto population. Almost 25 per cent of Toronto's adult population has a university degree compared to about 5 per cent of the Portuguese.

The relatively low level of educational achievement of many Portuguese is reflected in their occupational status. Compared to the rest of Toronto's labour force, comparatively few Portuguese are employed in managerial and professional occupations. In contrast, a considerably larger proportion of Portuguese are engaged in sales, service, and lower level manual employment, jobs that do not require high levels of education. As with education, there are differences between the Portuguese in West Central Toronto and Mississauga, with Mississauga's Portuguese being more engaged in managerial and professional occupations.

In spite of relatively low levels of education and occupational status the average income of Portuguese households is comparatively high, at least in Mississauga, where Portuguese household incomes are slightly above the Toronto average. This contrasts with West Central Toronto, where average household income for the Portuguese is much lower than for Portuguese in Mississauga. In part this reflects the lower socio-economic status of Portuguese in West Central Toronto and an older age structure with more retirees.

As noted earlier the Portuguese have a high propensity for home ownership, and this is reflected in Table 10.3. Home ownership among Portuguese households in Mississauga is very high: 88.5 per cent, compared to 66.4 per cent for the Portuguese in West Central Toronto. However, the latter is still higher than the overall level of home ownership in the Toronto CMA (63.1 per cent) and much higher than non-Portuguese home ownership in West Central Toronto (31.8 per cent) (Statistics Canada 2007c). The Portuguese in Mississauga also tend to live in newer single detached housing that is in a good state of repair and requires only regular maintenance. The very high level of Portuguese home ownership in Mississauga, primarily in relatively new single detached dwellings, confirms earlier evidence from the 1990 and 2003 surveys about the motivations of Portuguese for moving to Mississauga.

In sum the Portuguese who remain in West Central Toronto are more likely to be first generation, older, and of considerably lower socio-economic status than those who have moved to Mississauga. They are also less likely to be home owners and much less likely to live in single detached housing. For these families, however, a move to the suburbs is not a priority. The central city neighbourhood is the place where they feel comfortable, where they can live a Canadian life in a 'Portuguese way,' among those who share their culture, way of life, and language. Portugal Village and its environs is a re-creation of their homeland – an area where they can keep some of their cultural traditions alive in the New World.

Conclusion

What does the future hold for the Portuguese of Toronto? The answer to this question lies primarily with the new generations of Portuguese Canadians. Their assimilation is expected to increase in the years to come. However, at this stage in the life of the Portuguese community it is not clear the degree to which these new generations will preserve any of their ancestral culture and traditions. The long-term survival and integrity of Portuguese neighbourhoods and communities in Toronto and other Canadian cities may thus be problematic.

Many forces contribute to this uncertainty: the decrease in immigration of Portuguese to Canada; the departure of the first-generation Portuguese from the core to the suburbs; increasing levels of education among new generations of Portuguese; internal and external threats to the community, such as the arrival of other ethnic groups (including the Chinese in Toronto); inner-city revitalization/gentrification/redevelopment; and rising house prices in the inner city. To these forces we should add the wish of some families (mainly first generation) to return to Portugal's islands or to its mainland to retire. The changes that these Portuguese communities will experience within the next decades will be crucial for their survival and integrity, as well as the maintenance of Portuguese culture and traditions.

NOTES

1 For further details on the methods and socio-demographic characteristics of the Portuguese samples see Teixeira 1993 and 2007. Of the 110 Portuguese who participated in the first survey 97.3 per cent were born in Portugal and 70 per cent spoke Portuguese most of the time at home. Of first-generation respondents born in Portugal 60.7 per cent were born in the Azores. Most respondents, 67.3 per cent, arrived in Canada during 1966–75 and emigrated mainly for economic reasons (43.0 per cent) and to join family already living in Canada (40.2 per cent). Of the respondents, 79.1 per cent were already home owners and 59.1 per cent had lived in the city of Toronto before moving to Mississauga. Almost all of these (former) Torontonians lived in the core of the Portuguese community (see Teixeira 1993). In summer of 2003, thirteen years after the original interviews, Teixeira decided to re-interview the 110 Portuguese home buyers in Mississauga. The original respondents were sent a letter explaining the objectives of the study. Of these thirty-nine participated in a telephone survey. All interviews were conducted in Portuguese. All respondents were still living at the same house ('stayers') as in 1990 (see Teixeira 2007).
2 A. Sousa, interview with Carlos Teixeira, Toronto, 3 July 1989. Sousa is the owner of the first Portuguese restaurant in Toronto.
3 Concerning the Portuguese glazed tile, or *azulejo,* see Wheeler 1993.
4 Father A. de Melo, interview with Carlos Teixeira, Toronto, 21 June 1989; Father E. Rezendes, interview with Carlos Teixeira, Mississauga, 16 June 1989; and Father A. Cunha, interview with Carlos Teixeira, Toronto, 28 Aug. 1989.

5 According to leaders in the Portuguese communities of Mississauga and Toronto about 50,000 Portuguese live in Mississauga.

REFERENCES

Alpalhão, J.A., and Da Rosa, V.M.P. 1980. A *Minority in a Changing Society: The Portuguese Communities of Quebec*. Ottawa: University of Ottawa Press.

Anderson, G.M. 1974. *Networks of Contact: The Portuguese and Toronto*. Waterloo, ON: Wilfrid Laurier University.

Anderson, G.M., and Higgs, D. 1976. *Future to Inherit: The Portuguese Communities of Canada*. Toronto: McClelland & Stewart.

Breton, R. 1964. 'Institutional Completeness of Ethnic Communities and the Personal Relations of Immigrants.' *American Journal of Sociology* 70: 193–205.

Brettell, C.B. 1977. 'Ethnicity and Entrepreneurs: Portuguese Immigrants in a Canadian City.' In *Ethnic Encounters: Identities and Contexts*, ed. G.L. Hicks and P.E. Leis, 169–80. North Scituate, MA: Duxbury Press.

Krohn, R.G., B. Fleming, and M. Manzer. 1977. *The Other Economy: The Internal Logic of Local Rental Housing*. Toronto: Peter Martin Associates.

Lavigne, G. 1987. *Les ethniques et la ville*. Montreal: Le Préambule.

Lemon, J. 1985. *Toronto since 1918*. Toronto: Lorimer.

Li, P.S. 2003. *Destination Canada: Immigration Debates and Issues*. Toronto: Oxford University Press.

Lo, L., and S. Wang. 1997. 'Settlement Patterns of Toronto's Chinese Immigrants: Convergence or Divergence?' *Canadian Journal of Regional Science* 20: 49–72.

Marques, D., and J. Medeiros. 1989. *Portuguese Immigrants: 25 Years in Canada*. Toronto: West End YMCA.

Murdie, R.A. 1969. *Factorial Ecology of Metropolitan Toronto, 1951–1961: An Essay on the Social Geography of the City*. Research paper no. 116, Chicago: Department of Geography, University of Chicago.

Murdie, R.A., and C. Teixeira 2006. 'Urban Social Space.' In *Canadian Cities in Transition: Local through Global Perspectives*, ed. T. Bunting and P. Filion, 154–70. Toronto: Oxford University Press.

Ribeiro, M.A. 1990. *O Canadá e a presença Portuguesa*. Toronto: Correio Portugues.

Statistics Canada. 1973. Population and Housing Characteristics by Census Tracts. *1971 Census*. Toronto. Statistics Canada cat. no. 95-721. Released May 1973.

- 2001. Citizenship, Immigration, Birthplace, Generation Status, Ethnic Origin, Visible Minorities, and Aboriginal Peoples. www.statcan.ca.
- 2007a. Census Trends for Census Metropolitan Areas and Census Agglomerations (table). *2006 Census.* Statistics Canada cat. no. 92-596-XWE2006002. Ottawa. Released 4 Dec. 2007.
- 2007b. Population and Dwelling Count (highlight tables). *2006 Census.* Statistics Canada cat. no. 97-550-XWE2006002. Ottawa. Released 13 March 2007.
- 2007c. Custom Product EO1025. *2001 Census.* Ottawa: Statistics Canada.
- 2008. Ethnocultural Portrait of Canada (highlight tables). *2006 Census.* Statistics Canada cat. no. 91-562-XWE2006002. Released 2 April 2008.
Teixeira, C. 1993. 'The Role of "Ethnic" Sources of Information in the Relocation Decision-Making Process: A Case Study of the Portuguese in Mississauga.' PhD diss., York University.
- 2007. 'Residential Experiences and the Culture of Suburbanization: A Case Study of Portuguese Homebuyers in Mississauga.' *Housing Studies* 22 no. 4: 495–521.
Turner, D. 1973. 'The Portuguese find "making it" has a new twist.' *Toronto Daily Star,* 8 Dec., 1, A3.
Wheeler, D.L. 1993. *Historical Dictionary of Portugal.* Metuchen, NJ: Scarecrow Press.
Whyte, M. 2003. 'Going up market.' *Toronto Star,* 21 Dec., B1, B7.

11 The Portuguese Community in Quebec

VICTOR M.P. DA ROSA AND CARLOS TEIXEIRA

Quebec is the Canadian province with the highest concentration of Portuguese after Ontario. This can be explained by the Portuguese perception of common cultural and socio-economic conditions between Quebec and Portugal. Indeed, when one moves from Portugal to Canada, Quebec is a particularly suitable milieu for settlement, as cultural and geographical similarities ease the immigrants' adaptation. Moreover, the presence of members of the same ethnic group becomes a 'pull' factor, facilitating emigration of more Portuguese to Quebec. Similar to what was found by Anderson (1974) for the Portuguese of Toronto, immigrants living in Quebec usually made the decision to emigrate as a result of networks created by friends or family members.

Once in Canada Portuguese immigrants sought to reconstitute their families here. As was observed in Chapter 1, in the early 1950s Canada promoted an immigration policy based on sponsorship and family reunification, which helped to launch chain migration. This process reunited entire Portuguese families in Canada, a type of immigration that strongly influenced the occupational opportunities available for the new immigrants, as well as their areas of settlement (cf Anderson 1974; Lavigne 1987; Teixeira 1986, 1993, 2006).

This chapter examines the community life of Portuguese in Quebec; first, social characteristics, including occupations and education; second, areas and types of residence; and third, community life. The conclusion speculates on the future of the community.

Occupations and Education

On arrival Portuguese immigrants often took jobs very different from the ones they had had at home. Immigrants to Quebec in the early

1950s came to meet needs in agriculture and railway construction. Those who followed them came to join families or friends and on arrival found work in construction, services, and industry-related occupations (Anderson 1974).

When Portuguese women immigrated to Quebec they generally did not work outside the home, either because they had large families to look after or because their husbands, often for cultural reasons, did not want them to work. Most of these women were sponsored by their husbands, had little education (less than four years, on average), and had few skills other than housework. Consequently, those who took jobs tended to become garment workers, cleaners, or domestics. Because of their unfamiliarity with French and English and their lack of special skills, many took on repetitive piecework for low wages, often under demeaning conditions (Alpalhão and Da Rosa 1980; Labelle et al. 1987; Januário 1988; Lopes 2000).

Although unfamiliarity with Canadian labour legislation and lack of strong representation in unions (Alpalhão and Da Rosa 1980; Aguiar 1991) left both male and female Portuguese workers difficult to hire, they have made significant gains in the last decade in their struggle for equality and rights in the workplace (Nunes 1986; Giles 1992; Teixeira 1999). This being said, 2001 figures from Statistics Canada indicate that 48.5 per cent of the Portuguese in the Montreal Census Metropolitan Area (CMA) had less than a high school education. This is reflected in the group's employment picture, with 29 per cent in 'sales and services' occupations, 18 per cent in 'business, finance and administrative' occupations, and another 15.2 per cent in occupations unique to 'processing, manufacturing, and utilities' (Statistics Canada 2002).

The majority of the first-generation Portuguese have remained in unskilled and semi-skilled occupations, and Portuguese manual labourers have acquired the reputation of being hard-working, reliable, and thrifty. Most of these immigrants simply have not experienced upward mobility from their low initial 'entrance status' (Goldust and Richmond 1973; Reitz 1981). However, more recent Portuguese immigrants, particularly since 1975, and the Canadian born, appear less segregated occupationally. The new generations have greater opportunities in education (Marques 1992; Oliveira and Teixeira 2004). In general the second generation seems to experience upward mobility, with higher job status and better pay (Richmond 1986), but in spite of an increase in the number of self-employed members of the community, the general picture is not rosy. As Noivo writes, 'Unfortunately, findings suggest that the hopes and desires of the second generation will not be satisfied; the overall education, social, and economic lives of the third generation are alarming' (1997: 134).

Despite low job status and income pioneer Portuguese households attained a certain economic stability and often their ultimate 'dream' – owning a home. Often several members of the household contributed to the family income. The wife and the children (some of whom left school early to help the family finances) worked hard and sacrificed to improve their family's life. As a result Portuguese households have high levels of home ownership (Alpalhão and Da Rosa 1980; Lavigne 1987; Teixeira 1986, 2006). Portuguese have considerably improved their housing conditions, from boarding or renting when they arrived to owning homes in Montreal and its suburbs.

Residence

In 2001 most Portuguese in the province of Quebec were concentrated in Montreal, Laval, Gatineau-Hull, Champlain, St Thérèse-de-Blainville, and Quebec City (see Figure 1.4, p. 10). We estimate that almost 60 per cent of them come from the Azores. In this section we look at Montreal, neighbouring Laval, and Gatineau-Hull.

Montreal

The metropolitan region of Montreal has been the main pole of attraction for immigrants settling in Quebec since the early 1950s. Today, even though there are Portuguese in all the districts of greater Montreal, the majority are settled in a area bounded by Sherbrooke to the south, St-Denis to the east, Avenue du Parc to the west, and the CN/CP railway lines to the north (Figures 11.1 and 11.2). These neighbourhoods, known as Quartier St-Louis and Quartier Mile-End, have served as the reception area for several ethnic groups, including Jews, Poles, Greeks, and Italians.

Straddling the border of the city's two English and French communities, these neighbourhoods have affordable housing, employment close by, and accessible transportation. In the 1970s the area north of Sherbrooke was clearly the heart of the community. Within this area, and particularly in St-Louis, north of Sherbrooke. Portuguese residents have done a remarkable job of renovating their houses and improving the neighbourhood's quality of life, for example, in the Park of Portu-

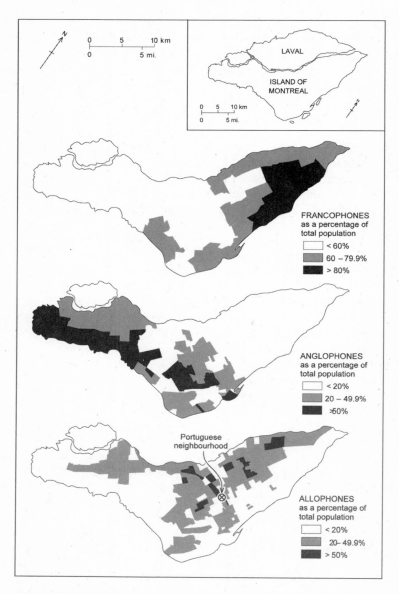

Figure 11.1. Geographical distribution of ethnic communities, Island of Montreal, 1996
Source: Lo and Teixeira 1998, adapted from Monière and Côté 1995: 162–3.

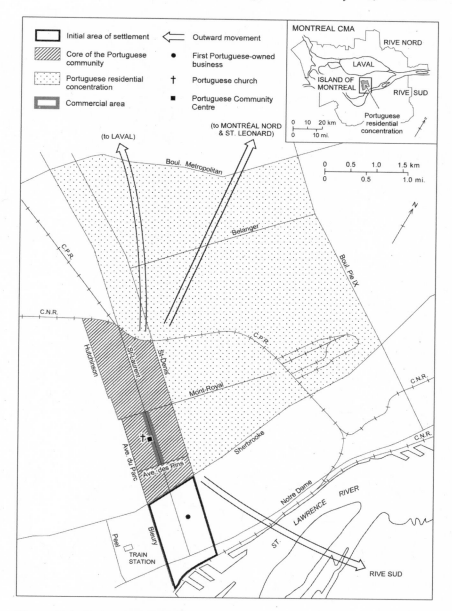

Figure 11.2. Portuguese in Montreal, 2007

gal, on St-Laurent between Avenue des Pins and Mont-Royal (Alpal-hão and Da Rosa 1980; Teixeira 1986).[1] One observer has stated, 'Les Portugais semblent monopoliser un espace assez précis. Ils l'occupent et ils l'aménagent. Commerces. Logements. Institutions. Ils signifient leur présence. Façades multicolores. Affiches en langue portugaise. Ils investissent. Restauration, Réfection ... ils sont là' (Lavigne 1987: 20).

Within the core of the community ethnic visibility becomes impor-tant, and a Portuguese ethnic atmosphere exists. The Portuguese, being a sociable people, have tried to re-create through their institu-tions their rich culture and traditions. Their institutions are not only meeting places but also a means of promoting the language and culture of origin, of sponsoring educational, social, and recreational activities, and of assisting immigrants who face language or other social problems.[2] From this perspective they help to bridge genera-tional and cultural differences among Portuguese Canadians as they assist them in adapting to their new home.

Da Rosa and Laczko (1984–7) identified four major types of organi-zations: mutual or benefit; recreational; religious; and educational. Among others, benefit societies, which are voluntary organizations, include the Centro de Acção Sócio-Comunitária de Montreal and the Caixa de Economia dos Portugueses de Montréal; recreational associ-ations, the Clube Oriental Português de Montreal, Associação Por-tuguesa do Canadá, Club Portugal de Montréal; religious associations, the Missão Portuguesa de Santa Cruz and the Igreja Evangélica Bap-tista; and educational associations, Escola Santa Cruz, Escola Por-tuguês do Atlântico, and Escola Secundária Lusitana.[3] At present we may consider regional organizations as a fifth type (e.g., Casa dos Açores, Rancho Folclórico Verde Minho, and Rancho Chamarrita do Faial). The institutional completeness of the Portuguese community is evident in the numerous social and religious institutions and ethnic businesses. In 2007 the Portuguese in Quebec had approximately 721 businesses, more than forty-six clubs and associations, five community schools, and four churches (data provided by the Portuguese con-sulate, 2007). Obviously, ethnic community institutions are necessary and must be preserved and encouraged. It seems nevertheless advis-able to promote exchanges and relations among different ethnic groups because this is essential to mutual adaptation and is also a means of combating ethnocentrism.

At the beginning of the twenty-first century the heart of the Por-tuguese community remains at the intersection of St-Laurent and Rachel, where the main church and community centre are located.

Some new arrivals settled farther west or north, and some families have gone as far as Villeray, far to the north bounded by Boulevard Métropolitain. The availability of better housing was often a major factor in this move. However, for sponsored immigrants, the choice was often made for them; they often lived with their sponsors or in housing belonging to them. Some Portuguese have moved to other neighbourhoods or to Laval and the South Shore (Teixeira 2006). The majority of these households are home owners.

During the first three decades of Portuguese settlement in Montreal the Portuguese showed distinct spatial patterns, which translated into geographical and social isolation from the host society. In fact, they showed particularly high levels of residential concentration. For first-generation immigrants this segregation was a major barrier to their blending into Montreal's mainstream society. Factors such as language barriers, cultural values, and limited sources of information for locating housing may explain the high concentration that characterizes the Portuguese community (Teixeira 2006).

In the last two decades the settlement patterns and distribution of the Portuguese population of Montreal have clearly changed (see Teixeira 1986, 2006). Several factors have contributed to these changes. Some of the new immigrants, particularly those who arrived after 1975, had better education, skills, and experience and so did not need to settle in the core of the community. Also, with chain migration many selected residences where their sponsors and relatives already lived. As well, some first-generation families became better off and could acquire their own houses, preferably in suburbs such as Laval and the South Shore. Thus the central city, particularly the core of the community, gradually became less attractive to the new immigrants.

Their slow dispersion is a fairly recent phenomenon. Since the mid-1970s residential patterns have changed as the Portuguese have become more dispersed over a larger area than ever before. Two patterns have emerged in this process: first, a northward movement along the traditional 'immigrant corridor'; and a second, a movement to the suburbs, especially Laval, in an intra-city migration that has involved some form of self-segregated resettlement (Figure 11.3).

These forces were largely responsible for the emergence of the new Portuguese settlements farther from the core in areas such as Anjou, Laval, Longueuil, Montréal Nord, and St-Leonard. This exodus shows up clearly in the 1976, 1981, and 1991 censuses (Figure 11.3, Teixeira 2006). This movement, however, had not yet noticeably lessened the viability of the core's ethnic institutions, businesses, and services.

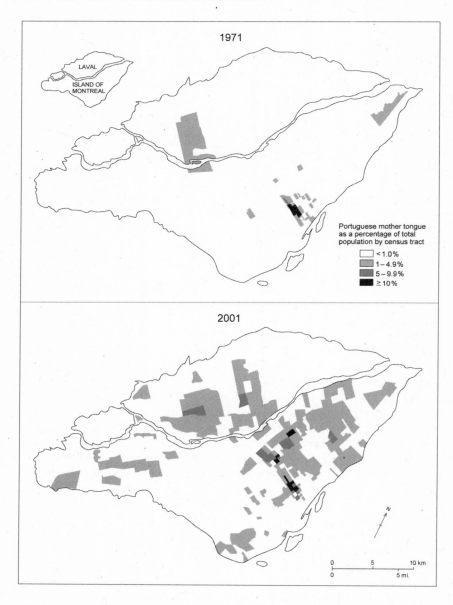

Figure 11.3. Portuguese mother tongue as percentage of population, Island of Montreal and Laval, 1971 and 2001
Source: Data from Statistics Canada, 1971 and 2001 Censuses.

Laval

Laval, particularly the neighbourhoods of Chomedey, Vimont, and Pont-Viau, has become the most important relocation area for Montreal's Portuguese. The movement out to Laval is a recent phenomenon (Figure 11.3). The Portuguese community in this suburb expanded from 635 people in 1971 to almost 6,000 in 2001 (Statistics Canada 1973, 2002), and community leaders estimate it numbers today between 10,000 and 15,000.

In 2001 the Portuguese were not evenly distributed in Laval. A questionnaire (Teixeira 1996, 2006), informal interviews, and census data indicate re-segregation in Laval, with some families particularly from the Azores living in or near existing pockets of Portuguese concentration. For instance, nearness to friends, relatives, and the Portuguese church affected choice of location. Almost every socio-cultural event centres on the Our Lady of Fátima church, which contains both the community centre and the Portuguese-language school. For other families relocation led to geographical dispersion. Thus two distinct and separated Portuguese communities seem to be forming in Laval (Teixeira 1996, 2006).

Gatineau-Hull

Another large Portuguese concentration in Quebec is situated in Gatineau, the twin city of Ottawa, the federal capital. Some of the first Portuguese to settle there did so in the early 1950s, following their departure from La Tuque region of Quebec, where they had worked in the lumber industry. Today the Portuguese population of the Gatineau-Hull region (not including Ottawa) is estimated at 3,500, the majority of whom come from the Azores and, more specifically, from the parish of Maia on São Miguel island.

Community Life

Leadership and Politics

Portuguese communities are differentiated on the basis of social class, politics, and regionalism (Anderson and Higgs 1976; Alpalhão and Da Rosa 1980). Class distinction – a strongly established tradition in Portuguese society – is still pronounced today among the Portuguese in Canada. The community may be divided into two major social groups:

The one to which the majority of the people belong is made of tens of thousands of members of the working class. They struggle every day facing a vast complexity of preoccupations in the fight for a position of survival and well-being which they culturally identified with factors of economic and financial nature. The other, to which the minority belongs, is made up of people who, because of the status they hold in the social, economic, educational and religious structure, fill positions of leadership and representation in the community ... [While] the Portuguese working class is not divided ... [the leadership is divided] since the attempts to unify our community may have been until now, of a merely individualistic and selfish nature. (Couto 1982: 8)

It is not surprising that the Portuguese have been described as a class-conscious community.

Portuguese Canadians have also been criticized, particularly by other Portuguese, for their lack of political unity and participation in the political and social life of their host society. However, opinions about Portuguese communities' unity or lack thereof are often contradictory and inconclusive. Some critics express concern, arguing that the lack of unity is a serious problem. Others see the lack of success in creating large-scale projects such as umbrella organizations to represent community interests, as being manifestations of the Portuguese 'personality.' For example, there has been some concern about the proliferation of small Portuguese clubs and associations in the last three decades, given the absence of clear leadership and the financial means necessary to support them; indeed some never develop beyond the stage of good intentions (Anderson and Higgs 1976; Alpalhão and Da Rosa 1980; Teixeira 1999; Lopes 2002).

The failure of certain projects and divisiveness within communities are, according to Alpalhão and Da Rosa (1980), a result of the individualistic temperaments or personal ambitions of certain 'pseudo-leaders,' and of regional differences among the Portuguese immigrants. But as the community comes of age and the new generations mature, some of these problems may vanish.

Portuguese participation in Quebec's political life, even in terms just of voting, has always left room for improvement, but some progress has been made in the last decade. The Portuguese community in Quebec, as well as in Canada in general, has been described as not being sufficiently cohesive and politically aware to defend and promote its own interests and rights within the political institutions of the host society (Alpalhão and Da Rosa 1980). Only in the 1990s was the first Portuguese school trustee, Clara Pires, elected in Montreal, representing the Commission des Écoles Catholiques de Montréal. At about the same time António de Sousa was elected councillor in Hull. In 1997 a Portuguese Canadian, Luís Miranda, was elected borough mayor of Anjou, for the first time. In the fall of 2008, Alexandra Mendes was elected as a member of the federal Parliament to represent Brossard-LaPrairie riding (Montreal South Shore).

First-generation immigrants have shown in the past what Alpalhão and Da Rosa (1980) termed a certain 'political backwardness,' even an aversion, for things political. First-generation Portuguese lived under the Salazar regime, which denied them experience and education in the political process. This translated into a low level of political participation in Canada. Until quite recently for first-generation Portuguese politics and community involvement have been minor concerns. Distrust or fear of authority of all forms was and is quite common among them. However, as Alpalhão and Da Rosa wrote, 'On the one hand, the Portuguese ethnic group is still first generation and thus is a population still in the process of adapting. On the other hand ... the majority of immigrants ... have been victims of the obscurantism of a dictatorial political regime which never encouraged them to participate in the social and political life of the community' (1980: 220).

Therefore, despite the many Portuguese living in Quebec and their concentration in particular urban neighbourhoods, few have registered to vote. The reduced presence of Portuguese representation at the provincial or federal level weakens the group's position vis-à-vis mainstream institutions. Nevertheless, in the last ten years Portuguese participation has increased, and it is worth mentioning that women in particular have become actively involved in Canadian political life.

Culture, Language, and Religion

To separate the Portuguese ethnic group from its culture and language of origin would be to dispossess it of its identity. In a survey done in Toronto, of all the ethnic groups polled the Portuguese felt the strongest about retaining their language and culture and passing them on to their children.[4] This phenomenon also occurs in other Canadian cities, including Montreal.

Through many formal and informal contacts with members of Montreal's Portuguese community we conclude that the Portuguese culture in Quebec is in transition, still adapting to a new milieu. The Portuguese language is also in a transitional phase, with the new generation using their parents' tongue at home less and less and almost exclusively to communicate with their grandparents, while preferring French and/or English when in public. Yet according to the 2001 census, after Ontario the largest number of people whose mother tongue is Portuguese is in Quebec , particularly in metropolitan Montreal (Statistics Canada 2002).

Already there is some evidence of a 'mother tongue shift' within Portuguese communities. For example, Veltman and Paré (1985) provide data on the linguistic evolution of the Portuguese in Montreal. They found that although Portuguese immigrants frequently use their own mother tongue, they do so most often in their contacts with family members. Generally unilingual on arrival, they frequently acquire a second language – French and/or English – and most of this learning process occurs in the workplace.

Veltman and Paré (1985) also looked at the linguistic integration of Portuguese youths in Montreal from four to twenty-four years old. They concluded that these young people employ their mother tongue only with their parents and grandparents, and French and English mainly with siblings or outside the home. Similarly Dias (1990) found that the first generation tends to be unilingual, and the second generation bilingual or trilingual. However, most Portuguese of Azorean descent feel little need to maintain their language, especially because they do not intend to return to their home islands. Mainlanders, in contrast, many of whom intend one day to return to Portugal, are more inclined to preserve their language and culture.[5] More recently Oliveira and Teixeira (2004) have shared the conclusions arrived at by Veltman and Paré (1985) and Dias (1990).

Yet in general Portuguese communities strive to maintain their language and culture. This is particularly evident in their creation of social, cultural, political, and religious institutions that use their language and transmit their culture and traditions to the new generations. These institutions dominate their socio-cultural life and not only preserve and promote their language and culture but also promote friendship and solidarity through a range of social, cultural, and recreational activities.

Some community members still wish to prepare typical Portuguese meals, and located in the core community are commercial suppliers of suitable products, many of them imported from Portugal. Groceries, bakeries, fishmongers, and restaurants with 'ethnic products' and a distinctly Portuguese atmosphere help to maintain a distinctive cuisine in Quebec. Most of these businesses are in the major urban cores of Portuguese concentration and provide not only familiar products but also services in Portuguese, thus easing immigrants' adjustment to their new country.

The Portuguese media in Quebec, particularly newspapers, are crucial in the transmission and preservation of the language and culture of origin. Both spoken and written media are well established, but like the community they serve the media are in transition. The most widely read community newspapers are *A Voz de Portugal, Lusopresse,* and *O Emigrante.* Both the press and television programs have started to dedicate more space to news about the local Portuguese communities, and this major source of information should continue as a cultural bridge between new and old immigrants while adapting to the needs of the younger generation, whose knowledge and use of the Portuguese language will certainly decline but who still take pride in their heritage.

Portuguese immigrants have developed a remarkable network of community schools throughout Canada. For first-generation Portuguese, whose knowledge of both official languages is minimal and who still use Portuguese at home, the teaching of Portuguese to their children remains important.[6] And throughout the years the Portuguese churches in Quebec have functioned not only as a cornerstone for the community but also as a key element for cultural and language maintenance.

Conclusion: Ethnic Commitment and Survival

The question of ethnic commitment and survival for the Portuguese in Quebec remains open. This ethnic group has been in Canada for a little more than a half century, and the majority of its members have come to stay. With varying degrees of loyalty to their cultural heritage, they seem to have adapted relatively well into the host society. However, Quebec urgently needs to make efforts to achieve an optimal degree of accommodation of ethnic minority groups.[7]

The existence of high geographical concentrations of Portuguese slowed assimilation. Instead, these ethnic neighbourhoods favoured socio-economic isolation. While Portuguese attachment to traditions can offer a valuable contribution to Quebec's ethnic mosaic, it has sometimes inhibited upward mobility. Is this the fault for the Portuguese? Perhaps. Already there is a feeling among community leaders that the Portuguese should strive for a higher level of involvement in the social and political life of the receiving society.

In most Portuguese communities in Quebec there are numerous signs that suggest the host society's acceptance of the newcomers, but not full assimilation. The move to the suburbs has been not a radical step toward assimilation but rather a movement toward gradual blending into Québécois society. Many families move in search of 'privacy' and are fluent in French and/or English. However, despite suburbanization, they tend to have frequent contacts with the core of the Portuguese community, visiting relatives and friends, shopping on weekends, and attending social events. In spite of being 'on the move' they show no sign of relinquishing attachment to Montreal's original Little Portugal.

Other structural factors include the constant decline in the number of Portuguese settling in Quebec, the gradual but apparently inexorable, long-term assimilation of the group into Quebec society; and the remarkable improvement of living standards in Portugal with its full membership in the European Union. All these factors together make us uncertain about the survival and the ethnic commitment of the Portuguese in Quebec.

It is impossible to predict the future of Quebec. Many scenarios exist, and it is within an ongoing variety of political and economic frameworks that the Portuguese must envisage the next decades. At this stage it is difficult to delineate the exact patterns of change that the Portuguese communities of Quebec will undergo during the lifetime of the present generations. For future generations the process of cultural identification may become the most problematic challenge. For many of them, whether to be Canadian, English Quebeckers, Portuguese Canadians, Portuguese, or Québécois will remain a continuing dilemma. New generations are being socialized to be Québécois just as other residents of the province are, which means that in due time they will lose the cultural traits their parents brought with them from Portugal.

NOTES

1 In 1975 Montreal's Order of Architects awarded its annual prize to the residents of the Portuguese community in recognition of their architectural innovations in the St-Louis district. In 1993 the Association des

Architectes Paysagistes du Québec honoured them for their work at the Park of Portugal, in the heart of the community.

2 A good example of this is the Portuguese Association of Canada, founded on 7 January 1956 and the first major Portuguese organization in Canada. It was set up to give immigrants the chance to meet one another. Its chief aim now is to bring Portuguese nationals together through cultural, artistic, sports, and recreational activities. Its achievements include the formation of a philharmonic orchestra and sports, folklore, and theatre groups.

3 Obviously this list is not exhaustive but merely provides a few examples of the diversity of Portuguese organizations.

4 See the newspaper survey 'The Portugueses sticking together through bad times,' published in the *Toronto Star*, 14 June 1992, A6–7.

5 According to *A Voz de Portugal* (1981, 5), only between 10 per cent and 15 per cent of Azorean children attended Portuguese-language schools.

6 There are three Portuguese community schools in Montreal (Escola Portuguesa de Santa Cruz, Escola Português do Atlântico, and Escola Secundária Lusitana), one in Laval (Escola Portuguesa de Laval), and one in Gatineau-Hull (Escola Portuguesa Amigos-Unidos de Hull).

7 As witnessed by Quebec's Government Consultation Commission on Accommodation Practices Related to Cultural Differences, co-chaired by Gérard Bouchard and Charles Taylor.

REFERENCES

Aguiar, L. 1991. 'Struggling on So Many Fronts: Attempting to Unionize a Textile and Garment Factory in Montreal.' MA thesis, McMaster University.

Alpalhão, J.A., and Da Rosa, V.M.P. 1980. *A Minority in a Changing Society: The Portuguese Communities of Quebec*. Ottawa: University of Ottawa Press.

Anderson, G.M. 1974. *Networks of Contact: The Portuguese and Toronto*. Waterloo, ON: Wilfrid Laurier University.

Anderson, G.M., and Higgs, D. 1976. *A Future to Inherit: The Portuguese Communities of Canada*. Toronto: McClelland & Stewart.

Couto, E. 1982. Keynote speech. In 'The Portuguese Community of Toronto: Needs and Services,' 5–12. Unpublished document prepared by the Portuguese Interagency Network, Toronto.

Da Rosa, V.M.P., and L.S. Laczko. 1984–7. 'Ethnic Organizational Completeness: A Discussion of Trends in Montreal's Portuguese Community,' *Gávea-Brown: A Bilingual Journal of Portuguese-American Letters and Studies 5–8*, nos. 1–2: 17–27.

Dias, M. 1990. 'Deux langues en contact: Le français et le portugais dans les communautés de Paris et de Montréal.' PhD diss., University of Toronto.

Giles, W. 1992. 'The battling women who fought for dignity.' *Toronto Star*, 10 Sept., G7.

Goldust, J., and A.H. Richmond. 1973. *A Multivariate Analysis of the Economic Adaptation of Immigrants in Toronto*. North York, ON: Institute of Behavioural Research, York University.

Januário, I. 1988. 'Les activités économiques des immigrantes portugaises au Portugal et à Montréal à travers les récits de vie.' MSc thesis, Université de Montréal.

Labelle, M., G. Turcotte, M. Kempeneers, and D. Meintel. 1987. *Histoires d'immigrées: Itinéraires d'ouvrières colombiennes, grecques, haïtiennes et portugaises de Montréal*. Montréal: Boréal.

Lavigne, G. 1987. *Les ethniques et la ville: L'aventure urbaine des immigrants portugais à Montréal*. Montréal: Le Préambule.

Lopes, D.N. 2000. *Peregrinação; Uma História das Comunidades Portuguesas do Canadá, 1953–1999*. Ponta Delgada: Direcção Regional das Comunidades, 2000.

Marques, D. 1992. 'Here to stay.' *Toronto Star*, 12 Sept., G1–3.

Monière, d., and R. Côté. 1995. *Québec 1996*. Montreal: Fidès.

Noivo, E. 1997. *Inside Ethnic Families: Three Generations of Portuguese-Canadians*. Montreal and Kingston: McGill-Queen's University Press.

Nunes, F. 1986. 'Portuguese-Canadian Women: Problems and Prospects.' *Polyphony* 8, nos. 1–2: 61–6.

Oliveira, A., and C. Teixeira. 2004. *Jovens Portugueses e Luso-descendentes no Canadá*. Oeiras: Celta.

Reitz, J.G. 1981. *Ethnic Inequality and Segregation in Jobs*. Toronto: Centre for Urban and Community Studies.

Richmond, A.H. 1986. 'Ethnogenerational Variation in Educational Achievements.' *Canadian Ethnic Studies* 18, no. 3: 75–89.

Statistics Canada. 1973. Population and Housing Characteristics by Census Tracts. *1971 Census*. Toronto. Statistics Canada cat. no. 95-721. Released May 1973.

– 2001. Citizenship, Immigration, Birthplace, Generation Status, Ethnic Origin, Visible Minorities, and Aboriginal Peoples. www.statcan.ca.

– 2002. 2001 Census of Canada. Population and dwelling counts, 93F0051XIE. www12.statcan.ca.

Teixeira, C. 1986. 'La mobilité résidentielle intra-urbaine des Portugais de première generation à Montréal.' MSc thesis, Université du Québec à Montréal.

- 1993. 'The Role of Ethnic Sources of Information in the Relocation Decision-Making Process: A Case Study of the Portuguese in Mississauga.' PhD diss., York University.
- 1996. 'The Suburbanization of Portuguese Communities in Toronto and Montreal: From Isolation to Residential Integration?' In *Immigration and Ethnicity in Canada*, ed. A. Laperrière, V., Lindstrom, and T.P. Seiler, 181–201. Montreal: Association for Canadian Studies.
- 1999. 'Portuguese.' In *An Encyclopedia of Canadian People*, ed. P.R. Magocsi, 1075–83. Toronto: University of Toronto Press.
- 2006. 'A Comparative Study of Portuguese Homebuyers' Suburbanization in the Toronto and Montreal Areas.' *Espace, Populations, Sociétés* 1: 121–35.
Veltman, C., and O. Paré. 1985. *L'insertion sociolinguistique des Québécois d'origine portugaise*. Montreal: INRS – Urbanisation.
A Voz de Portugal. 1981. 'O Ensino da Língua Portuguesa no Quebeque: Apenas 10 a 15 por cento de Crianças Açorianas vão à Escola de Sábado,' 12 Mar., 5.

12 The Portuguese in British Columbia: The Orchardists of the Okanagan Valley

CARLOS TEIXEIRA

In the second half of the twentieth century Canadian society was rendered culturally and racially heterogeneous by successive waves of immigration: first primarily from western European countries such as Portugal, and later from a more diverse range of source countries in Asia, Africa, Latin America, and the Caribbean. One of the defining features of this immigration was its urban character, with most immigrants choosing to settle in the major urban centres of Montreal, Toronto, and Vancouver (Murdie and Teixeira 2006). Portuguese immigrants have been representative of this process, with most settling in the immigrant reception areas of urban Canada where they formed institutionally complete ethnic neighbourhoods – Little Portugals – with an appreciable number of diverse social and economic organizations and an established business structure.

It should nevertheless be acknowledged that important numbers of Portuguese immigrants arrived and settled in rural Canada as well. This settlement choice is not surprising, as Portugal has traditionally been an agricultural economy, and most Portuguese immigrants to Canada came originally from rural areas (Anderson and Higgs 1976). In fact it was as a result of the stagnation of Portugal's agricultural economy in the 1950s that the first Portuguese came to Canada, when the Portuguese government encouraged emigration as a solution to the country's unemployment (Anderson and Higgs 1976; Teixeira 2000–2). Through chain migration entire Portuguese families arrived in Canada, and British Columbia came to host the third most important concentration of Portuguese settlement in the country, after Ontario and Quebec (see Chapter 1).

The Portuguese immigrants who settled in British Columbia were representative of immigrants to Canada in general with regard to their preference for urban settlement. Eventually, more than three-quarters of the province's Portuguese population settled in major urban areas. As a consequence of this urban orientation there has been a notable lack of research dealing with the important Portuguese presence and business activities in rural Canada (see Joy 1977–8, 1989; Munzer 1981; Teixeira 2001–2).

Immigration has been widely recognized as a primary engine of economic, social, and cultural change for Canada. Indeed, both scholars and policy makers have acknowledged the positive impact that immigration has on the economic growth and development of Canadian cities (Hiebert 2000; Teixeira, Lo, and Truelove 2007). Various factors and barriers have contributed to immigrant participation in the self-employed sector of the economy, and entrepreneurship has thus long been a characteristic immigrant economic activity. But surprisingly little scholarly research has been undertaken on immigrant entrepreneurial experiences in rural Canada (see Barrett, Jones, and McEvoy 1996; Teixeira 2001–2).

With respect to the Portuguese entrepreneurs of rural British Columbia it is necessary to pay particular attention to the agricultural industry of the Okanagan Valley. As one observer notes, 'Although part of the Canadian government's immigration programme was intended to bring Portuguese farmers to Canada in the 1950s, it was only in the Okanagan Valley that this programme was successful' (Koroscil 2000: 155). Due to a shortage of farm workers in the Okanagan Valley in the 1950s the first Portuguese immigrants came to the region to work as fruit pickers. Soon, however, to the surprise of many native-born Canadians, the Portuguese channelled their savings into developing their own businesses in the region and in a relatively short time became owners of their own orchards (Joy 1989).

This chapter examines the entrepreneurial behaviour and experiences of Portuguese immigrants in the agricultural sector of the Okanagan Valley economy, with a particular focus on the areas of Penticton, Oliver, and Osoyoos (Figure 12.1). The development and operation of these Portuguese immigrant entrepreneur businesses are explored, with attention paid not only to the history but also to the future of the Portuguese entrepreneurs in the Okanagan Valley orchard industry.

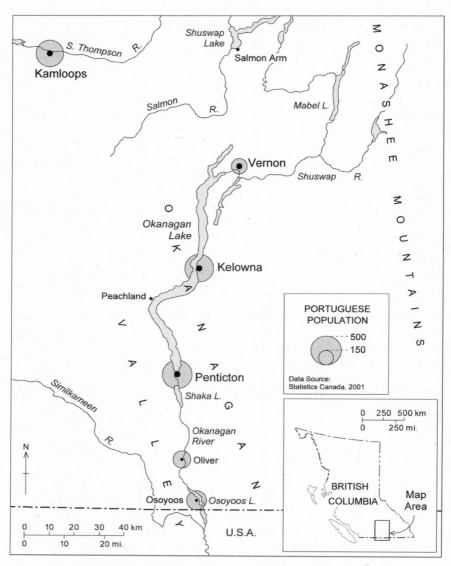

Figure 12.1. Population of Portuguese ethnic origin, Okanagan Valley, 2001
Source: Data from Statistics Canada 2001.

Methodology

This study relies on information collected in two phases. In the first, in May 2004, I conducted thirty-two informal interviews with key leaders of the Portuguese communities of Penticton, Oliver, and Osoyoos and with Portuguese orchardists in order to obtain a better understanding of the way these entrepreneurs operated their businesses and the major challenges they faced in the market. I also had the opportunity to visit the three main Portuguese ethnocultural organizations of the study communities: the Luso-Portuguese Canadian Multicultural Society of Penticton, the Okanagan Portuguese Club of Oliver, and the Portuguese Canadian Cultural Society of Osoyoos. The information collected from these informal interviews played a very important role in allowing me to build a questionnaire that I administered to Portuguese orchardists in the same communities in May–June 2005.

The second phase data collection relied on that questionnaire. With the help of key leaders from the study communities, I identified all Portuguese owners of orchards in the areas and delivered questionnaires to them (Figure 12.2). I also contacted three local Portuguese ethnocultural organizations and the two main local fruit co-ops (Sun Fresh Co-op and Okanagan Similkameen Co-op Grocers Association) and asked for their cooperation in the promotion of the study to their members. A total of eighty-one questionnaires were distributed (eighteen in Penticton, twenty-eight in Oliver, and thirty-five in Osoyoos), of which fifty-nine were completed: thirteen from Penticton, twenty-one from Oliver, and twenty-five from Osoyoos.

The questionnaire had fifty-eight closed and open-ended questions within the following four broad categories: (1) respondent's background; (2) business establishment – history and employment; (3) community resources in starting and operating the current business; and (4) business activities/practices and the market.

From Rural Portugal to the Rural Okanagan Valley

Acute labour shortages in the agricultural sector, and particularly the tree fruit industry, in the Okanagan Valley in the 1950s prompted the Canadian government to encourage labourers from southern Europe to migrate to the Valley. The first Portuguese immigrants arrived in 1955. On their arrival in the Okanagan, Annamma Joy reminds us,

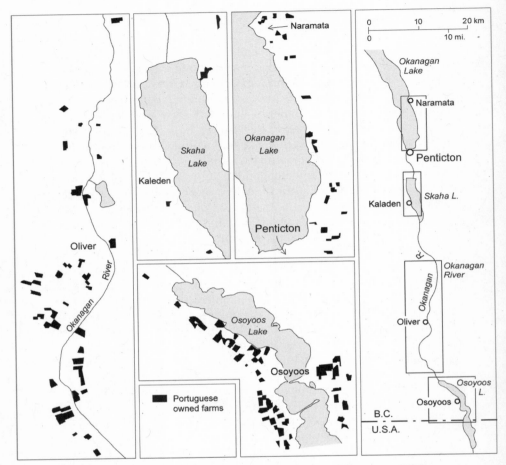

Figure 12.2. Portuguese-owned farms, Penticton, Oliver, and Osoyoos, 2005
Source: Okanagan–Kootenay Sterile Insect Release Program 2005.

serious doubts were raised as to the assimilation of the Portuguese in Canada ... In the Okanagan, the coming of the Portuguese was viewed as a mixed blessing. While the farmers in the district were very glad to have the reliable help, non-farmers were concerned about the numbers of unskilled labourers and their relatives moving into small settlements [Penticton, Naramata, Oliver, and Osoyoos] ... [also] ... there were occasional outbursts of resentment from locals when the Portuguese formed little groups on the street corners and spoke in their mother tongue.' However, while there may have been some unease upon the Portuguese immigrants' initial arrival in the Valley, it should be emphasized that sources indicate there 'was a concerted effort by the locals to enable the Portuguese and other newcomers in the area [Oliver] to settle.' (Joy 1989: 49)

In contrast to Portuguese immigrants who settled in Canada's major urban areas (e.g., Montreal, Toronto and Vancouver) and formed geographically well-delimited and compact ethnic neighbourhoods ('Little Portugals'), the lifestyles and settlement patterns adopted by the Portuguese immigrants who chose the Valley as their home did not result in any formation of Portuguese neighbourhoods:

They [Portuguese] were scattered all around the town [Oliver and Osoyoos] ... Although they were newcomers, in many ways distinct in terms of clothing, food, and language, they were first considered as good and trustworthy workers, then small orchard owners, subsequently large orchard owners, and finally good citizens ... [T]heir commitment to the local-residential unit was the main reason they were accepted in the community ... By working on and subsequently buying the land, they avoided the formation of ethnic neighbourhoods ... [and] demonstrated commitment to the local unit rather than to their ethnic group. Being a member of the 'community' meant subordinating ethnic or cultural loyalty to the local-residential unit. (Joy 1989: 154–6)

This settlement strategy is particularly interesting for how it differs from the strategies adopted by Portuguese in urban Canada.

The first group of fewer than thirty immigrants arrived in the Okanagan Valley in 1955, and their numbers gradually increased. According to British Columbia Statistics about 800 people in the Okanagan-Similkameen Regional District declared Portuguese as their mother tongue. Within this large area the majority are concentrated in Penticton (175), Oliver (120), and Osoyoos (130). However, according to key Portuguese informants, the number of Portuguese of first generation and their descendants in the region may more accurately be as high as 1,500. It is interesting to note that in these three areas the Portuguese language ranked high as one of the most spoken languages (top five single mother tongue): in fifth place in Penticton (4 per cent) and in third place in both Oliver (14 per cent) and Osoyoos (14 per cent) (British Columbia Statistics 2001).

The fifty-nine respondents from Penticton, Oliver, and Osoyoos form a homogeneous cultural group. All were of the same ethnic background and had the same mother tongue. With the exception of two respondents all were first-generation immigrants, born in Portugal (96.6 per cent). The majority (70.2 per cent) were born in mainland Portugal, 26.3 per cent were from the Azores islands (primarily from São Miguel and Terceira), and the remaining 3.5 per cent were from the island of Madeira. Most of these respondents came from rural regions of Portugal (e.g., the northern parts of the country, and particularly from Beira Baixa). More than two-thirds arrived in Canada during 1955–9 (33.9 per cent) and 1960–9 (35.7 per cent). Those who arrived in the 1950s can be considered the 'pioneers' of Portuguese immigration to the Okanagan Valley. José da Costa, whom I interviewed, is one of these pioneers. He reflects on his – and the Portuguese community's – beginnings in the Valley: 'I arrived in Halifax from Portugal April 2, 1955. I took the train and I arrived in Kelowna a few days later – April 7. With another eleven Portuguese we were distributed in different places in the Valley to work in the orchards and/or farms. Myself and Alfredo Farinha we went to Oliver while the others – Joao Chique (Vernon); Antonio da Costa and Antonio Marques (Kelowna); "Alentejano" [nickname] (Penticton); Jose Eugenio, Joao Meange, and "Algarvio" (nickname) (Osoyoos); Jose Antunes, "Sofredo," and "Alentejano" [nicknames] (Keremeos) – were dispersed along the Valley ... but we kept in touch.'

Another successful Portuguese pioneer in the orchard business was Joe Fernandes, who became the first Portuguese immigrant to buy an orchard in Osoyoos in 1959. He initially operated the orchard with the assistance of his wife, Maria, and their seven children. Fernandes became one of the most well-known Portuguese in the South Okanagan and an icon in the Portuguese community of Osoyoos, in large part for his successful entrepreneurial adventures outside the orchard business. As his daughter, Laura Garcia, explains in an interview,

My father came to Canada in 1953 to work in Quebec and Ontario and in 1955 he crossed Canada by train and found work in Kitimat. Then he moved to Osoyoos where in 1959 he bought his first orchard, a seven acres orchard for $7,000 ... He was the first Portuguese to buy an orchard in Osoyoos ... and in 1960 our family left Madeira to join him here. He farmed for many years growing fruit and vegetables and established a very successful fruit selling businesses ... He became known across Canada and brought many tourists and attention to Osoyoos ... for example in one newspaper from Vancouver (*Vancouver Sun*, Sept., 1992) we could read: 'Osoyoos – His Own Banana Republic: Immigrant Fruit-stand Farmer Creates a Little Bit of Portugal in Middle of British Columbia' ... He kept his banana farm going for many years until his death in 1993. He was then 73 ... the family closed the banana farm one year later.

The success of these Portuguese pioneers was repeated by later Portuguese immigrants in the southern Okanagan Valley. In 1987 it was reported that 'of the 420 commercial orchards in the Oliver area almost 25 per cent are owned by Portuguese Canadians; of the 223 Osoyoos commercial orchardists 44 per cent are of Portuguese Canadians' (Koroscil 2000: 161). This proportion of Portuguese ownership of the industry is all the more remarkable when we consider the comparative youth of this community. This being said, however, almost two decades later, in 2005, the number of Portuguese-owned orchards had decreased to only twenty-eight orchards in Oliver and thirty-five in Osoyoos. Clearly, the role of the Portuguese in this industry seems to be in transition.

Like their counterparts in the rest of Canada the large majority of Portuguese emigrated to Canada for economic reasons. Forty-three respondents (72.9 per cent) indicated that they had come to join members of their families already established in the country or the Okanagan Valley, and thirteen respondents (22.0 per cent) had arrived with a labour contract to work in the agriculture and/or orchards. The well-known factor of sponsorship and family reunification characterizes the immigration of Portuguese to the study areas, and we may thus conclude that the choice of the Valley as their final destination to live and work was a family affair –largely determined well in advance of migration by members of the nuclear or extended family already established in the region. Not surprisingly, family members already established in the Valley played a determining role for many Portuguese immigrants in finding their first residence and first job on arrival – most of the time in the fruit industry.

It is interesting to note that out of the fifty-nine respondents thirty-two (54.2 per cent) declared that when they came to Canada and to the Valley it was with the idea of staying only temporarily. The main goal was to make some money and better their lives and then return to Portugal. Yet they never did leave.

By 2005, when the surveys were administered, only two respondents (3.4 per cent) indicated that they were planning one day to return to Portugal; one of those planned to spend 50 per cent of his retirement time in Portugal and 50 per cent of it in the Valley. Two other respondents (3.4 per cent) also indicated that they might retire outside of the study areas, with a preference for Vancouver, Victoria, or Kelowna: cities where their children live or because of accessibility to better health care and hospitals. These numbers reveal that whatever their original intent, this group of Portuguese immigrants have come to stay in the Valley. At the time of the survey the average Portuguese respondent was sixty years old and thus close to retirement, so their plans can be said to have matured over time.

More than two-thirds of the respondents, 69.5 per cent, have completed only primary level education (four years of education in Portugal). It is therefore not surprising that some still face major difficulty communicating in English. It is interesting to note that this group of immigrants had no experience with business when in Portugal. With the exception of five respondents (8.5 per cent), none had been in business or self-employed before moving to Canada.

We may speculate that, given this lack of a business background, the interest in entrepreneurship among this group may be due in part to the orchard industry being connected to the land. Indeed, more or less from their time of arrival, purchasing their own land became almost an obsession for this hard-working group of immigrants. This may be a rural manifestation of a phenomenon noted in urban centres such as Toronto, where the Portuguese group has displayed a remarkably high level of land/home ownership; many Portuguese residences in Little Portugal also feature back gardens filled with vegetables and other plants. Even in Canada's big cities the rural roots of Portuguese immigrants are clearly apparent. For members of the group living today in the Okanagan Valley it is evident that land ownership has not only economic but also symbolic significance as the attainment of their Canadian dream.

Survey Results

Going into Business: The Orchard Industry in the Okanagan Valley

For the majority of our respondents (94.9 per cent) the orchard they owned at the time of the survey represented their first business experience on Canadian soil. However, 74.6 per cent have been in the business for more than twenty years and are therefore established entrepreneurs. As noted by Joy the Portuguese 'had a step-like progression from the position of farm workers to medium-sized farm owners. Each progressive stage was characterized by their special efforts to improve and enhance their lifestyle. Farming was a lucrative occupation for them because unlike other farmers, they did not hire any outside labour: it was a family concern. Since they had bought land when it was not expensive, they made a profitable investment' (1989: 153–4).

Why were these Portuguese immigrants attracted to self-employment in the orchard industry? The questionnaires administered to orchardists in Penticton, Oliver, and Osoyoos reveal their most important motivations as a strong desire to work for themselves, followed by the wish to own a piece of land in their new country. Forty-two respondents (71.2 per cent) referred to these two options as their main reasons for going into the fruit tree industry. Another eighteen (30.5 per cent) cited their own or their families' prior involvement in agriculture in Portugal. Agriculture for them represented what they termed a 'family tradition' as they moved from being farm workers in Portugal to being farm workers in the Valley, where they ultimately achieved ownership of their own orchards (Table 12.1). These motivations and desires were clearly expressed:

'I arrived in 1957 ... and in the mid-1960s most of my Portuguese friends were buying orchards in Oliver and Osoyoos. I was poor in Portugal but my dream was to own my own piece of land here.'

'The Okanagan Valley is like Algarve in Portugal ... when I decided to stay [permanently] here my first goal was to work to myself and to own land that I could one day pass to my children.'

It can be concluded that for these Portuguese immigrant entrepreneurs, being a fruit tree grower in the Valley was a natural extension of their family traditions and culture in Portugal. Land ownership and

Table 12.1
Reasons for entry into orchard business, 2005

	Penticton (N = 13)		Oliver (N = 21)		Osoyoos (N = 25)	
	N	%	N	%	N	%
To be self-employed/control destiny	3	23.1	7	33.3	13	52.0
Like to farm/wanted to own land	7	53.9	8	38.1	4	16.0
Family tradition/familiar with business	7	53.9	4	19.1	7	28.0
Economic independence	1	7.7	2	9.5	4	16.0
Language barriers elsewhere	1	7.7	2	9.5	1	4.0
Lack of jobs elsewhere	1	7.7	1	4.8	1	4.0
Other	1	7.7	0	0.0	1	4.0

Note: N = number of respondents. Percentages do not sum to 100 because entrepreneurs frequently mentioned more than one reason.
Source: Author's questionnaire survey, 2005.

success in business became important signifiers of status for this group. This impetus was so strong that, as Munzer observes, it led to 'economic competition, status rivalry and jealousy' (1981, 98) among some Portuguese orchardists in the Valley.

By remodelling or improving their houses and buying orchards with their savings the Portuguese valorized the land and were, in consequence, viewed favourably by other Canadians: 'They earned the respect in the eyes of their employers. They were not seen as renters because they were concerned with property value, living conditions, and environment ... The idea of converting a cabin into a home [by adding better plumbing and electricity] was a significant step ... In short, self-help and family cooperation made it possible for these farmers not only to buy land but also to make economically feasible. Further in a decade the value of the land had doubled' (Joy 1989: 142).

When asked why they chose the southern Okanagan Valley, and particularly Penticton, Oliver, and Osoyoos, to establish themselves, thirty-one respondents (52.5 per cent) indicated that the presence of family members and Portuguese friends played a determining role in their choice of where to buy land and start a new business. Another thirty respondents (50.8 per cent) also indicated the good location of the area – particularly the beauty and the weather conditions, which reminded them of Portugal, as well as the quality of the land (Table

Table 12.2
Reasons for selecting Oliver, Osoyoos, or Penticton as orchard site, 2005

	Penticton (N = 13)		Oliver (N = 21)		Osoyoos (N = 25)	
	N	%	N	%	N	%
Family members/friends living in the Valley	7	53.9	8	38.1	16	64.0
Location/good land and prices	7	53.9	9	42.9	14	56.0
Labour contract (through immigration)	2	15.4	5	23.8	2	8.0
Other	1	7.7	2	9.5	1	4.0

Note: Percentages do not sum to 100 because entrepreneurs frequently mentioned more than one reason.
Source: Author's questionnaire survey, 2005.

12.2). With regard to the price of land ownership, some respondents cited as a reason for their location being the good prices that they paid for their land/orchard. Considering that the majority of Portuguese orchardists bought their orchards in the 1960s and '70s we can specu-late that they bought at the right time and for a relatively good price. This is particularly the case if we compare their costs with today's very high market prices for land that seems to define the current real estate market of the south of the Okanagan Valley (see Penner 2005; Madison 2006).

Table 12.3 presents the main barriers experienced by some of our entrepreneurs as they established their orchard businesses: language barriers and/or culture shock (including different agricultural prac-tices); getting financing; and marketing and/or market price issues. Language barriers (lack of knowledge of English) and the resultant culture shock were by far the most significant barriers for almost two-thirds of our respondents.

These immigrants also had to adapt to different agricultural prac-tices in Canada: : 'In the Okanagan Valley, the formation of agricultural cooperatives and mechanization of agriculture is a response to the constraints and problems faced by farmers who are drawn into the industrial context' (Joy 1989: 109). These practices were new to Por-tuguese orchardists. It must be understood that although agricultural work was a cultural tradition for members of this group, under the Salazar regime in Portugal in the 1950s when they emigrated, mecha-

Table 12.3
Barriers experienced by Portuguese immigrants when establishing current business, 2005

	Penticton (N = 6)		Oliver (N = 11)		Osoyoos (N = 19)	
	N	%	N	%	N	%
Language barriers/culture shock	4	66.7	9	81.9	9	47.4
Getting financing	2	33.3	3	27.3	8	42.1
Marketing/market prices	4	66.7	1	9.1	5	26.3
Other	1	16.7	0	0.0	2	10.5

Note: Percentages do not sum to 100 because entrepreneurs frequently mentioned more than one barrier. The number of respondents reflects those who responded to this portion of the survey, not the total sample.
Source: Author's questionnaire survey, 2005.

nization and agricultural cooperatives were unknown. They were therefore confronted by a steep learning curve in adapting to Canadian farming methods and technologies:

> They utilized the most up to date machinery and they kept pace with the changing orchard management practices that were introduced into the industry. In Portugal if they had a small orchard most of the work would have been accomplished with hand implements and not orchard machinery unless they worked on orchard estate. The major change that the Portuguese orchardists had to adapt to in the Okanagan was the noninterplanting of vegetables between the tree fruits and vineyards. In Portugal, on small orchard acreage where land use was intensive interplanting was a common practice. In the Okanagan, on most orchard parcels, interplanting did not take place because the space between the tree fruits and vineyards was needed for farm machinery use. (Koroscil 2000: 160)

Although this type of business requires substantial capital to buy land and thus start operations, surprisingly only thirteen respondents out of the total fifty-nine from the three study areas declared having encountered problems getting financing to buy the land they own today (22.0 per cent). Based on informal interviews with key leaders of the Portuguese communities in the study areas, I can conclude that one of the defining characteristics of the Portuguese orchardists in the

Valley was their heavy reliance on members of their nuclear and/or extended family, including Portuguese friends, to obtain the minimum funds required by financial institutions for the financing to buy land. These loans were often made in a very informal way by relatives and/or friends, in some cases without signed documents. This strategy allowed Portuguese immigrants to become self-employed after only a short time in the Valley.

A system of 'pool savings' was quite common, revealing the role played by cultural tradition and trust among members of this ethnic group: 'Financing ... is raised by a unique system of pooling savings. The Portuguese lend to each other with only verbal agreement, and they do not charge each other interest. When one sceptical Canadian said, "Suppose the borrower dies, you'll never see your $2,000 again," the reply was: "If he dies, he loses his life. All I lose is my $2,000" ... The instinct of the Portuguese is for the land. The money is incidental' (Fraser 1964: 35).

Of course this strategy proved successful. Often the Portuguese would farm their own ten-or fifteen-acre parcels of land and rent out the other ten acres to other farmers. Through hard work and frugal financial management – with the assistance of other group members – the Portuguese became successful entrepreneurs (Koroscil 2000: 162). After five decades or so in the Valley the Portuguese entrepreneurs became established land and business owners. The cultural importance among the Portuguese of owning their own land and homes serves to explain both their speed of entry into the real estate markets of the Okanagan Valley and their success in their chosen field of entrepreneurship.

Community Resources and Economic Success

An important characteristic of immigrant businesses in urban Canada is their size – small and family oriented – with extensive use of family and co-ethnic labour (Teixeira, Lo, and Truelove 2006). How do Portuguese orchardists in rural British Columbia fit this picture, with respect to the number and ethnic background of their employees? Table 12.4 indicates that only twenty-two respondents (37.3 per cent) (ten in Penticton, six in Oliver, and six in Osoyoos) had full-time employees. Most orchards owned by Portuguese ranged from being a one-person operation to a 'family-oriented' operation with two to five full-time employees. However, due to the nature of this business – sea-

Table 12.4
Business by number of people employed full time, 2005

	Penticton (N = 10)		Oliver (N = 6)		Osoyoos (N = 6)	
	N	%	N	%	N	%
One-person operation (1 employee)	6	60.0	3	50.0	3	50.0
Family business (2–5 employees)	4	40.0	3	50.0	2	33.3
Small to medium size business (6–15 employees)	0	0.0	0	0.0	0	0.0
Large, diversified business (>15 employees)	0	0.0	0	0.0	1	16.7
Total full-time employees	19	100.0	9	100.0	27	100.0

Note: The number of respondents reflects those who responded to this portion of the survey, not the total sample.
Source: Author's questionnaire survey, 2005.

sonal, with heavy labour during the pruning and the harvest seasons – a large number of Portuguese orchardists (thirty-eight, or 64.4 per cent) in the study areas also relied on part-time employees (Table 12.5). The respondents also indicated that most of these part-time employees were temporary migrant workers coming mainly from Quebec, Mexico, or other parts of Canada.

Given that family members and co-ethnic labour have traditionally played a crucial role in the operation, success, and survival of small ethnic business (see Barrett, Jones, and McEvoy 1996), it is not surprising Portuguese orchardists in the three study areas relied extensively on family members (71.2 per cent) as well as on employees from the same ethnic background (78.0 per cent) to run their orchards. The ethnicity of full-time employees seems to have been a major criterion in the Penticton, Oliver and Osoyoos entrepreneurs' hiring decisions.

Portuguese immigrant women also played a very important role in the running and success of Portuguese family-oriented orchard businesses in the Okanagan Valley: 'The Portuguese women worked ... In the initial years, they worked along with their husbands as pickers. When the men bought their own orchard (small farms at first) they had to continue helping their husbands. The only way they could save money to buy more land was not to use hired help. The family therefore worked as a unit. But with the increase in size of the orchards and

Table 12.5
Business by number of people employed part time, 2005

	Penticton (N = 7)		Oliver (N = 12)		Osoyoos (N = 19)	
	N	%	N	%	N	%
One-person operation (1 employee)	1	14.3	3	25.0	2	10.5
Family business (2–5 employees)	3	42.9	6	50.0	13	68.4
Small to medium size business (6–15 employees)	3	42.9	3	25.0	2	10.5
Large, diversified business (>15 employees)	0	0.0	0	0.0	2	10.5
Total part-time employees	31	100.0	43	100.0	165	100.0

Note: The number of respondents reflects those who responded to this portion of the survey, not the total sample.
Source: Author's questionnaire survey, 2005.

the returns on them, there was really no need for the women to work. The women, thus freed from orchard work, secured jobs in the packing house ... This act of moving out of the house by women can be seen as an indicator of acculturation' (Joy 1989: 130).

Portuguese children were also very important in the operation of these ethnic businesses. As Laura Garcia, the daughter of a successful Portuguese orchardist from Osoyoos, recalls, 'As a kid, you got up before school and worked on the orchards, went to school, and then worked some more hours when you got home' (Watts 2004: 46). It should also be noted that Portuguese children played an important role in acting as language interpreters for their parents in Canada.

This context leads us to ask two questions. Why was there such heavy reliance on members of their own ethnic group? And how important are those employees for successful running of the business? To explore these issues respondents were asked to comment on both the importance and the advantages of having employees of the same ethnic background.

Most entrepreneurs (forty-three, or 72.9 per cent) cited Portuguese employees as 'very important' or 'important' to the operation and success of their orchards. Table 12.6 reveals that the major advantages of having Portuguese as employees were seen to be their reputation as hard working, reliable, and trusty, followed by their knowledge of the

Table 12.6
Major advantages of having employees of same ethnic background, 2005

	Penticton (N = 8)		Oliver (N = 14)		Osoyoos (N = 21)	
	N	%	N	%	N	%
Hard working/reliable people	5	55.6	9	64.3	13	61.9
Communication/language	3	37.5	5	35.7	10	47.6
Broad knowledge of farming	4	50.0	5	35.7	8	38.1
Other	1	12.5	1	7.1	2	9.5

Note: Data based on percentage of entrepreneurs who indicated ethnic employees were 'very important' or 'important.' Percentages do not sum to 100 because entrepreneurs frequently mentioned more than one reason. The number of respondents reflects those who responded to this portion of the survey, not the total sample.
Source: Author's questionnaire survey, 2005.

Portuguese language (making it easy for their employers to communicate with them) and their broad knowledge of farming.

Along with heavy reliance on full- and part-time employees of their own ethnicity did this group of Portuguese entrepreneurs rely on other ethnic community resources for information, advice, and contacts as well? Respondents were asked which resources, if any, they used when starting or operating their current business. Some 67.7 per cent of all resources used by the fifty-nine Portuguese entrepreneurs were from the same ethnic background. By far the most important were relatives and Portuguese friends, followed by non-Portuguese organizations at 13.6 per cent. Both relatives and Portuguese friends occupied a central role in the business lives of the respondents by recommending employees and clients, providing information on the selection of the business site, offering mutual aid and assistance in initial training in fruit growing, and providing some capital to establish and/or expand their current business (Table 12.7).

Portuguese entrepreneurs were also closely involved in community networks. Fifty-six respondents (94.9 per cent) declared being 'highly' or 'somewhat' involved in the socio-cultural life of their local Portuguese community. Of those 71.2 per cent indicated being a member of and/or participating actively in the life of their Portuguese community's socio-cultural associations and/or religious organizations.

These results indicate that Portuguese entrepreneurs in the fruit tree

Table 12.7

Importance of ethnic (Portuguese) sources in establishment/operation of current business, 2005

	Penticton (N = 8)		Oliver (N = 14)		Osoyoos (N = 18)	
	N	%	N	%	N	%
Recommending employees	6	75.0	12	85.7	18	100
Providing information about business site	4	50.0	9	64.3	16	88.9
Providing information about market/ climate for business	5	62.5	9	64.3	11	61.1
Providing mutual aid/assistance/ training	5	62.5	5	35.7	13	72.2
Providing capital to establish/expand current business	3	37.5	5	35.7	4	22.2
Other	2	25.0	2	14.3	3	16.7

Note: Data based on percentage of entrepreneurs who indicated 'ethnic' sources were 'very important' or 'important' in the establishment/operation of current business. Percentages do not sum to 100 because entrepreneurs frequently mentioned more than one reason. The number of respondents reflects those who responded to this portion of the survey, not the total sample.
Source: Author's questionnaire survey, 2005.

industry were highly involved in networks of kinship and friendship and community ties that were instrumental in establishing and running these labour-intensive businesses.

Business Evaluation: Present and Future

Being self-employed in the orchard business can be both satisfying and frustrating. Which aspects of Portuguese current business are the most satisfying to those involved and why? Most Portuguese entrepreneurs (fifty-two, or 88.1 per cent) enjoyed the independence of running their own business, followed by working the land and growing fruit in what they consider to be a good environment and lifestyle (78.0 per cent).

What aspects of the current business dissatisfy them the most? It is interesting to note the elements of dissatisfaction with self-employment among some of our respondents. Some 86.5 per cent complained about the long hours, in conjunction with the hard work involved with low fruit prices in return. Another 81.4 per cent complained about the uncertainties and fluctuations in the fruit market prices, making the orchard business sometimes unattractive and its future unpredictable. The following quotations reveal their views about operating problems:

> 'When fruit prices are high, I am very satisfied ... but government red-tape and low prices for fruit is a major problem for this business ... we never know how much we are getting paid for our product.'

> 'The fruit market uncertainty [is] due to unfair trade [with the United States] and the import practices that affect the viability of my own business and the fruit industry here.'

> 'Long hours, low pay, and hard work ... the uncertainties of the weather conditions like frost, rain ... and one of the hardest part now is the shortage of employees.'

Here Portuguese immigrants echo the concerns of the industry as a whole. Joe Sardinha, a Portuguese orchardist and also the president of the BC Fruit Growers Association, expressed similar concerns about the future of the fruit industry: 'There are many opportunities for branding B.C. products and promotion and the industry strategy has to include industry sustainability. We believe we grow the best apples in the world, but the fact that borders are open and unrestricted is making it tough' (Watts 2006: 23).

Despite the numerous challenges of running an orchard in the very competitive fruit tree industry in Okanagan Valley today (Penner 2005; Seymour 2005; Steeves 2005; Madison 2006), Portuguese entrepreneurs evaluate their businesses very positively. In all three study areas almost all respondents said that they were 'very successful' or 'successful' (100 per cent in Penticton, 85.7 per cent in Oliver, and 96.0 per cent in Osoyoos). The large majority of Portuguese entrepreneurs in this part of rural Canada – the Okanagan Valley – feel they have done well and succeeded in their industry.

A number of factors have contributed to their success. By far the most frequently cited factors were (1) family members; (2) business location; (3) good reputation and the business relationship with customers and the community; and (4) business practices and/or marketing strategies (Table 12.8). Respondents were also asked for the two most important factors in the success of their businesses. Top of the list

Table 12.8
Factors in success of orchard business, 2005

	Penticton (N = 13)		Oliver (N = 21)		Osoyoos (N = 25)	
	N	%	N	%	N	%
Family members	10	76.9	17	81.0	23	92.0
Business site/location	9	69.2	16	76.2	22	88.0
Good reputation/business relationship	10	76.9	15	71.4	21	84.0
Business practices/marketing strategies	10	76.9	14	66.7	16	64.0
Portuguese employees	5	38.5	10	47.6	15	60.0
Customers (including non-Portuguese)	3	23.1	9	42.9	12	48.0
Other	2	15.4	2	9.5	3	12.0

Note: Data based on percentage of entrepreneurs who indicated 'very important' or 'important.' Percentages do not sum to 100 because entrepreneurs frequently mentioned more than one reason.
Source: Author's questionnaire survey, 2005.

was family members (61.0 per cent), distantly followed by business location (28.8 per cent).

Respondents were also asked about the outlook for their orchard business in Penticton, Oliver, or Osoyoos. It is interesting to note that they were divided in their responses. Only one Portuguese respondent, from Osoyoos, noted that the business was growing, whereas twenty-eight (47.5 per cent) rated it stable. About one-third of all respondents (twenty-one, or 35.6 per cent) were pessimistic about the future, declaring that business was getting worse (Table 12.9). When this last group was asked to elaborate, some respondents emphasized that the first generation of Portuguese orchardists was getting older and retiring, and the new Canadian-born Portuguese generations were simply not interested in following in their footsteps:

'More bad years than good in the past decade ... [Also] the new Portuguese generation [born in Canada] wants nothing to do with the fruit business and a lot of the old generation is getting out.'

'Portuguese are selling to East Indians ... a lot of hard work and expenses and their children do not want this type of business. It is simple as that.'

Table 12.9
Future of Portuguese orchard business in Oliver, Osoyoos, or Penticton, 2005

	Penticton (N = 13)		Oliver (N = 21)		Osoyoos (N = 25)	
	N	%	N	%	N	%
Growing	0	0.0	0	0.0	1	4.0
Stable	9	69.2	11	52.4	8	32.0
Worse	3	23.1	5	23.8	13	52.0
Don't know	1	7.7	5	23.8	3	12.0

Source: Author's questionnaire survey, 2005.

'I don't know what to say ... They [Portuguese] are old, retiring ... I have three sons and none so far showed interest in keeping the business ... it's sad after all these years.'

Another group of respondents showed their concern about the competitive nature of the fruit industry, particularly with regard to free trade and the United States. They bemoaned the unpredictability of the market, especially low returns from fruit growing in the Valley today:

'Dumping of fruit from USA at below of cost of production ... [and] poor government support doesn't help this business at all.'

'Urban pressures and reduction of farm land to housing ... other interests rather than fruit. Some farmers are cashing on it ... Many farmers are also already converting to grapes ... Worldwide the fruit market is very competitive with China coming into the picture.'

'Labour increased [salaries] and the returns decreased ... In 1974 I used to pay $2 per hour [to employees] ... now [2005, it] is $15 per hour ... In 1974 they used to pay 33 cents a pound and now 25 cents a pound.'

Within this context of uncertainty and lack of confidence in the fruit industry it is unsurprising that about half the respondents (57.6 per cent) in the three study areas (seven in Penticton, eleven in Oliver, and sixteen in Osoyoos) indicated they were going out of

Table 12.10
Business plans over next five years, 2005

	Penticton (N = 13)		Oliver (N = 21)		Osoyoos (N = 25)	
	N	%	N	%	N	%
To go out of business/retirement	7	53.8	11	52.4	16	64.0
To seek additional capital investments	2	15.4	4	19.0	4	16.0
To hire more employees	1	7.7	4	19.0	3	12.0
To move to another kind of business	1	7.7	3	14.3	3	12.0
Other	3	23.1	2	9.5	2	8.0

Note: Percentages do not sum to 100 because entrepreneurs frequently mentioned more than one reason.
Source: Author's questionnaire survey, 2005.

business in the next five years for personal reasons or retirement. As Table 12.10 shows very few are planning to expand their businesses in the future by seeking additional capital investments or hiring more employees.

Evidence from this study indicates that Portuguese orchardists who are moving toward the age of retirement are also planning their exit from the orchard businesses. However, they are divided on what to do with the land they own: sell it and cash in, or pass it on to their children. When asked the key question – 'When you retire, do you hope to pass this business on to your children or to other members of the family?' – only nineteen respondents (32.2 per cent) (five in Penticton, nine in Oliver, and five in Osoyoos).

Almost half of the respondents (47.5 per cent) said no, and another twelve (20.3 per cent) simply replied 'don't know,' suggesting that they are leaving the decision to their children. Respondents who would like to pass on their land explained why:

'I would like to leave it to my son because I love my farm and land.'

'I love this location and I would like it to remain in the family ... I also would like to retire and live on the property.'

'Feel so good to pass to my children and remain in the family. We came to Canada because of them ... a better future.'

In these responses we can see something of the deep attachment of Portuguese immigrants to the land and their new home in Canada. However, it is interesting to note that those who did not intend to leave their land to family members reveal the transformation in education and opportunity that is also defining the new generations of the Portuguese group in Canada:

'My children have education and went to other jobs ... They looked for a different career and lifestyle which I don't blame them.'

'My son is pursuing his own career and I will not interfere there ... [Also] I don't want my children to arrive at 40 and suffer as I do from my back problems. This is a very tough type of job ... I used to work from sun to sun.'

Perhaps nothing so symbolizes that the Portuguese community of the Okanagan Valley is a community in transition as the changing cultural imprint on the landscape of the south Okanagan Valley. Colourful roadside fruit and vegetable stands once dotted the landscape of the region, and for years, the signs on the stands, featuring Portuguese family names, were markers of the group's presence in the region and the industry. These markers are changing however, as Koroscil observes: 'In the 1970s and early 1980s the roadsides of Oliver and Osoyoos were dotted with stands. Every Portuguese farmer who owned an orchard operated a fruit and vegetable stand in front of their house ... The young people left in the family were no longer willing to run a stand ... The "signs" on the stands that remain also reflect the changing attitude of the new generation. The first generation of Portuguese were eager to use their surnames on their property and enterprises such as Ferreira's Fruitstand and Moreira's Fruitstand. However, the second generation use their Christian names such as Tony's Fruit and Vegetable Stand and Danny's Drive-In' (2000: 164–5).

Other respondents made the case that transition is simply the new reality of the life cycle and demographics of the orchard industry (Steeves 2008). It is particularly interesting to note that one group of immigrant entrepreneurs seems to be being replaced by another with the arrival in the Okanagan of new farmers from the Punjab region of India (Seymour 2006). In the words of one respondent, 'Let's be realistic ... Changing demographics have been led by a new influx of immigrants to the Okanagan Valley. Many orchards were at one time operated by Portuguese families. These farms have since been sold to Indo-Canadian families that now operate approximately 55 per cent of the fruit orchards valley-wide. The young Portuguese families have benefited from higher education opportunities and have moved on to non-farming careers, leaving the parents to sell the farming upon retirement.'

The dilemmas faced by the Portuguese in the southern Okanagan Valley mirror those of Portuguese across Canada as the first generation of immigrants nears or enters retirement and the new generations look to new horizons and possibilities. The Portuguese are clearly on the move; the only question remains, 'To where?'

Conclusion

In 2005 an article in the *Oliver Chronicle* celebrated the community's recognition of the achievements of one Portuguese orchardist. In a way the article represents the life cycle and achievements of this remarkable group as a whole: 'As a 12-year old boy fresh from Portugal in 1964, Jack Machial's first job the day after his family's arrival in the Okanagan was picking cherries in an Oliver Orchard. On Tuesday, November 15 [2005], this fifth-generation farmer whose background leaned toward olives and ground crops in a mountainous Portuguese region, stood on the podium at the Penticton Trade and Convention Centre with his wife, Adelia, and accepted the prestigious Golden Apple Award – an award recognizing excellence in the tree fruit industry. It was given out at the 37th annual BC Fruit Growers Association's Horticultural Forum' (Johnson 2005: 1).

This Portuguese entrepreneur is representative of his many fellow immigrants who arrived in the Okanagan Valley in the 1950s and 1960s and, with the help of co-ethnic family and friends and through hard work, became established members of their industry and the region's business community. As this group has matured, however, it is now facing a range of new dilemmas as the Portuguese community in the region experiences transition.

Results from this survey echo earlier research in Canada, which identified ethnic/community resources as of crucial importance for Portuguese in the establishment and successful running of their businesses (see Joy 1989; Teixeira 2001–2). However, while the responses indicate the success of this group they also reflect the dilemma Portuguese entrepreneurs face today as both their industry and their community undergo transition. The Portuguese are strongly drawn to the land and to ownership of property as a cultural value, but they also acknowledge the uncertainties of the fruit industry and the hard work it demands. Many of the immigrant entrepreneurs wish to pass their land on to children or other family members, but this prospect is unlikely. More likely, perhaps, is that the Portuguese role in this Valley industry will be assumed by a new group of immigrants to Canada. With the decrease of Portuguese immigration to Canada in the last two decades, and particularly to the Okanagan Valley, it will be up to the new Portuguese generations – born and raised in Canada – to decide whether to continue the family tradition of working the land.

The transition being experienced by the Portuguese community and its entrepreneurs in the Okanagan Valley may be of wider significance given the preponderance of immigrant settlement in Canada's three major metropolises and the stated interest of government leaders in extending the economic benefits of immigration throughout the rest of the country. As findings from this study indicate the settlement of new immigrants has had clear positive benefits to the rural economy of this region. This research is therefore of clear and present interest to both academics and policy makers, and points to the need for further research to develop a better understanding of ethnic entrepreneurship and of the business strategies employed by immigrants pursuing new lives and economic success in rural Canada.

ACKNOWLEDGMENTS

I wish to thank all Portuguese orchardists who participated in this study and shared with me their entrepreneurial experiences in the Valley, as well as the 'key' informants from the Portuguese communities of Penticton, Oliver, and Osoyoos for their warm welcome reception and for helping in different stages of the data collection. I am in debt to all. This research was funded through a Social Sciences and Humanities Research Council (SSHRC) OUC/UBCO internal research grant.

REFERENCES

Anderson, G., and Higgs, D. 1976. *A Future to Inherit: The Portuguese Communities of Canada*. Toronto: McClelland & Stewart.

Barrett, G.A., T.P. Jones, and D. McEvoy. 1996. 'Ethnic Minority Business: Theoretical Discourse in Britain and North American.' *Urban Studies*, 33: 783–809.

British Columbia Statistics. 2001. Profile of Immigrants in B.C. communities 2001 – Okanagan – Similkameen. Vancouver: Ministry of Community, Aboriginal, and Women Studies.

Fraser, D. 1964. 'Immigration.' *Saturday Night*, 34, 35.

Hiebert, D. 2000. 'Immigration and the Changing of the Canadian City.' *Canadian Geographer* 44 (1): 25–43.

Johnson, W. 2005. 'Jack & Adelia Machial: Golden Apple Award Winners.' *Oliver Chronicle* (Oliver, BC), 23 Nov., 1–2.

Joy, A. 1977–8. 'The Portuguese in the Okanagan Valley: Inter-ethnic Networks and Community Adaptation.' *RIKKA* 4: 67–71.

– 1989. *Ethnicity in Canada: Social Accommodation and Cultural Persistence among the Sikhs and the Portuguese*. New York: AMS Press.

Koroscil, P.M. 2000. *British Columbia: Settlement History*. Vancouver: Simon Fraser University.

Madison, D. 2006. 'How Full Is Our Valley: Can We Support Our Exploding Population and Development?' *Okanagan Life* (Apr.): 40–4.

Munzer, R.P. 1981. 'Immigration, Familialism and In-group Competition: A Study of the Portuguese in the Southern Okanagan.' *Canadian Ethnic Studies* 13: 98–111.

Murdie, R.A., and C. Teixeira 2006. 'Urban Social Space.' In *Canadian Cities in Transition: Local through Global Perspectives*, ed. T. Bunting and P. Filion, 154–70. Toronto: Oxford University Press.

Penner, D. 2005. 'Okanagan wineries pour big money into development.' *Vancouver Sun*, 10 Sept., A3.

Seymour, R. 2005. 'Growers fight back: Apple orchardists ponder anti-dumping complaint against U.S.' *Daily Courier* (Kelowna, BC), 28 July, A1, A4.

– 2006. 'Indo-Canadians see more future in orchards.' *The Okanagan Saturday* (Kelowna, BC), 4 Feb., A3.

Statistics Canada. 2001. Citizenship, Immigration, Birthplace, Generation Status, Ethnic Origin, Visible Minorities, and Aboriginal Peoples. www.statcan.ca.

– 2002. 2001 Census of Canada. Population and dwelling counts, 93F0051XIE. www12.statcan.ca.

Steeves, J. 2005. 'Agriculture – Orchardists here left out of subsidy handouts.' *Capital News* (Kelowna, BC), 25 Nov., A9.

– 2008. 'Aging orchardists need to think about farm succession.' *Capital News* (Kelowna, BC), 20 Jan., A10.

Teixeira, C. 2001–2. 'The Portuguese Presence in Canada: An Overview of Five Decades.' *Gávea-Brown: A Bilingual Journal of Portuguese-American Letters and Studies* 22–3: 5–28.

Teixeira, C., L. Lo, and M. Truelove. 2007. 'Immigrant Entrepreneurship, Institutional Discrimination, and Implications for Public Policy: A Case Study of Toronto.' *Environment and Planning C: Government and Policy* 25: 176–93.

Watts, A. 2004. *Osoyoos Visitors' Guide.* Osoyoos: N.p.

– 2006. 'Fruit growers assess how to save the industry.' *Capital News* (Kelowna, BC), 23 Aug., A4.

PART FOUR

History, Cultural Retention, and Literature

13 Value Conflicts and Cultural Adjustment in North America

ONÉSIMO TEOTÓNIO ALMEIDA

In 1986 I was invited to give a keynote address at a conference on the Portuguese community of Ontario, held in Toronto.[1] The organizers suggested that perhaps I could say something based on my experience with the Portuguese communities in the United States, not only in New England but also in California. Having written this essay with a particular Portuguese community in mind, it is not without hesitation that I submit a 'talk among family' to be reprinted in this volume. What follows is essentially my address with minor revisions, additions, and notations of factual change.

The Portuguese communities in Canada are at least a hundred years more recent than those of the United States. However, this may be their biggest difference. At the deep level of cultural structures they seem to experience a similar struggle for adjustment and adaptation as people mostly of rural origin adapt to an urban, industrial society and as they try to reconcile southern European/Iberian, Catholic values and an Anglo-American world.

Fully aware of the complexities involving generalizations about cultural groups, with the inherent risks of stereotyping, I offer a broad look at the Portuguese communities in Canada based on my decades of extensive contacts with the Portuguese communities in the United States and my long-standing attempt to understand Portuguese culture. Thus the impressionistic observations in the first part of this essay are at least recurrent enough to confirm my sense that they run deep in our culture; there is indeed common ground. I attempt, second, to support these observations with others by researchers studying the Portuguese in the Americas and Europe. A basic assumption of this work is that one can talk about cultural backgrounds and that it is possible to detect the underlying structure of a value system and the hierarchy of values of a cultural group, however generalized this may be.[2] Third, I speculate about the future of the Portuguese on this continent.

A Caveat

The more I read about a group such as the Portuguese, be it in writings from outsiders (most of them non-Portuguese) or insiders (the Portuguese themselves), and the more contact I have with the Portuguese not only in Portugal, in the Azores, or in Madeira but also in immigrant communities in the United States, Canada, Bermuda, France, and Venezuela, the more I become convinced the majority of the Portuguese share some basic values. I say the 'majority,' for I do not believe that there exist homogeneous cultural groups. Of course there are differences among Portuguese, some of them quite significant. Who would deny that there are differences between the *lisboetas* and the *transmontanos* or the *açorianos*? But even within one of these groups one finds distinctions. Among the Azoreans, for instance, there are the *micaelenses*, who are distinct from the *picarotos*, and both in turn differ from the *terceirenses*.

The point is that one can go on finding differences until one reaches the individuality of each member of the group. But that happens only if we compare the elements of a group with each other. If we take the group as a whole and compare it with another group taken as a whole, it is then that we find the similarities shared by the members of each group. It is only when we compare the Spaniards as a group with the Portuguese as a group that the differences between a *transmontano* and an *algarvio* become minimal and often unimportant.

By the same token, if we compare the Iberian peoples, taken as a unity, with the Germans, we will find quite a few striking differences. I recall here Roger Brown, the Harvard psycholinguist, who said, 'Sometimes a college student who has been talked out of his stereotypes in a psychology course is amazed to discover on his first trip abroad, that the Germans really are different from the Italians' (1958: 365).[3]

Common Ground

However, enough of these general considerations. Let me use a few lines taken from a newspaper clipping in my collection. It is from a story reporting a study of a Portuguese immigrant community made by a group of social scientists. As the reporter puts it, the Portuguese are discreet, not given to delinquent habits or to xenophobia, and seem absent from all the national debates on immigration. Lately the Portuguese have joined forces to defend their language and culture, but their leaders have no visible profile outside the community. They are 'good immigrants,' and they have dozens of organizations and associations of all sorts. No other immigrant community has produced as many clubs, most of them mainly for soccer and religious feasts.

However, the reporter goes on to note, the young generation rejects such organizations, as they often do the Portuguese language and culture. The adults feel themselves divided between Portugal and their new immigrant home and visit Portugal as often as they can, but their children shy away from their past and the small world of their parents. They do not keep up ties, nor are they interested in bringing to the Portuguese community their own experience, which could both help to promote unification of its interests and give it visibility in the country at large, in the process attracting attention to some of its needs.

Now you are going to think that this must have been taken out of the *Toronto Star*, the *Globe and Mail*, or a French-Canadian newspaper. Wrong. Your next guess would be the *New Bedford Standard Times* or the *Providence Journal*, perhaps the *Boston Globe*, or even the *New York Times*. None of the above. It is French, yes, but from Paris. The newspaper was *Le Monde*, and the group described was the Portuguese community in France. But it certainly looks as if *Le Monde* is talking about us in Toronto or in the United States.[4]

Three Viewpoints

This false supposition serves to confirm my earlier statement that it is legitimate to speak about generic (in the sense of widespread) characteristics of a cultural group. Countless people familiar with the Portuguese, not to mention the Portuguese themselves, still would accept as roughly accurate the following characterization by the Portuguese anthropologist Jorge Dias in 1959:

> To describe the traditional national character in a phrase, we can say that the Portuguese is a mixture of dreamer and man of action, or better still, an active dreamer, who has a certain practical and realistic basis. Portuguese activity does not have its roots in cold-blooded will but is nur-

tured on imagination and is deeply reflective. They share with the Spanish the aristocratic disdain for small-minded gain, for pure utilitarianism and comfort, and the paradoxical taste for ostentation of wealth and luxury. But they do not have a strong abstract ideal like the Spanish, or a pronounced mystic tendency. The Portuguese are above all, profoundly human, sensitive, loving and generous without being weak. They do not like to cause suffering, and avoid conflicts, but can be violent and cruel when pride is hurt ...

There is, in the Portuguese, an enormous capacity for adaptation to ideas and people, but this does not imply lack of personality ...

They do not have the exuberance and noisy spontaneous joy of the other Mediterranean peoples. They are more inhibited because of their great sense of the ridiculous and fear of the opinion of others. They are, like the Spanish, strongly individualistic, but have a profound basis of humanitarian feeling. The Portuguese do not have a strong sense of humor, but a critical and mocking spirit which can be sarcastic and destructive.[5]

To preclude the possibility of misunderstanding, let me say here that the great Portuguese ethnologist Leite de Vasconcelos (1958), in a three-volume work on Portuguese cultural traits and manifestations, noted studies had shown that Portuguese children were as intelligent as their American, Belgian, and British peers. But he observed that a particular study showed that while they actually ranked higher than the American, Belgian, and British children in verbal and abstract intelligence, their practical intelligence, where long periods of concentration were necessary, was not as good. Portuguese children were quick in reaction but worse at keeping their attention fixed for long periods. In other words, the Portuguese were quick in comprehension but showed little persistence in sticking to one thing. In Portugal the impartial spirit of enquiry was rare; people preferred to be either for or against something. The Portuguese, a poetic people who considered themselves amorous, liked to succeed without effort and to shine before their friends. Leite de Vasconcelos also observed that their lively intelligence was ruined by emotion and sentiment.

Although he deemed the Portuguese people as a whole to be gentle, sociable, and quiet, Vasconcelos also believed that irony, disenchantment, sadness, *saudade* (a melancholy yearning and nostalgia), and individualism were characteristic of them. Their volitional characteristics included patience, passivity, fatalism, a desire for profit, carelessness, and neglectfulness. Foreigners thought the Portuguese a hospitable, smiling, and docile people who worked as little as possible to make easy money and gain a superficial sense of importance. While northern Portuguese were hardworking and serious (at least more so than their compatriots), everywhere there was a non-European sense of time. Vasconcelos also noted that other observers added to the lot of national defects parasitism, extreme credulity coupled with a certain fatalism, megalomania, moral insensitivity, a spirit of indecision coupled with a proclivity to contradictory actions, and a spirit of routine coupled with a love of novelty and change. Finally, he also found that since the sixteenth century our fellow countrymen had exhibited a strong tendency to consider anything foreign, particularly French, better than anything indigenous, and were consequently imitative.[6]

A foreigner, Paul Descamps, does not seem off the mark when, commenting on some Portuguese cultural traits, he asserts that the Portuguese are lacking not in initiative but in perseverance. He thinks that they have no sense of time or of the consequences of their actions. Although he detects a tendency toward anarchic individualism, he concludes that the Portuguese are 'unstable communitarians rather than true individualists': their main bonds of social solidarity are based on family, clan, and patronage (in Robinson 1979: 25).

These three portraits differ in many ways, but they overlap in a remarkable number of characteristics. It goes without saying that none of those characteristics need be linked to genetics. Many powerful theories have been circulating for a long time that offer plausible reasons for their existence. Some of them reach back to the Greeks. Aristotle, for one, attributed to the Mediterranean sun and pleasant climate a strong power over the emotions of the region's people. But we do not have to get into such explanations at this moment.[7] It suffices to stress here that no single theory can account for the diversity of cultures. Attempts at identifying the differences aim simply at mapping them out. One can often identify connections and underlying structures. In some cases it may seem possible to glimpse the roots of a particular characteristic of a culture.

A Great Coherence

After extensive research in various regions of Portugal some contemporary Portuguese anthropologists have found 'a great coherence' in

the Iberian world. In a debate following a conference on Iberian identity held at the University of California, Berkeley, in which the Portuguese anthropologists João de Pina-Cabral and Rui Feijó participated, Pina-Cabral stated, 'I am convinced that if we look at the
different ways in which people organize their lives, we could find
something that would amount to an Iberian ethnographic region ... I
think it is important that the Iberian Peninsula, the Portuguese
Atlantic Islands, the Balearics, the Languedoc, and the French Pyre-
nees are all areas that, from a sociological point of view, present great
coherence. This is something which people who, in Portugal, are concerned with regionality, such as Rui Feijó or myself, cannot ever forget'
(1989).

Rui Feijó responded, 'We came to look for Iberian identity, and we
came out with an idea that there are different levels and different
meanings of identity in Iberia, and this is quite important. But if we
have come up with this idea of diversity, Iberia still stands, as João de
Pina-Cabral was saying, as something which might be profitably considered as a whole – not separate as Spain and Portugal – for further
comparative study' (1989).

The important fact here is the consistency of the portrait made of us
as a group – one that depicts us as having similar cultural traits –
because, if accurate, it may be of some consequence in our lives as we
become part of a new culture outside Iberia. Indeed, it is perfectly fine
to enjoy the sun, spend all one's free time with friends, not be a slave
to time (*gozar a vida*, as we say), and so forth, as long as one accepts the
consequences of such a style of life. Back home in Portugal it is easier
to do so, since this is a shared ideal, but in a foreign land, an excessive
adherence to such alleged cultural habits may hamper us as a whole.
It may prevent us from attaining the objectives in life that most of us
consider important. If the need to adapt to the new culture (for
example, new patterns of work, concepts of time, possibilities for
family life in North American contexts) is understood by Portuguese
immigrants immediately on their arrival in the United States or
Canada – as represented by the (positive) stereotype of the hard-
working Portuguese – other necessary adaptations are not so easily
understood.

One example: today's societies, particularly technologically
advanced ones such as Canada's, demand that their members, if they
want to succeed, attain a high level of education. Personal advance-
ment is accomplished through dedicated study and hard work, activi-

ties that are incompatible with the spending of evening after evening chatting with friends or playing cards at the local club. But since education is finally becoming a priority among many Portuguese families, and a route that many young people and even many adults have lately chosen to accept, let me point out one area where our cultural habits have not allowed us to advance very far.[8]

One of the characteristics of modern societies is that individuals join associations according to their specific interests.[9] The interests of such groups are fostered by collective action. Thus objectives that are beyond the powers of the individual are attained through the collective efforts of the group. Unfortunately, this is a weakness of ours if we compare our efforts to those of other cultural groups. We seem to be able to join efforts in causes that strongly shake our emotions: religious events, sports, feasts, and fundraising for victims of tragedies or diseases that produce outpourings of sympathy. When our emotional side gets activated, we experience intense moments of togetherness. Yet if the event or the cause lasts too long, we are not able to keep our emotions aroused. When the unifying emotion is gone, the crowd breaks up into smaller and smaller groups, which then work at counter-purposes to one another. Therefore, when a project requires persistent work over a long span of time and results are not immediately visible; or when the cause itself does not continue to inspire strong emotions such as in supporting a local political candidate or working to improve the educational level of a particular group; or when the final objectives are seen as ethereal, then the Portuguese fail to gather enough interested people to carry out the task – that is, if it gets started at all.[10]

During the revolutionary period in Portugal after 1974, someone said that if you have two Portuguese you have three political parties – a line similar to one I used a few years ago as the title of an article for a new Portuguese newspaper in California, where there already existed a small and rather weak Portuguese newspaper. Instead of joining efforts to make a single, stronger paper, one group had decided to create a new one. The title of my column was 'Where There Is One Portuguese Newspaper, Let There Be Two.' The seeming clairvoyance of this line became clear a few years later when the 'new' newspaper split in two.

I am sure that this is a familiar phenomenon in Canada. To figure out how telling this example is, just count how many Portuguese newspapers there are in Toronto alone. Or take a look at the programme of an exhibition entitled *Portuguese Canadian Press in a Multicultural Society,* which took place at the John P. Robarts Library, University of Toronto, in 1995. Twenty-five newspapers, six magazines, and twenty-two bulletins were appearing regularly in Canada in that year.[11]

We Portuguese are very much affected by our emotions. It is difficult for us to keep cool during the small incidents that always arise in social life. Instead of controlling our reactions and thinking of long-range objectives, we feel that we must react, that we must straighten things out right away and call people by the names they deserve. Then we join with the few who agree with us and proceed to form still another organization, which, once formed, will consume the energies of its members in cold or open war with the other existing groups. And so time goes on. And so energies are wasted. And so we lose opportunities that could benefit us. Once in a while we stop to look at the score and become frustrated. We accuse everybody else of not doing anything and then get together in conferences to talk about how we can and should change things. But usually such conferences are momentary traces. After all the enthusiasm and the earnest celebration of our togetherness, we go right back to our old destructive habits.

Assimilation Ahead?

But none of this has to be. In fact, already many things are changing. The children of the immigrants from the 1950s and 1960s are changing the scenery. Both in the United States and in Canada groups are working to overcome these pitfalls of our adjustment to urban and modern life. There are organizations that have come a long way and are now gaining significant influence in the larger communities of which they are a part. In the United States these include immigrant assistant centres (such as the ones in Fall River, New Bedford, and Cambridge), the Luso-American Education Foundation in California, the Portuguese-American Business Association of Southeastern New England, and the Portuguese-American Scholarship Foundation.[12] In Canada the proliferation of social, civic, and cultural organizations is also encouraging: the Portuguese-Canadian National Congress, the Alliance of Portuguese Clubs and Associations of Ontario, the Federation of Portuguese-Canadian Businessmen and Professionals, and the Chambre du Commerce Portugais du Québec are just a few examples. A visible and growing trend is toward unification of the once parochial organizations. We Portuguese are, in general, a very traditional people, and there is nothing wrong with that. But if we choose to emigrate, for whatever reasons, we must also be willing to change in ways that are going to better our chances and increase our opportunities to fulfil our human needs and desires. The choice is never to change merely for the sake of change. It is not even necessarily a matter of changing aspects of culture that, considered individually and per se, are 'inferior' to those of the new culture.[13]

It is simply a matter of realizing that in a new cultural context some very basic elements of our culture have inevitably changed (and I am not speaking only about snow and incredibly low temperatures). In these new contexts some of our old ways – as good as they may be in another cultural context – may even have detrimental effects and inhibit attainment of some long-range goals that we, as human beings, consider valuable. We must be rational enough, sometimes, to put our very lively emotions and those little tricks that give us very small victories over our peers into parentheses, so that we may better ourselves in the long run. I hope that we may deepen our understanding of our collective cultural traits, not in order to downgrade our ethnic group but to improve it. Ronald Inglehart said that 'an awareness of the fact that deep-rooted values are not easily changed is essential to any realistic and effective program for social change' (1997: 19). The advice of Socrates – know thyself – remains for us a potent admonition.

Conclusion

The anthropologist Estellie M. Smith (1974) has called Portuguese-American communities 'the invisible minority,' capturing sharply their discreet presence outside the strong world of their working and family life. A survey of writing about three Portuguese communities in Canada confirms my long-held impression that the same could be said about Portuguese-Canadian communities. Not so long ago *L'Européen* dedicated the main feature of one of its editions to the Portuguese in France. On the front cover the article was entitled 'Les Portugais de France: Une intégration réussie, une fierté retrouvée,' or 'The Portuguese of France: An Achieved Integration, a Recovered Pride' (Malaurie and François 1998). The opening paragraph quotes an unnamed French minister as having called 'invisible' the 800,000 Portuguese in France.[14] Since it is unlikely that he read Estellie Smith the convergence of opinion seems to confirm the main contention of this essay – that there is 'a great coherence' in the world of Portuguese communities outside Portugal. If that is the case we have now one more reason to hope that the signs of a successful integration and of a recovered pride already visible in the Portuguese communities of Canada and the United States are confirmation that they are following the path of the Portuguese in France.

Biological laws are taking their toll. A young generation of Portuguese-Canadians is replacing the Portuguese born. They are growing up in a different environment from that of their parents. Yet talk of assimilation *tout court* may be premature. Portuguese neighbourhoods are still lively and English does not need to be spoken for survival. Just like in the United States, France, or Venezuela it is possible to eat in various Portuguese restaurants; shop at Portuguese bakeries, markets, furniture stores, and car dealers; go to events every weekend in Portuguese clubs; fill a year-round schedule with festivities of all sorts; attend mass in Portuguese at Portuguese churches; be involved in social organizations; attend concerts of Portuguese artists; watch Portuguese television and read Portuguese newspapers – both local and from Lisbon or the Azores; go to soccer games played by Portuguese players; visit a Portuguese doctor; and even go to mainstream stores, hospitals, and government offices, including the police, where one is served by Portuguese-speaking clerks and officers. Portugal's life was recreated with dynamism and resilience; enthusiasm, *saudade*, and cooperation; and thousands of labour hours being donated to the club or the church. Over the years the laws of demographics apply, however, and change has slowly been taking place. The Portuguese are here as Portuguese, even though one sees increasing signs of integration. Almost paradoxically, though, the more this happens the more visible to outsiders these communities are. The expression 'invisible minority' may in fact be a misnomer, or at least a misleading concept.

Along these sixty years of presence in Canada the Portuguese have come a long way. Less and less insular, they are more and more visible; more connected to the Azores and Portugal, thanks to television, the Internet, and much cheaper phone calls – I like to speak of the Atlantic River – yet more rooted in Canadian soil in all aspects of life. Their communities form several nuclei still very far from each other, with not much uniting us at the national level, almost like the Azores were before they became an autonomous region; that is, when each island lived almost locked unto itself. Geography works against their communities. However, thanks to the communication channels and easy mobility of the modern world, many Portuguese Canadians frequently cross paths at events in Portugal and in the communities, or read each other's writing and about each other in the newspapers that the Internet makes accessible to all. The majority still feel Azorean and Portuguese, but they also share a sense of belonging to this immense Canada and to the continent on which it sits. Sixty years are almost a life for most of them.

Geographical dislocations carry with them dislocations of identity, we all know. The Portuguese have not escaped that rule. So they will continue to integrate, but their resilience and strong attachment to the past will allow them to remain Portuguese for a while longer.

NOTES

1 I gave the address on 24 October 1986.
2 This used to be looked on with suspicion. Things have changed with the publication of books such as Geert Hofstede's *Culture's Consequences: International Differences in Work-Related Values,* which argues that 'people carry "mental programs" which are developed in the family in early childhood and reinforced in schools and organizations, and that these mental programs contain a component of national culture. They are most clearly expressed in the different values that predominate among people from different countries' (1984: 11). Charles Hampden-Turner and Fons Trompenaars state that in a 'survey of 15,000 executives we found that culture of origin is the most important determinant of values. In any culture, a deep structure of beliefs is the invisible hand that regulates economic activity. These cultural preferences, or values, are the bedrock of national identity and the source of economic strengths – and weaknesses' (1993: 4). Obviously these authors refer to trends and statistically significant patterns.

No culture is uniform, and no value is held across the board by every single member of a cultural group. No culture forms a harmonious, cohesive whole, nor are its values static. No reference to 'culture' and 'values' in this essay should be understood as support for any sort of essentialism. Postmodern discourse tends to emphasize internal diversity, contestation, conflict, negotiation, and so on, sometimes in an extreme form, as if throwing the baby out with the bath water. It is precisely against this other extreme that I believe it is still legitimate to refer to the underlying and shared values of a particular culture.

3 Collective names such as 'Portuguese,' 'French,' and 'Italians,' may not be rigorous, scientific terms, but we still use them, even though with a

grain of salt – not just in our daily language, and not only the non-scientists. Social scientists, for instance, use them frequently. William Watson, of McGill University, author of *Globalization and the Meaning of Canadian Life* (1998), wrote in an article entitled 'Identity in My Own Back Yard,' 'It's not very sophisticated, I know, to categorize people according to the weather they have to cope with. But it's how we Southern Canadians categorize the Inuit, Californians, Congolese, Jamaicans, Siberians, Arabs and many others' (Montreal *Gazette*, 11 Jan. 1999). In regard to the Portuguese, for instance, I have written extensively against attempts to construct an essentialist version of Portuguese culture. See, for instance, my 'Filosofia portuguesa – alguns equívocos' (1985).

4 From different angles and different political viewpoints various studies of the Portuguese in North America seem to agree on the overall characteristics of these communities. See, for instance. Huff 1989; McLaren 1990; and Feldman-Bianco 1992.

5 Jorge Dias, 'Os elementos fundamentais da cultura portuguesa,' appeared originally in *Actas do colóquio internacional de estudos luso-brasileiros* and has been translated in Robinson (1979: 24). I am always hesitant when dealing with generalizations such as this. I take them globally rather than literally, but I cannot reject them outright, for, as impressionistic as they are, just like an impressionistic painting they still capture a portrait. For a theoretical justification of this position, see my study 'On Distinguishing Cultural Identity from National Character' (1996).

6 These findings by the noted Portuguese ethnologist are scattered throughout his voluminous study. I use here the English synopsis in Robinson (1979: 24–5).

7 For the particular case of the Azoreans, who constitute the largest part of the Portuguese community in Ontario, or for that matter in Canada, I have attempted a detailed analysis of their culture in 'A Profile of the Azorean' (1980).

8 Education became a priority in Portugal soon after the revolution of 1974. Curiously this emphasis occurred much sooner and is more widespread than among the Portuguese communities in the United States or Canada.

9 Some authors prefer to use the adjectives 'industrialized' or 'capitalist.' 'Modern,' however, seems to be a broader, more neutral term.

10 I have expanded on this topic in 'The Portuguese and Politics: A Look at the Cultural Roots of a Distant Relationship,' a paper I presented at a conference on Portuguese-American communities and political intervention, sponsored by the Portuguese American Leadership Council of the United States (PALCUS), at the University of Massachusetts, Dartmouth, in the autumn of 1996.

11 See the exhibition catalogue *Portuguese Canadian Press in a Multicultural Society* (Marujo, Teixeira, and Marques 1995). For further information on the Portuguese press in Canada, see Teixeira 1999.

12 As if to confirm what I have stated above, two of these associations have ceased to exist, and another is struggling to survive. Two promising ones, however, have emerged: PALCUS, in Washington, DC, aimed at uniting the community nation-wide for political intervention, and the Portuguese-American Scholarship Foundation.

13 Even if North America is composed of many cultures, from the point of view of the Portuguese immigrant it is not the differences that are striking but the similarities vis-à-vis the culture in which he or she was brought up.

14 *L'Européen* says that the Portuguese in France 'make France' (*font France*) in their own way, but without saying a word – so discrete that in 1986 the Commission for the Reform of the Nationality Code did not include them in the public debate. None of their leaders had been invited. *L'Européen*, 13 May 1998, 16 and 18.

REFERENCES

Almeida, Onésimo T. 1980. 'A Profile of the Azorean.' In *Issues in Portuguese Bilingual Education*, ed. D. Macedo, 113–64. Cambridge, MA: National Assessment and Dissemination Center.

– 1985. 'Filosofia portuguesa – alguns equívocos.' *Cultura, história e filosofia* 4: 219–55.

– 1996. 'On Distinguishing Cultural Identity from National Character.' *Proceedings of the Fifth Conference of the International Society for the Study of European Ideas, at the University for Humanist Studies*. CD-ROM. Utrecht, The Netherlands.

Brown, R. 1958. *Words and Things*. Glencoe, IL: Free Press.

Feijó, Rui. 1989. 'Socio-cultural Differentiation and Regional Identity in Portugal and Spain.' In *Iberian Identity: Essays on the Nature of Identity in Portugal and Spain*, ed. R. Herr and J.H.R. Polt, 231. Berkeley, CA: Institute of International Studies.

Feldman-Bianco, B. 1992. 'Multiple Layers of Time and Space: The Construction of Class, Ethnicity, and Nationalism among Portuguese Immigrants.' In *New York Academy of Sciences Annals*, 145–74. New York: New York Academy of Sciences.

Hampden-Turner, C., and Trompenaars, F. 1993. *The Seven Cultures of Capitalism: Value Systems for Creating Wealth in the United States, Britain, Japan, Germany, France, Sweden, and the Netherlands*. London: Piatkus.

268 Onésimo Teotónio Almeida

Hofstede, G. 1984. *Culture's Consequences: International Differences in Work-Related Values*. Beverly Hills, CA: Sage Publications.

Huff, T.E. 1989. 'Education and Ethnicity in Southeastern Massachusetts: Issues in Planning and Policymaking.' New England Board of Higher Education *Bulletin* (Aug.): 2–7.

Inglehart, R. 1997. *Modernization and Postmodernization: Cultural, Economic, and Political Change in 43 Societies*. Princeton, NJ: Princeton University Press.

Malaurie, G., and P.O. François, eds. 1998. 'La fierté retrouvée des Portugais de France.' *L'Européen* (13–19 May): 16, 27.

Marujo, M., C. Teixeira, and D. Marques. 1995. *Portuguese Canadian Press in a Multicultural Society*. Exhibition catalogue. Toronto: Robarts Library, University of Toronto.

McLaren, P. 1990. 'The Antistructure of Resistance: Culture and Politics in Toronto High School.' In *Customs in Conflict: The Anthropology of a Changing World*, ed. F. Manning and J.M. Philibert, 387–412. Lewiston, NY: Broadview Press.

Pina-Cabral, João. 1989. 'Sociocultural Differentiation and Regional Identity in Portugal.' In *Iberian Identity: Essays on the Nature of Identity in Portugal and Spain*, ed. R. Herr and J.H.R. Polt, 230. Berkeley, CA: Institute of International Studies.

Robinson, R. 1979. *Contemporary Portugal: A History*. London: George Allen & Unwin.

Smith, Estellie M. 1974. 'Portuguese Enclaves: The Invisible Minority.' In *Social and Cultural Identity: Problems of Persistence and Change*. Proceedings of the Southern Anthropological Society no. 8, ed. Thomas K. Fitzgerald, 80–91. Athens, GA: University of Georgia.

Teixeira, C. 1999. 'Portuguese.' In *Encyclopedia of Canada's Peoples*, ed. P.R. Magocsi, 1075–83. Toronto: University of Toronto Press.

de Vasconcelos, J.L. 1958. *Etnografia portuguesa: Tentame de sistematização*. 3 vols. Lisbon: Imprensa Nacional.

Watson, W. *Globalization and the Meaning of Canadian Life*. Toronto: University of Toronto Press.

14 Literature of Portuguese Background in the Context of Literature in Canada

ISABEL NENA PATIM

António Augusto Joel's study 'Literature of Portuguese Background in Canada' remains a landmark in the understanding of the Portuguese contribution to Canadian literature and to literature produced in Canada, both by resident Portuguese writers and by Canadian writers of Portuguese descent. According to Joel, literature of Portuguese background in Canada (LPBC) 'faces a problem that also affects other writing in this country: it fails to achieve the status of mainstream literature' (2000: 223). He ascribes the marginal status of this literature, in the Portuguese case, to content, form, and language-related factors. With respect to the first of these, the writing 'relates exclusively to homeland ways of life, emerging as ethnographic exercises of memory and nostalgia rather than literature'; with respect to the second, some writing assumes 'the form of chronicles, being published primarily within so-called ethnic newspapers either in Canada or elsewhere' (223). What is more, texts that 'do achieve an acceptable literary form' may nonetheless be framed as marginal because of their content. With respect to the third factor, the works 'appear in the Portuguese language, without the involvement of any Canadian publisher' (223).[1] As Joel points out these characteristics help to create 'a self-imposed segregation, sometimes cast within the tradition of a single writer who epitomizes the homeland's literature' (223).

This chapter looks at the contribution of Portuguese immigrants and second-generation Portuguese Canadians to literature in Canada. Portuguese experiences in Canada represented in narratives written or published in this country fall into three main categories. First, I look at prose representations of immigrant experience that explore the feeling of being neither here nor there, best expressed as the 'paradox of nowhere,' a phrase coined by Joel (2000: 228). Second, I draw on representations of postsettlement, or second-generation experiences. Unlike first-generation Portuguese experiences, these reflect the day-to-day life and relationships of Portuguese immigrants in Canada. Third, I explore third-generation Portuguese experiences in Canada, as illustrated by the narrative of second-generation Portuguese-Canadian writer Erika De Vasconcelos. Finally, I develop an analysis of LPBC within the broader context of literature written and published in Canada.

Representations of Portuguese Experiences in Canada in Writing

The terms 'ethnic fiction,' 'immigrant fiction,' 'minority writing,' or 'multicultural fiction' (all used in contrast to 'mainstream literature'), when used in reference to literature produced or published in Canada, account for the diversity and plurality of voices and writing in this country. Some writers and writing will be either included or excluded from the corpus (and from bibliographies, anthologies, and encyclopedias) depending on the terminology and criteria adopted in order to define literature in Canada. The tendency to label literature 'of ethnic background,' according to Joel (2000: 224), has brought about several studies and bibliographies of Portuguese writing that have identified and defined such literature, and these remain significant sources for any study of the field.[2] Yet Teixeira and Lavigne's two bibliographies of literature of Portuguese background in Canada, in English and Portuguese respectively, do not include recent authors whose contributions are remarkably important (Teixeira and Lavigne 1992, 1998). Similarly Joel (2000: 224) makes only a single reference to a Canadian author of Portuguese descent currently writing narrative works of fiction in English and publishing in Canada, Erika De Vasconcelos.[3] De Vasconcelos's first novel, *My Darling Dead Ones*, was first published in 1997, and her second, *Between the Stillness and the Grove*, published in 2000, confirms the writer's concern to go beyond immigrant experience per se. Her focus is not on the act of migration itself but on the process of a woman discovering who she is, i.e., her self (Alfano 1998).

Joel's study is framed by two criteria. He selected only prose texts that related to or described 'first-, second-, or even third-generation Portuguese experiences in Canada' and that represented the diversity of contributions to LPBC (Joel 2000: 224). He therefore set aside many of the titles compiled by Teixeira and Lavigne in 1998. Employing Joel's diachronic approach to the three categories I outlined above will facilitate a clearer understanding of first- and second-generation Portuguese-Canadian contributions to literature in Canada.

The Paradox of Nowhere

Joel studies two titles illustrating first-generation experience: the 1993 short story 'Dollar Fever: The Diary of a Portuguese Pioneer,' by C.D. Minni, a writer of Italian background; and a 1976 novel entitled *Os bastardos das pátrias*, by Lourenço Rodrigues. He points out that although these texts were written more than two decades after the first official arrival of Portuguese immigrants in Canada in 1953, they are set at that time (Joel 2000: 225). 'Dollar Fever' takes place in 1954–5, while *Os bastardos* spans 1956 to 1974; their fictional spaces are those of the journey from Portugal to the host country, Canada.

Both illustrate the arrival and settling of first-generation Portuguese immigrants and share the 'same idea of solitude and family loss' (Joel 2000: 228). Leaving family and community contributed to feelings of displacement and loneliness, setting the terms of survival, often portrayed in Canadian literature as a theme, along with other themes such as the climate, the dimension and vast distances of the host country, and the alien landscape. But it is the human factor that 'conveys the sense of difference or strangeness above all, the lack of human feelings towards immigrants, who were treated like numbered or tagged objects' (226). Aware of this treatment on arrival the immigrant characters in the fiction express feelings of revolt, shame, and dishonour. If for some newcomers these feelings fed the desire to return home after some time of hard work and savings, others believed after some time in their new country, with its different world views, that they would never readapt to the lives and world views of their homeland. Immigrant characters also express the feeling of being 'simultaneously strangers in their own country of origin and in their adopted country,' an ambiguity captured in the expression 'paradox of nowhere.' Shaping one's existence 'neither here nor there' but here and now, it literally becomes 'nowhere' else but in memory.

Negation and Negotiation of the Old Self

To illustrate second-generation Portuguese experience in Canada Joel draws on Laura Bulger's book of short stories, *Paradise on Hold* (1987), first published in Portuguese as *Vaivém* (1986), and on the novel *Um poeta no paraíso* (1994), by Manuel Carvalho. Bulger's compilation reflects the day-to-day life of Portuguese immigrants in Canada rather than focusing on 'the social confrontation or cultural clash' of the pioneers and their anxiety facing departure and arrival (Joel 2000: 229). Changes in relationships within the family either in Canada or back in the homeland; adoption of the new values and culture of the host country; changes in lifestyle; the integration of family members into the new society at different rhythms or to differing degrees; the prospect of returning to Portugal or remaining in Canada; and related anxieties, hopes, and dilemmas are some of the themes of these stories.

Nevertheless, issues of identity and change, as portrayed by characters in the book, may not be shaped so much by adoption of new values and cultures as by 'negation of the old self' (Joel 2000: 229). It is in the context of adaptation to a new culture and the path to integration enabled by citizenship that Joel approaches Manuel Carvalho's *Um poeta no paraíso*. Unlike Bulger's book of short stories it was published only in Portuguese. Though Carvalho is a first-generation Portuguese Canadian, his novel reflects on second-generation Portuguese experiences in Canada that eventually overcome the paradox of nowhere. According to Joel, 'the sense of a fantastic and magical reality' pervades the narrative and establishes it as mainstream literature, widening the appeal of a book on the day-to-day life of Portuguese immigrants in Montreal (2000: 232).

The sense of the fantastic and magical is conveyed by the character Luís Vaz de Camões, the outstanding and well-known sixteenth-century Portuguese poet. In the story he survives a shipwreck and emerges from the sea in twentieth-century Montreal. At the point of arrival he becomes as three characters: Luís, Vaz, and Camões. The idea of survival is associated with the fragmentation of the self, and thus with the different forms of negotiation between the old self and the new country and its cultural identity. In Joel's opinion this novel clears the path for a move by LPBC toward the mainstream, which is later confirmed by Erika De Vasconcelos. The author of *My Darling Dead Ones* and *Between the Stillness and the Grove* in fact plays a leading role among second-generation Portuguese-Canadian writers.

Poetry and the Stream of the Sea

Like the theme of survival, issues of identity are portrayed in Canadian literature frequently and in multiple forms. In texts illustrating first-generation Portuguese experiences in Canada, the sense of identity may rely on memory and the sense of loss, along with a desire to retain a vanishing heritage. In texts that describe third-generation Portuguese experiences in Canada identity may rely on a longing for their heritage once integration has been eased by birth and citizenship and adaptation of cultural identity is assumed. As Joel explains, the issue 'is not one of integration in the host country's culture, but on reintegration in the ancestral country and culture' (2000: 232–3). Likewise, survival is not the struggle to survive in a new society or environment, as in literature about the first generation, or a negotiation of self as new values and cultures are adopted, but an acknowledgment of the past and the family roots.

The presence of the Portuguese and of Portugal finds multiple expression in De Vasconcelos's first narrative fiction, which is in fact metafiction, or *biografictione*. Studying that presence helps us to understand the conflicts in this novel as in some way disconnected from the act of migration per se.[4] Three languages (English, French, and Portuguese), and three locations (Montreal, Toronto, and Beira), are involved in the quest of the main character, Fiona, for self-discovery and indeed for self itself. Fiona anchors the narrative, and the story skips back and forth in time (present and past) and space (Portugal and Canada). Born in Canada she is one of the two daughters of immigrant parents, Leninha and Joaquim, and thus represents the second generation of Portuguese Canadians. The novel weaves the story of three generations of women and their family relationships. Intergenerational relationships are the source of the conflicts in the novel, whereas the acknowledgment of the past and of family roots holds the key to understanding her own identity and to survival (Patim 2004).

While the conflicts in *My Darling Dead Ones* may be disconnected from the act of migration, in *Between the Stillness and the Grove* migration is clearly the key for self-knowledge and survival. It is presented as an alternative to silence and suffering on the path to self-knowledge and growth. Portugal features in this novel as a place of self-imposed exile and self-*re*discovery. The main character, Dzovig, escapes from communist Armenia to Portugal when her lover Thomas dies. At the same time she is escaping an intergenerational conflict, that between father and daughter. While coming to terms with her past she develops new relationships in Portugal and reconfigures her priorities and boundaries. Reading Portuguese poetry also helps her in this process and Fernando Pessoa (1888–1935) is her chosen author. We believe De Vasconcelos uses the multiple voices and identities of the Portuguese writer and critic Fernando Pessoa – best known as a poet under his real name, but also under the chief heteronyms Alberto Caeiro, Ricardo Reis, and Álvaro de Campos but also as a prose writer under the semi-heteronym Bernardo Soares – to show the countless possibilities for Dzovig in her self-*re*discovery process while in Portugal. Dzovig is attracted to the surname Pessoa because it means 'literally, person. Anyone, or everyone' (2001: 6). When Dzovig reads his books, the poet gets into her mind and they talk to each other. 'You read my mind,' Pessoa tells her (2001: 326). The fragmentation of Pessoa's self helps De Vasconcelos to express the fragmentation of the character Dzovig.

As in De Vasconcelos's first novel, time and space are structured in three parts: in this case, the past is set in Armenia, the present is set in Portugal, and the future is projected onto Canada, where the character decides she will go to. While it could be said that in *My Darling Dead Ones* De Vasconcelos explores her sense of place and her self by rooting her characters in both Canada (the 'here') and Portugal (the 'there'), in *Between Stillness and the Grove* the writer acknowledges her sense of time and her self by uprooting her characters from their homeland (the past) and re-rooting them both in Portugal (the present) and Canada (the future).

LPBC in the Context of Canadian Literature

Teixeira and Lavigne's bibliography surveys LPBC from 1953 to 1996, whereas Joel's socio-literary study analyses literature of Portuguese background in the context of contemporary literature in Canada, and specifically of Canadian literature in English.

Readers, scholars, and academics attempting to define Canadian literature face several challenges. How does one define national identity? What literary forms and literary influences are Canadian? And what are the characteristics of the national literature? This debate has never suggested that literature in Canada per se does not exist, but while some have tried to frame this diversified and multiple body of work within categories, others question the need to frame it at all, no matter how useful it might be to define the field. The debate itself, however, has in fact helped to define and assert the position of the literature.

At the outset of writing in Canada, travel and exploration narratives such as David Thompson's *Narrative of His Explorations in Western North America 1784–1812* not only helped to determine the physical space but also placed the self in that new geographical landscape: 'By charting, naming and defining this space, the explorer initiates a kind of indigenization that shifts the European "Self" from the position of outsider to the position of imaginative ownership' (Macfarlane 2003: 358). Writing from the perspective of an 'outsider,' to a certain extent continues in nineteenth-century literature of immigration, but it is inverted: the 'normal' is no longer the voice of the narrator or character faced with the exotic landscape; now the character must face the necessity of having to fit into that landscape, as strange and different as it may be. The question becomes 'Who am I now that I'm here?' instead of 'Where's here?' (Macfarlane 2003). This literature involved (re)defining not only the self but also home.

Such (re)definition of self and of identity is rooted in a juxtaposition, in the presence of two nations within a single identity – and the same could be said of Portuguese Canadians. That terminological process can be useful to identify the diversity and multiplicity of voices in the Canadian body of literature, but it has also prompted inclusive and exclusive definitions of identity, namely the concept of 'hyphenated identity,' which has been called into question by some writers and critics. Several anthologies have been published following this criterion of juxtaposition, but so far none has been published on 'writing by Portuguese Canadians,' 'Canadian literature of the Portuguese diaspora,' or 'Canadian writers of Portuguese descent.' Volumes such as those could be understood as the expression of a human being's utmost need for 'home' and 'belonging.'

The 1960s were a milestone for Canadian literature as theoretical frameworks emerged. Historical, geographical, and thematic models determined the inclusion or exclusion of texts within anthologies that attempted to present the body of 'Canadian literature.' The work of some authors and critics remains seminal for our understanding of Canadian writing: Northrop Frye's *Anatomy of Criticism* (1955) and *The Bush Garden* (1971), and Margaret Atwood's *Survival* (1972). Karen E. Macfarlane explains the contribution of Frye and Atwood to legitimizing the study of Canadian literature, but at the same time she points to a shift in more contemporary studies: 'Contemporary debates in the field of Canadian literary study have shifted the focus from an emphasis on "canonical" texts to include works and voices that have traditionally been excluded or marginalized in the formation of this conception of this national literature' (2003: 357). Shifting from thematic approaches to Canadian literature to the study of issues shared by

Canadian works portrays 'the ways in which Canadians write and write themselves' (357).

It is in this context that we understand the way in which Canada's two Portuguese-language writers, Lourenço Rodrigues and Laura Bulger, are included in Michael Batts's *Encyclopedia of Literature in Canada* (2002). When we look for Portuguese-Canadian writers under 'Portugal,' we are sent to 'multicultural voices,' an organizational process that confirms the importance of Joel's study to LPBC.[5] These two references are obviously framed within a specific criterion, as 'multicultural voices' includes writers in a language other than English or French who have published their work while living in Canada (Patim 2004: 110).

More recent discussions of the theme of identity in literature have been partly influenced by postcolonial literary theory. This issue is presented thus by Macfarlane: 'So perhaps Canadian culture is not clearly *post*-colonial, but is negotiating a complex position between the postcolonial and the colonial. Whether Canadian literature can be defined as post-colonial is, I think, a separate debate' (2003: 372). As the critic explains, the Canadian literary canon excludes some texts and is thus engaged in 'a type of colonial relationship with the texts it excludes.' If some anthologies and encyclopedias help to form the canon, several others are a counterpart to it by giving expression to multicultural voices. Eventually an anthology of LPBC will include texts illustrating first-, second- and third-generation experiences of the Portuguese in Canada, of first- and second-generation Portuguese Canadians, and of Portuguese residents in Canada, and writing in Portuguese, French, or English, bringing together 'mainstream' literature and 'ethnic' or 'immigrant' literature. De Vasconcelos's two novels, as representatives of contemporary LPBC, could be approached as postmodern Canadian literary texts.

John Clement Ball examines how postmodernism has been deployed to refer to a historical period that is largely contemporary, to an artistic style identified as parodic, self-conscious, and fragmentary, and to a world view of the dominant cultural mode of global capitalism of the end of the twentieth century (2002: 895). Postmodern literature shapes cultural anxieties, fragmented structures, divided and undetermined selves. These selves are confronted with realities that co-exist in a space and time, in a global sphere, at a speed never experienced before, and almost within a juxtaposition of time and place. Canada somehow contains the particular conditions needed to produce the postmodern text: a multicultural population, a decentralized geography, and a cultural ambivalence toward the English and the Americans. The Canadian expression of the postmodern draws, for example, on the rejection of binary oppositions (Cheetham and Hutcheon 1991), and a postmodern approach to the narratives of third-generation Portuguese in Canada would thus be particularly suitable.

Conclusion

The issue of whether a Canadian literature exists is imbued with the varied terminology used to account for the multiplicity of voices emerging with each text written and published in this country. Empowered by literary theory and criticism, the body of Canadian literature is in itself a representation of experiences in Canada. It is in this sense that we understand the literature of Portuguese background in the context of literature written and published in Canada: those literary works contribute to the celebration of Canada, of multiculturalism in the field of literature, and to the growing cultural diversity of the country.

The diversified body of Canadian literature illustrates multiple voices but shares common issues. Chronologically evolving from definitions of space (through naming and charting) to definitions of the self (through issues of identity and redefining self and home), geographical ambivalence is often shaped in the literary text. The Portuguese have contributed to the multiplicity of voices that make up Canada's multiple geographies and identities as portrayed in literature.

I acknowledge Joel's remarkable contribution to the understanding of LPB in Canada and assume that LPBC can be understood as a process that is still evolving. Though Erika De Vasconcelos, born and living in Canada, remains the single Canadian author of Portuguese descent to whom he refers, her work radiates with the newness of her contribution to Canadian literature. Analysing De Vasconcelos's work in light of the three main factors Joel identifies as conferring on LPBC a marginal status within the body of Canadian literature confirms the innovation of her novels: neither content, nor form, nor language make them less Canadian than any other text.

Language and the context of publication have in the past excluded the contriution of the Portuguese to literature in Canada. Lourenço Rodrigues and Manuel Carvalho published their works in Portuguese, whereas Laura Bulger opened a linguistic path for Erika De Vasconcelos by publishing her short stories in both Portuguese and English. Vasconcelos's novels, however, were written in English and published by a Canadian publisher, and thus represent a new moment in LPBC, as the marginalizing effect of form and language is no longer an issue. Content, too, is given new status as conflicts in both novels are disconnected from the act of migration per se. The literary quality of Carvalho's *Um poeta no paraíso* had already set it on the path to mainstream literature despite its language, and De Vasconcelos's illustration of Portuguese culture and literature continues that process, making her work precious for second-generation Portuguese Canadians.

Self-discovery and family relationships are the sources of conflict of De Vasconcelos's novels. In *My Darling Dead Ones* Portugal features as the homeland for first-generation Portuguese in Canada and as the longed-for heritage for second-generation Portuguese Canadians. In *Between the Stillness and the Grove* Portugal is featured as a place of exile for the immigrant character who chooses to live there. Whereas in the first novel Portugal is the place to discover the past and Portuguese roots, in the second it is the country in which the immigrant character Dzovig wants to forget her past. As De Vasconcelos illustrates in her second novel, the redefinition of self and of identity goes beyond linguistics and homeland. If her first novel shapes representations of Portuguese experiences in Canada, the second illustrates experiences of immigrants in Portugal. Both intertwine the themes of quest, self-discovery, and survival. They raise a question that is central to Canadians, Portuguese, or any other nationality: 'Who am I now that I am here?' The theme of survival, dear to Canadian literature, is also illustrated in LPBC as it emerges from the struggle to survive in a global society and not only in the host country.

To understand the contribution of LPBC to literature in Canada it is best to point to contemporary studies of Canadian literature that include works and voices traditionally excluded or marginalized. More relevant than applying traditional thematic approaches to Canadian literature is simply to identify issues shared by Canadian literary texts written by authors of different origins. Canada's multicultural identity has been expressed through numerous authors of numerous backgrounds.

Erika De Vasconcelos is one of those voices of contemporary Canadian writers, whether as a Canadian writer of Portuguese descent or as a voice of multicultural Canadian writing. Her work contributes to a celebration of Canada's growing cultural diversity and, in a sense, sustains or at least does not oppose, Canada's self-image as multicultural community. The shift in contemporary debate about Canadian literary study as it begins to include works and voices previously omitted from the body of Canadian national literature also promotes the value of LPBC in Canada and of De Vasconcelos's work in the context of contemporary literature in Canada.

NOTES

1 Joel gives as examples Carvalho 1997; de Melo 1994, 1996; Joel 1995; and Vincente 1995.
2 Mentioned examples of studies and bibliographies include Baden 1979; Miska 1990; Teixeira and Lavigne 1992, 1998; and Simone 1995.
3 Joel limits his study to work prose texts, and only to those that relate or describe Canadian experiences, criteria that cause him to set aside titles compiled by Teixeira and Lavigne (1998). He therefore refers only to De Vasconcelos's first novel, as a narrative that illustrates third-generation Portuguese experiences in Canada.
4 Memories, personal experiences, and stories conveyed to De Vasconcelos by ancestors are already fiction of fiction, and are in turn put into fiction by the writer.
5 As William New explains in the Preface, the encyclopedia interprets the term 'literature in Canada' but doesn't define 'Canadian author,' as it includes Canadian-born writers, temporary Canadian residents, immigrants, and expatriates (New 2002).

REFERENCES

Alfano, M. 1998. 'Interview. By the Force of Their Own Will: The Women of *My Darling Dead Ones.' Paragraph: The Canadian Fiction Review* 23: 3–9.
Baden. N.T. 1979. 'Portuguese-American Literature, Does It Exist? The Interface of Theory and Reality in a Developing Literature.' *MELUS* 6, no. 2: 15–31.
Ball, John Clement. 2002. 'Postmodernism.' In *Encyclopedia of Literature in Canada*, ed. W.H. New, 895–8. Toronto: University of Toronto Press.
Batts, M. 2002. 'Multicultural Voices.' In *Encyclopedia of Literature in Canada*, ed. W.H. New, 764–9. Toronto: University of Toronto Press.
Bulger, L. 1987. *Paradise on Hold: Short Stories.* Toronto: Bramble House.

Carvalho, M. 1994. *Um poeta no paraíso*. Laval: Éditions Luso.

– 1997. *Parc du Portugal*. Laval: Éditions Luso.

Cheetham, M., and L. Hutcheon. 1991. *The Condition of Postmodern: Trends in Recent Canadian Art*. Toronto: Oxford University Press.

De Vasconcelos, E. 1998. *My Darling Dead Ones*. Toronto: Vintage Canada.

– 2001. *Between the Stillness and the Grove*. Toronto: Vintage Canada.

Joel, A. 1995. 'Impressões do Outro Lado: Chronicles.' *A Voz de Chaves* 8.

– 2000. 'Literature of Portuguese Background in Canada.' In *The Portuguese in Canada: From the Sea to the City*, ed. C. Teixeira, and V.M.P. Da Rosa, 223–35. Toronto: University of Toronto Press.

Macfarlane, K.E. 2003. 'Issues and Contexts: Canadian Literature in English.' In *Profiles of Canada*, 3rd ed., ed. K.G. Pryke and W.C. Soderlund, 355–81. Toronto: Canadian Scholars' Press.

de Melo, F.F. 1994. *Os visitantes da América e reminiscências*. Toronto: Olive Press.

– 1996. *Nadine: A Sereia dos corais e reminiscências*. Toronto: Olive Press.

Minni, C.D. 1993. 'Dollar Fever: The Diary of a Portuguese Pioneer.' In *Home and Homeland: The Canadian Immigrant Experience*, ed. P. Fanning and M. Goh, 48–62. Toronto: Addison-Wesley and Rubicon Publishing.

Miska, J. 1990. *Ethnic and Native Canadian Literature: A Bibliography*. Toronto: University of Toronto Press.

New, W.H. 2002. Preface to *Encyclopedia of Literature in Canada*, ed. W.H. New, vii–x. Toronto: University of Toronto Press.

Patim, I.M.S.N. 2004. 'The Presence of Portugal and the Portuguese in the Fiction of a Canadian Writer of Portuguese Descent: Erika De Vasconcelos' *My Darling Dead Ones*.' *Portuguese Studies Review* 11 no. 2: 109–32.

Rodrigues, L. 1976. *Os bastardos das pátrias*. Lisbon: Distribuidora 'O Século.'

Simone, R. 1995. *The Immigrant Experience in American Fiction: An Annotated Bibliography*. Lanham, MD: Scarecrow Press.

Teixeira, C., and G. Lavigne. 1992. *The Portuguese in Canada: A Bibliography*. Toronto: Institute for Social Research, York University.

– 1998. *Os Portugueses no Canadá: Uma bibliografia (1953–1996)*. Lisbon: Direcção-Geral dos Assuntos Consulares e Comunidades Portuguesas.

Vincente, A.S. 1995. *Vida e tradições nas Aldeias Serranas da Beira*. Montijo: Sograsol.

15 Reflections on a Society in Rapid Transition

JOHN WARKENTIN

Geography and history books are of their time; they reflect the major scholarly concerns and approaches of their period. That is very true of these essays on the Portuguese-Canadian community, published near the beginning of the twenty-first century. Another aspect of time resonates throughout the book. This is a study of an immigrant group from Europe that has been in Canada for barely a half century, hardly into its second and third generations in its new homeland. Everywhere before us in these essays we see cultural differences originating in the former home country, the social and economic stresses of adapting to very new cultures and circumstances, and generational contrasts as new lives are created in a new land. We are presented with a society in rapid transition: the Portuguese have been just long enough in Canada that the jagged processes of adaptation and acculturation are still very apparent, so that they can be observed and analysed by scholars. Most of the contributors are part of the Portuguese-Canadian community, or closely associated with it. They illuminate the community to itself while it is going through a testing passage, an ongoing transformation. These studies, too, have a wider interest that extends well beyond the Portuguese-Canadian community because they confront universal problems experienced by many immigrant groups. The community has strong ties to the past, as is to be expected, but inevitably it is forced as time hurries along to move increasingly into current life in Canada. That shift, that tipping point, is the excitement of this volume, and most of my reflections are centred on the way it is portrayed through the chapters.

The Portuguese migration to Canada came at a critical time in Canadian social history. It was part of the large migrations of the 1950s to '70s, very shortly after the Second World War when people emigrated from Europe and the Caribbean to Canada. There had been very large previous migrations, especially before the First World War, when immigrants moved both onto the land and into cities, in a period when Canada welcomed settlers to open up new agricultural lands, help build railways, and work in new mines and factories. These newcomers arrived at a time when the general assumption was that they would all be assimilated into the general population after two or three generations. In the decades before the Second World War conformity to the existing society was simply assumed, though even then there was apprehension that newcomers might not fit in. But the Portuguese arrived at a different time, when such attitudes had imperceptibly begun to change. Gingerly, Canada was on the path to multiculturalism. Why this happened is not easy to explain because many complex factors were at work, but Canadians after the Second World War did turn into a more welcoming people. Vital changes in attitude occurred in the larger society as it began to reinvent itself and become more inclusive. At the same time, of course, arriving immigrants had to make much more fundamental cultural changes in their own lives than any that the host society was experiencing.

During the 1950s and '60s, when Canada was changing its attitude to newcomers, I lived in two strongly Mennonite communities on the Prairies, a mixed community of Ukrainian and British Canadians (also on the Prairies), and in the cities of Winnipeg and Toronto. In later years I have reflected on what I observed and experienced. The Second World War and its immediate aftermath had a profound influence on Canadians. Service men and women had met with different cultures in Europe and Asia, and the people at home, too, learned of a wider world through the news from distant countries, much of it from the sharp immediacy of radio. The rebuilding of Europe and parts of Asia after the war made Canadians very much aware of other peoples, and this knowledge helped open minds. A liberating factor was that service men and women had observed the relaxation of pubs and the joys of wine, which contrasted with prevailing puritanical attitudes in many parts of Canada. This was a time of liberation, and a freer, more accommodating attitude was also made easier by fairly consistently prosperous times after the war. Roads were built, autos acquired, airlines expanded, travel increased, movement was in the air, the ground was laid for a more open society. Such feelings were propelled by Canadian awareness that colonial people in Asia and Africa were striving for self-government; newspapers and magazines were full of stories about the creation of new postcolonial countries such as India and Pakistan. All this was made more vivid by radio, and after 1952 by television. Other examples of societies or groups struggling for justice were evident: the fight against racism in the United States, the battle of French Canadians against the economic dominance of British Canadians in Quebec and their crucial struggle to protect the French language, and the fight for women's rights. Canada was changing. (Sadly, even at this time of awakening, the welfare of Canadian First Nations, Inuit, and Métis peoples was effectively ignored.)

As a result, there was a new awareness of the need for accommodation, for adjustments on all sides, for respect for cultures other than your own. This was a crucial change; Canada moved from unilateral assimilation to the larger society toward what has become known as acculturation, where essential cultural characteristics of the different immigrant societies are respected within a multicultural or pluralistic society. Portuguese immigrants began to arrive just before and during the time when this change from assimilation to acculturation was underway. Indeed, whether conscious of it or not, they were part of the process that brought about cultural change in the larger Canadian society. The experience of most of these immigrants was also very different from earlier generations, when many immigrants moved onto the land in relatively isolated areas and established pioneer farms. They had limited awareness, let alone contact, with the larger society. Most Portuguese immigrants moved into cities, where outside their homes and institutions they and then their children met many other social groups, or at least became aware of them. The newly arrived settlers changed in this process, but they, along with the many newcomers from other countries, helped bring about change in the larger society as well, which has slowly reconstructed and transformed itself into a more tolerant society. Although it is often overlooked by immigrants in the stress of individual experiences in the process of change, this is one of the great contributions made to Canada by the immigrant societies.

In my reflections on the essays I follow the organization of the book wherever possible. I turn now to the chapters on the Portuguese diaspora by Rocha-Trindade and on historical and geographical perspectives by Teixeira and Da Rosa. The Portuguese are a people in motion, as we learn from Rocha-Trindade, settling and establishing roots in many parts of the world and in many different countries. A sense of adventure, of seeking knowledge, of acquiring fortune and territory were early impulses in the way Portuguese searched out other parts of the world, and much later this turned to seeking economic betterment when they emigrated to nearby countries, or travelled across the South Atlantic, and then the North Atlantic.

The early story of Portuguese exploration and colonization is a highly significant component of fifteenth-century European expansion overseas. Portugal led the way in navigating around the southern shores of Africa to reach the Indian Ocean and the Far East. Shortly thereafter the Portuguese were active in the New World and established colonies, along with Spanish, English, French, and other Europeans in what became known as the Americas and the New World. Invading Europeans subdued native peoples, destroyed many cultures, and resettled enormous tracts of land. In the early sixteenth century Portuguese colonists in the New World founded Brazil, and in 1822 the colony became an independent Portuguese-speaking country. A vast land of great resources, today it has a population of 184 million. Portuguese emigrating to Brazil have the great advantage of living in a Portuguese-speaking country. In fundamental contrast to Brazil the large populations of Portuguese origin in the United States and Canada do not live in New World countries originally founded by Portuguese pioneers. There was a long time lag in the movement of Portuguese emigrants to the United States and Canada, compared to the founding of colonial Brazil, and they arrived as immigrants in these northern countries long after the land had been taken from the aboriginal peoples and resettled, mainly by Spanish, French, and British colonists. In the case of Canada, Portuguese immigrants moved into a country where English and French was spoken and where there were long-established governments, cultural institutions, and societies. They were faced by existing strong cultures, not relatively weak aboriginal societies, and much change was required, as other essays make clear.

The Portuguese-Canadian population distribution across the country parallels that of other post–Second World War migrations. Teixeira and Da Rosa describe how in the last half of the twentieth century most immigrants headed for the larger urban centres, where the jobs were. It was a time of economic expansion, especially in the construction and service industries. This accounts for the large number of Portuguese Canadians in Ontario, concentrated in Toronto; in Quebec, mostly in Montreal; and in British Columbia, mainly in Vancouver. There are smaller numbers in Alberta, mainly in Edmonton, and in Manitoba, especially in Winnipeg. Some Portuguese immigrants who first went to jobs in smaller resource towns when they arrived were also caught up in the general Canadian rural-to-urban demographic shift, and soon made a second move to join growing Portuguese-Canadian communities in major cities. Family homes were established, community institutions founded, and Portuguese-Canadian localities in the large cities quickly emerged. There have been considerable internal migrations within the larger cities, but the Portuguese-Canadian imprint is firmly impressed, and their communities have become an integral part of the broader urban life in those centres. In future years a measure of Portuguese-Canadian integration into the larger Canadian society will be the extent to which Portuguese Canadians mirror general internal Canadian demographic shifts, as some young people move to rapidly growing sections of the country such as Alberta. However, the current Portuguese-Canadian population distribution is well rooted in different parts of the country: a stable and integral part of the Canadian fabric in the early twenty-first century. One region where Teixeira and Da Rosa find future demographic shifts in the Portuguese-Canadian population more difficult to predict is in Quebec, a topic they discuss later in the volume.

Newfoundland and the White Fleet

In the North Atlantic Ocean in the twentieth century the Portuguese White Fleet represented a particular and very distinctive economic and cultural contact between Portugal, a country on Europe's western edge, with Newfoundland and Labrador, a province on Canada's eastern edge. To put this association in perspective Portugal of course had a much earlier and very much stronger link across the South Atlantic Ocean with South America, where they established their flourishing colony of Brazil. Nevertheless, the White Fleet represents an important connection in its own right between two cultures, North American Newfoundlanders and European Portuguese, that were engaged in the same primary economic activity, the deep sea Atlantic fishery. The descriptions in these chapters by Doel, Andrieux, and Collins of the White Fleet and the cultural contact between Portuguese sailors and Newfoundlanders are of particular importance because the contact no longer exists. The authors provide a historical record of two societies interacting in an enterprise that attained heroic dimensions because of its inherent dangers. There is romanticism about gathering food from a source that moves, a contrast with farming where you are rooted in one place and till your own land fixed in space.

None of the other essays in this book mention the White Fleet, nor did I expect to find such a reference. This does not mean that the White Fleet and the experiences of its crews on shore in St. John's are unimportant. They are. It is in the future that the greatest significance of the White Fleet for the Portuguese-Canadian community may lie, not simply as a part of history but as a symbol of Portuguese energy in wresting a livelihood from the sea in the challenging conditions off eastern Canada's coast. The very need for a hospital ship on the high seas points to the dangers involved. Future Portuguese-Canadian writers or filmmakers may make use of the Fleet in their creative work, so that it becomes an icon of what their forebears accomplished in North Atlantic waters. Just as significant would be the White Fleet as a factor in the destruction of the North Atlantic cod fishery by fishermen from many countries, including Portugal. I expect the White Fleet will in time become more important in the Portuguese-Canadian mind because the experiences of the fishermen, the Newfoundland response, and the history of the environmental tragedy are the stuff of which stories and films are made and from which moral lessons drawn.

Immigration from Portugal to Canada

Cultural comparisons between ethnic groups, and between a particular group and the larger society within which it exists, are inevitable, but it is wrong to establish an informal league table of cultural superiority or inferiority. Cultures are simply different. Unfortunately when immigrant groups arrive in a country, feelings of inferiority and discouragement may arise, especially when language barriers make it difficult to communicate with members of the host society. One of the most difficult of all transitions is to adjust to another culture, as all immigrants are required to do, and it is unfortunate that in this process, as described by Oliveira in his essay on cultural retention, young Portuguese Canadians for some reason appear to have lost respect for the original mother culture. Why that is so is hard to fathom. True, the young are impatient to move on with their own lives, which they see as being part of the larger host society, but the question of denying the culture of the mother society remains. From what Oliveira writes this may be related to normal generational tensions in any family. It is not so much a matter of youth spurning the Portuguese mother culture as it is resentment of the patriarchal attitudes of an older generation convinced it always knows best. This is especially the case since this was occurring within the much more open, volatile, host society emerging within Canada in the critical years after 1960. Make no mistake: within the larger Canadian society there was a revolt of the young with respect to those over thirty, and Portuguese-Canadian society was forming its own character within this maelstrom. Forcing mother culture retention on the young simply arouses resentment when a seemingly more exciting culture is outside the door of the parental home.

Every family works out its own solution in these cultural adjustments. Unfortunately there are no training centres to show how to cope with cultural interaction and exchange, so no wonder there were serious problems as each Portuguese-Canadian family worked its way through this transformational change in their new country. For this most serious of issues of coping with different cultures there was no guidance, even as all energy was devoted to getting a job to put bread on the table, learning the rudiments of a new language, and keeping a family together. To the young the old mother culture seems irrelevant; it is not so much belittled as simply of little significance in the new life around them. In the great migrations of the early twentieth century to Canada, settlers were largely left to fend for themselves once on the land, and they made their way as best they could into the new world around them. In the migrations of the last part of the twentieth century to urban centres, of which the Portuguese are a part, there have been more support systems, in large part because Canada had by then introduced many more such institutions for society as a whole including, for instance, old age pensions, unemployment insurance, medicare, and provisions for learning a second language. However, in the matter of accommodating to cultural change within families it has been much like the old days; families just had to work this out themselves.

On relations between Portuguese Canadians of mainland origin and Azoreans, a matter discussed by Oliveira, there plainly is fear or resentment of the other and disparagement of what you don't know. The relationship between mainlanders and Azoreans is a regional prejudice rather than an ethnic prejudice, based on accent and alleged differences in educational aspirations. Baseless feelings of superiority and resentment are fearsome things, difficult to eradicate. All one can say is that over time, attitudes do change. On the Canadian Prairies there was once thought to be a pecking order among ethnic communities, and shockingly disparaging remarks would appear even in print about different immigrant groups in the heyday of social Darwinism. Such ethnic discrimination on the Prairies has changed over time, and members of groups that were maligned are now a respected part of general society.

Canada, too, has experienced regional prejudice. In the past many people in central Canada expressed a pronounced and unthinking condescension toward Newfoundlanders, usually never having been to that region. That has changed as more and more central Canadians have got to know the island and its people. It took time. However, there is still far to go in Canada when we think of disrespectful attitudes toward First Nations peoples in our society. Undoubtedly the wall between mainlanders and Azoreans too will recede and fade away, vexing as it may be, since it has led to a lack of self-esteem and a turning inward on the part of Azorean Canadians.

Another issue raised by Oliveira, implicit in some of the ideas just discussed, is the feeling of many Portuguese immigrants that Portugal is a backward or irrelevant country. Such feelings are not unknown among former colonies that look for cultural approval and accreditation to the centre of the empire that once ruled them. Or they may look for cultural approval to the next higher centre in the metropolitan hierarchy, as is true in North America. There is absolutely no reason for Portuguese Canadians to think this way about their homeland. Countries, it is true, have their admirable and not so admirable sides, their good and bad historical episodes. To deny such ups and downs is to deny life. Immigrants should have a good knowledge of the history and geography of both their former and present country to place them in perspective within the world.

The next two chapters are studies of contending forces: just treatment versus corporate and government power. The fight for better wages and increased security in their jobs by Portuguese-Canadian cleaning women who work in office towers and government offices, as described by Miranda, is remarkable in a number of ways. It underlines how important the second wage earner is in an immigrant family, when, paradoxically, in some instances the cleaning women were the prime wage earners. It also shows how people are willing to work together to secure a just wage in a society in which that has been held out as a promise but not in fact been forthcoming. It is the service worker who is sacrificed in the competitive struggle for lowest bids between cleaning firms tendering for jobs in big buildings. Perhaps the most rewarding thing revealed in this essay is the quick and resolute way in which the cleaning women assumed responsibility for improving their own wages and working conditions under very precarious personal circumstances. This emergence of leaders and general self-responsibility within a vulnerable group of workers is similar to the way in which leaders rose to the occasion within grassroots groups in Canada during the Great Depression of the 1930s, by organizing cooperatives. Within every community there are potential, if unknown, leaders, and dire circumstances bring them out to work for the betterment of their community. The strike necessitated a revision of how the Portuguese cleaning women were perceived; they were not militant yet they stood up for themselves against powerful forces, demanded respect, and received it.

Aguiar's essay on the Portuguese-Canadian community's mobilization against deportation raises the question 'When is a country really your country?' It shows how officials who apply the law and people in a community may hold contrary perceptions. Too often such questions do not concern us until there is a crisis, and just such a crisis is examined here. This too is a case study of how power is mobilized within the Portuguese-Canadian community, especially since an important implicit point is that the community is always intent on ensuring that it has a positive image within the host society. Such sensitivity is characteristic of most ethnic groups in Canada, and this appears to continue for generations, long after a group has settled in Canada. This case study provides a good insight into how, under effective leadership, a community will rally around and seek justice for one of their own. In this case although the deportee had besmirched the community name by his criminal acts, nevertheless because of his particular personal circumstances his treatment by the letter of the law was seen to be unjustly harsh. Different kinds of power are astutely described, but it should be borne in mind that despite old-boy networks and the resulting privileged access to those in power, we are all equal before the law in a democratic state. One can argue that old-boy contacts are sources of power, yet it is also true that a mobilized ethnic group is a source of lobbying power intended to sway decisions. The essential point, however, is that a potent Portuguese-Canadian group sought natural justice in a cause, and the larger Portuguese-Canadian community also came to believe it warranted support. Otherwise it would not have rallied behind the cause.

Multiculturalism in Canada has engendered conflicting views. Increasingly it is highly regarded, especially as in recent years it has become apparent that European countries find difficulty in integrating various ethnic groups, but concerns are still expressed that multiculturalism leads to ghettoizing. In her comparative study of the extent to which Portuguese-origin communities in Boston and Toronto participate in government, Bloemraad argues that Canadian social agencies that provide support to ethnic groups under the aegis of official multiculturalism have encouraged Toronto-area Portuguese Canadians to participate more fully in politics than Boston-area Portuguese Americans.

Although a democracy such as Canada offers many opportunities to participate and serve in various levels of government, there is a perception in the Portuguese-Canadian community that its members have not been quick to take advantage of them. The 'invisibility' that allegedly is characteristic of Portuguese Canadians implies that the community has missed out on government support it might have received. It is probably true that it would have been easier to address some social issues and negotiate particular matters for the community's well-being if access to power had been easier. Still, it does not appear that there were severe injustices that were not eventually solved. On a more positive note one hopes that for the benefit of both the Portuguese-Canadian community and all Canadians, persons of outstanding ability in the Portuguese community will rise to the opportunities before them and enter politics, not for the sake of power but to serve. That is what appears to be happening, as both Aguiar and Bloemraad argue, and for reasons that the latter explains.

Portuguese Communities and 'Little Portugals'

The drive of Portuguese immigrants to own homes in Canada as soon as they possibly can is understandable. In acquiring homes people put down roots in a new land, a deep sentiment similar to the homestead mentality of immigrants in earlier eras who moved onto the land and established farms and farm homes. But it goes beyond that: owning a home shows commitment to the new country; it is a landmark achievement. The subsequent movement to nearby areas where larger homes are available is a normal expansion into improved housing once the means to do so exist. It is the characteristic human aspiration for betterment. Teixeira and Murdie describe this process in Toronto, and they also emphasize how a distinctive Portuguese-Canadian locality, Portugal Village, was established there. A telling phrase, quoted by the authors, captures why the village was so desirable and significant in the community: it was 'where they can live a Canadian life in a "Portuguese way," among those who share their culture, way of life, and language.' The continuing westward momentum, leapfrogging all the way to Mississauga, was a major social shift because Mississauga is the quintessential Canadian suburb, based on the car, and moving there means adopting the total North American car culture. The move is understandable because it extends the continuing commitment to family through acquiring a newer, larger house, and above all a property with more surrounding space. As Teixeira and Murdie found in their survey, the suburban life is much enjoyed. But there is severance and a cost. For older family members the former service centre of Portugal Village can still be reached by car, but the equivalent intimate village ambience has not been re-created in Mississauga. The Portuguese-Canadian cultural cement in Mississauga is not that of an actual physical village but the network of spatial interaction made possible by visiting, with two churches providing a focus as well.

Teixeira and Murdie say it is too early to tell what will happen to the old Portugal Village. It is likely that some aspects of it will remain, both to serve the remaining Portuguese-Canadian community wherever they happen to live in Toronto and because of the demands of the larger Toronto community, which has become used to a distinctive Portuguese-Canadian physical presence centred on food. Multicultural Toronto as a whole would be the less if Portugal Village faded away. An object lesson here is Winnipeg, with a tiny Portuguese-Canadian population. Enlisting the help of city planners, a highly active business improvement group is hoping to create a Portuguese Village out of a few existing Portuguese restaurants, a bakery, and other shops located on a major street, as a means of rehabilitating a rundown area and bringing people back. It is doubtful that Toronto would allow the substantial existing Portuguese Village to fail, although there will undoubtedly be changes to make it more attractive as a destination to visit.

In their study of Portuguese Canadians in Quebec, Da Rosa and Teixeira portray the way the community functions. In Montreal Portuguese immigrants moved into a classic central reception area for new immigrants, where other ethnic groups had lived before and then moved on. Local community organizations were soon established, and perhaps, it is suggested, help account for the aloofness of Portuguese Canadians from the host society. Community leadership is important in immigrant societies, and class divisions within the Portuguese community, carried across the Atlantic, are revealed between those who continue to fill leadership roles and ordinary workers. However, changes are occurring within the community, as there is gradual acculturation to the larger society. Some adaptations are easier than others. The community accepts marriage outside the Portuguese-Canadian community, for instance, but preferably within the Roman Catholic faith. As in Toronto there is considerable movement from the original central community to larger lots and better homes. Among the factors driving this is a search for privacy while retaining ties to the old neighbourhood.

Da Rosa and Teixeira feel more unease about the future of the Portuguese-Canadian population in Quebec than Teixeira and Murdie do about its future in Ontario, where the issue of survival is not even mentioned. This is because a number of linguistic and cultural options are open to Portuguese Canadians living in Quebec. Quebec's status within Canada and the waxing and waning of the Quebec separatist movement are also important. Factors that also appear to be significant in considering the continued viability of the Portuguese-Canadian community in Montreal are the sense of place, of living in specific parts of the city, and the city's vital cosmopolitanism. Such factors become more and more important as one generation of Portuguese Canadians follows another in Montreal, forming bonds inside and outside the cultural community.

For more than a century in many parts of Canada the rural saga of beginning as a wage labourer, acquiring farm property, operating a family farm successfully, and then in the end after many years on the farmstead seeing your children leave the farm for urban jobs has been played out. Among the Portuguese-Canadian orchardists in interior British Columbia this experience has been raced through within one shockingly fast generation, as Teixeira explains in his analysis of fruit growing in the Okanagan Valley.

Through hard-slogging family labour and frugality, and with mutual support within their own community, many Portuguese Canadians acquired orchards and then demonstrated horticultural skill and business acumen in operating them successfully. A love of the land was fulfilled in these orchards. This was not subsistence farming, and the fruit growers faced and overcame the commercial problems and stresses that confront all farmers in the market system. What was accomplished in one generation is remarkable, but succession, passing the land on to the next generation, can be a problem. For many Portuguese-Canadian farmers who spent much effort creating and maintaining a successful orchard it has been a grave disappointment that their children have left the land, with no member of the family wanting to come back and carry on for another generation. In this as in so many other matters Portuguese Canadians are experiencing the same social forces as the larger society about them.

History, Cultural Retention, and Literature

It is very difficult to describe the general characteristics of a people or a country. For instance, much attention has been given by many writers to describing the Canadian identity, and still it remains elusive. But the attempt to describe the personality of a country is always renewed because people and communities are different in different parts of the world. When a person moves from one country to another, from one culture to another, great adjustments have to be made. Almeida cautiously presents some generalizations on Portuguese values and characteristics as portrayed by three people: a Portuguese anthropologist, a Portuguese ethnologist, and a non-Portuguese observer, augmented by his own observations. He carefully concedes that the Portuguese hold some values and characteristics in common. Immigrants to new lands, where the migrants will rub up against new societies and different cultures, will of course carry such cultural attributes. Almeida believes that if people are willing to emigrate in order to fulfil their desires, they must also be willing to change their ways in the new land. The degree of this accommodation is of course a matter of great debate in many countries, including Canada.

Almeida makes the critical and judicious point that Portuguese immigrants should be aware that cultural accommodations in the new country have to be made, and that these accommodations should be made sensibly. There are choices. Immigrants have a right to retain as much of their culture as they wish to keep. Good traditions should not be blindly thrown away, nor should new traditions be thoughtlessly adopted that do not conform to deeply held and sound values. There will be debate on what values are important and worthwhile, and there is serious generational conflict about this as has been described in other chapters.

Moreover, some adjustments are easily made, others not so easily. Almeida reinforces the view that cultural change is happening because of 'biological laws,' i.e., through generational change. As these changes occur, the old inward-looking attitude, in which Portuguese Canadians characterized themselves as an 'invisible minority' within Canada, is being discarded and there is greater participation in Canadian public affairs as earlier chapters point put. Furthermore as these adjustments continue, tensions and antagonisms among Portuguese Canadians that were brought from the Old World are ameliorated and fade away within the new society.

From within this new society a creative literature is slowly emerging. Patim situates this literature of Portuguese-Canadian background within contemporary conceptions of Canadian literature. Significant themes discussed in the social science essays in this book appear in memoirs and stories, such as the challenge of settlement, sense of loss, perception of a new identity, and adaptation to a different culture. In their stories Portuguese-Canadian writers have presented the theme of generational change starkly. As is to be expected in the creative writing produced by the first generation there are accounts of the experience of migrating, of loss of identity, and the challenge of trying to identify with a new country. By the third generation, however, the themes turn to reflections on the ancestral country and culture, and on the development of the individual. In these later works the cultural milieus of Portugal and Canada serve as background, not foreground. I expect, however, that Portuguese-Canadian writers in the future will continue to make use of the immigration experiences of their ancestors in their stories, a time of turmoil, anticipation, and apprehension, just as authors from different ethnic backgrounds in the larger Canadian society do.

Looking Forward

The Mennonite community on the Canadian Prairies, which dates back to migrations of the 1870s, regarded itself as 'Die Stille im Lande,' the quiet or unobtrusive ones in the land. These settlers deliberately came to Canada from South Russia to try to live a life secluded within their own community insofar as possible. Even in a relatively isolated rural area this proved impossible, as the outside world in a commercial farming region and a public education system affected the community more and more. The most conservative Mennonites left

Canada for other countries where the outside society would not have as great an impact, but the majority stayed, and the younger generation increasingly participated in the wider society, went to high school and university, and entered the professions. Individuals began to take part in public affairs, a few in time achieved office in provincial governments and the federal cabinet, and in 2007 a Mennonite became the premier of a province, the first to do so. This shows the power of acculturation over time, and persons from all immigrant communities in Canada, and of course from the aboriginal population, can expect similar experiences, right up to achieving the prime ministership of the country.

The perception by Portuguese Canadians that they are an invisible minority in Canada is also changing rapidly. As these essays show members of the community have already attained important public office in the larger society. It is true, however, that leaders in the Portuguese-Canadian community wonder whether the community as a whole makes effective use of the opportunities in Canadian society. The mere fact that this introspection is taking place is a good sign. Efforts are being made to rally the community toward greater achievement, especially in education. In its first decades in the new country the Portuguese-Canadian community's tightly focused cultural investment was in getting solidly established, providing for the family, and securing a good family home. That is understandable, and we have seen how well that goal has been achieved. Now the cultural investment is broadening, and includes securing a better education, moving into the professions, and into positions of greater responsibility in business and public affairs. In this the Portuguese-Canadian community is not alone. More and more emphasis in the larger society is placed on the need for higher education in order to get good jobs, and this can only reinforce the cultural change already taking place within the Portuguese-Canadian community about the importance of schooling.

Thus the community is preparing anew for its future within Canada, where it will retain its identity based on its European heritage and distinctive experience while participating fully in Canadian civic life. This book contributes to that process.